The Mind and Its World

Ever since Descartes made his sharp distinction between the mind and the body, the idea that the mind is essentially separable from the world and even from the body it inhabits has exerted an enormous influence on philosophy, psychology, cognitive science and artificial intelligence: the mind, the argument runs, is 'in the head'.

In *The Mind and Its World*, Gregory McCulloch argues that this claim is in fact untenable. Tracing the history of the idea from Descartes through Locke, Frege and Wittgenstein to behaviourism and contemporary forms of Cartesianism, he demonstrates that the philosophy of mind has yet to resolve many of the problems arising from its adoption and adaptation of Descartes' position.

McCulloch argues that these issues can only be resolved through a non-Cartesian approach, and in the second part of this book he develops such an alternative. The resulting position is externalist and holds that the mind is separable neither from the body nor from the environment in which this body lives.

The Mind and Its World provides a clear and accessible introduction to a cluster of contemporary controversies in the philosophy of mind and language. Written mainly for students with no previous knowledge of the subject, it will also make stimulating reading for specialists in the field.

Gregory McCulloch is Reader in Philosophy at the University of Nottingham. He is the author of an acclaimed book on the philosophy of language, *The Game of the Name*. His recent introduction to the early Sartre, *Using Sartre*, is also available from Routledge.

The Problems of Philosophy

Founding editor: Ted Honderich
Editors: Tim Crane and Jonathan Wolff, *University College London*

This series addresses the central problems of philosophy. Each book gives a fresh account of a particular philosophical theme by offering two perspectives on the subject: the historical context and the author's own distinctive and original contribution.

The books are written to be accessible to students of philosophy and related disciplines, while taking the debate to a new level.

* Also available in paperback

The Mind and Its World

Gregory McCulloch

London and New York

First published 1995
by Routledge
11 New Fetter Lane, London EC4P 4EE

Simultaneously published in the USA and Canada
by Routledge
29 West 35th Street, New York, NY 10001

© 1995 Gregory McCulloch

Phototypeset in Times by Intype, London

Printed and bound in Great Britain by
Mackays of Chatham PLC, Chatham, Kent

British Library Cataloguing in Publication Data
A catalogue record for this book is available from the British
Library.

Library of Congress Cataloging in Publication Data
McCulloch, Gregory.
The mind and its world/Gregory McCulloch.
p.   cm. – (Problems of philosophy)
Includes bibliographical references and index.
1. Philosophy of mind.   2. Ontology.   I. Title.   II. Series.
III. Series: Problems of philosophy (Routledge (Firm))
BD418.3.M364   1995   94–33896
128′.2–dc20   CIP

ISBN 0–415–07330–9 (hbk)
ISBN 0–415–12205–8 (pbk)

To Helen Dick,
and the memory of Ursula Nicol

There was a time when thought was defined independently of language, as something intangible and ineffable that pre-exists expression. Today people fall into the opposite error. They would have us believe that thought is only language, as if language itself were not spoken.... Each element of the system refers to a whole, but this whole is dead if nobody takes it up for his own purposes, makes it work.... In the system of language there is something that the inert cannot provide by itself, the trace of a practice.

Sartre

Speaking at the level of spontaneous phenomenology, it is undeniable that we perceive one another as 'thinking that the weather is muggy', 'believing that she will miss her train', and so on. These are phenomenologically real *conditions. But as soon as we ask whether a Thai speaker who believes that a 'meew' is on a mat is in the same psychological state as an English speaker who believes a 'cat' is on a mat, we run out of spontaneous phenomenology and begin to babble our favourite 'theory'.... Rather than think of the propositional attitudes as having a phenomenological reality which springs from the possibility of asking oneself if one really got the other person or the text right, one looks for a reduction of the propositional attitudes to something that counts as more 'basic' in one's system of scientific metaphysics.*

Putnam

Contents

Contents

Contents

Acknowledgements

I am grateful to Tim Crane and Bob Kirk, who both commented on the penultimate draft and saved me from numerous infelicities and worse. Thanks are also due to Steve Hunt, Simon Matthew, Alex Miller, Peter Millican, Tom Stoneham and Tim Williamson, who all made helpful suggestions; and also to Adrian Driscoll and Ted Honderich, for inviting me to write the book.

What follows is nothing like an exercise in anti-realism, and Michael Dummett is only mentioned in a few passing notes. But he is, through his writings, a major influence on this book, in that I have learned more about how to *do* philosophy from him than from any other source. I should also mention here the extent to which I have benefited over the years from having to maintain my views in the comradely but corrosive philosophical environment induced by my colleagues Robert Black and Bob Kirk: and for that I am grateful. For the actual doctrines embraced I think I owe most to the work of Frege, Putnam, Sartre, Wittgenstein and – at a further remove – Evans and McDowell.

Introduction

This book contains an introduction to a history of a problem in the philosophy of mind, and an attempt at a solution. The problem concerns the place of *mind* in the general scheme of things, and the history starts with Descartes. This is not because he was the first philosopher to write about this issue, but because he gave it a very distinctive focus, a focus that has stayed with the subject ever since. Descartes is fundamental in the philosophy of mind in the following very strong sense: one could come to a pretty full understanding of all that has happened in the subject since he wrote, even if one ignored everything that had gone before. Naturally, deeper understanding and specialisation require one to look further, but it is very striking how far one can go in the philosophy of mind just by starting with Descartes and considering the reactions to him. Good or bad, this is a fact of intellectual life.

Perhaps the best-known feature of Descartes' philosophy is his claim that the mind is an immaterial substance, with its corollary that the mind is separable, not only from the body it inhabits, but from the whole world of material bodies. In a sense, the issue of the separability of mind from 'its' body in particular, and all bodies in general, is the problem addressed in what follows. But it is important to realise that a very great deal of this issue remains unresolved even after Descartes' immaterialism has been rejected. Nowadays it is quite common for philosophers to proceed as though the first step, that of rejecting immaterialism and affirming the materiality of the mind, is the crucial one: that the remaining issues concerning how the material mind relates to the body it inhabits or informs are mostly a matter of detail, which even if tricky to get right are not as metaphysically profound as the first step. One principal moral of what follows is that this is a mistake. Many of the questions that arise given Descartes' view survive the transition to a materialistic framework, and as I hope to demonstrate, leave to be resolved metaphysical issues which are at least as deep as that settled by the first step away from immaterialism. Vanishingly *little* is settled when immaterialism is rejected.

The other principal moral drawn is that these outstanding issues should be resolved in a non-Cartesian manner. Although it is customary now to reject Descartes' immaterialism, it is almost as customary to adopt a form of materialistic Cartesianism, according to which the mind is, essentially anyway, a (material) thing to be found in the head. This is the most common contemporary form of *Internalism*, the view that an individual's mental characteristics are wholly constituted by what goes on within the skin of that individual, so that matters in the individual's physical or cultural environment have no bearing on the identity-conditions of these mental characteristics. Against this, I recommend an *Externalist* position which combines elements of Wittgenstein, and a dash of existentialism, in making embodiment partly constitutive of having a mind; and which blends this with Fregean themes to yield an accommodation of Putnam's influential views on natural kinds and our thoughts about them. According to the resulting position, the mind is separable neither from the body nor from the surroundings in which this body lives and moves.

Part I

CHAPTER I

Descartes and Cartesianism

Descartes is the most influential figure in the philosophy of mind. After him, it has been reasonable to expect philosophers of mind to answer three questions:

Q1: What kind of thing, if anything, is a mind?
Q2: How do minds and the mental fit into the broader scheme of things, and in particular how do minds relate to the material world, especially those bits of the material world which 'have' minds?
Q3: What are mental characteristics – what is it to think, feel, imagine, and so on?

The three questions are not wholly independent, most obviously because options for accounting for mental characteristics are limited by accounts of what sort of thing a mind is, and because in dealing with these two matters one might implicitly settle the other concerning the relations between the mental and the overall scheme of things. Nevertheless, there is often significant room for manoeuvre in these enterprises. Descartes made striking contributions to all three, and the account of his views given in the present chapter sets the scene for the rest of the book.

1 Cartesian Dualism

As regards the first two questions, Descartes set out, as he puts it in the subtitle of his *Meditations*, to demonstrate 'the distinction between the human soul[1] and the body' (PWDii: 12). His view was that minds are immaterial things or substances which have no spatial dimensions, and whose essence is to think, whereas

3

bodies are material substances, incapable of thought, whose essence is to occupy space. By this he meant all bodies – bushes, rocks – and not just the bodies which 'have' minds. This view is known as *Cartesian Dualism*:

> I recognise only two ultimate classes of things: first, intellectual or thinking things, i.e. those which pertain to mind or thinking substance; and secondly, material things, i.e. those which pertain to extended substance or body. (PWDi: 208)

One immediate and important implication of this view is that a human person is an amalgam of two things, immaterial mind and material body, which happen to be joined together but which *could be separated in principle*. This might come about, for example, were the body to die and decompose and the mind continue to exist, on earth or elsewhere. We shall see that this in-principle separability of the mind from the body it inhabits continues to be very common for a variety of reasons, even among those who are not fully-fledged Cartesian Dualists.

Descartes' approach to the third question above goes as follows:

> By the term 'thought', I understand everything which we are aware of as happening within us, in so far as we have awareness of it. Hence, thinking is to be identified here not merely with understanding, willing and imagining, but also with sensory awareness. (PWDi: 195)

Later, he adds

> All the modes of thinking that we experience within ourselves can be brought under two general headings: perception, or the operation of the intellect, and volition, or the operation of the will. Sensory perception, imagination and pure understanding are simply various modes of perception; desire, aversion, assertion, denial and doubt are various modes of willing. (PWDi: 204)

His view here incorporates the claim that thinking and other intellectual activities involve mental items called *ideas* of which we have 'inner awareness' (PWDi: 216). And at least some ideas represent things distinct from themselves, such as items in the material world. Thus on Descartes' view, to think about Paris

4

would be to entertain in an appropriate way an idea of Paris, or Paris-idea. But whereas the idea is mental, and thus in a mind, the city of Paris is a distinct thing, to be found, not in any mind, but on the river Seine.[2] We shall see that this view has been just as influential as Descartes' account of the mind–body distinction, and that it too can survive, in essentials, rejection of many of Descartes' specific doctrines.

2 Mind–body relations

Cartesian Dualism suggests the following question. If mind and body really are separate things, then how are we to account for the fact that they are, nevertheless, related to one another in various ways? This question has a very general version, as well as a number of specific ones. At its most general, the question raises the problem which many see as the key objection to Cartesian Dualism: how can individual immaterial minds and material bodies *interact causally*? For example, I may decide to make a cup of coffee and as a result go to the kitchen and start to prepare it. Here we apparently have a mental cause (the decision) and a bodily effect (coffee-making activity). Equally, I may spill some hot water on myself and feel a sharp burning sensation. Here we have a bodily cause (the contact of water on skin) and a mental effect (my feeling). Moreover, these are not just odd isolated causal exchanges, but rather belong to a whole network which constantly criss-crosses between the mental and the bodily realms. My coffee-making behaviour causes taps to release water which wets the floor which makes someone slip and curse . . . , and my feeling of being burnt causes my exclamation which vibrates the air and wakes someone up . . . Many, including Descartes, have found it hard to understand or explain how causal networks like these, involving physical law, energy transfer, and so on, can include immaterial substances with no spatial dimensions. Descartes often went into great detail about the bodily occurrences which he supposed to underlie action and perception:

> First, in so far as our senses are all parts of the body, sense-perception, strictly speaking, is merely passive . . . [it] occurs in the same way in which wax takes on the impression from a seal . . . Second, when an external organ is stimulated by

an object, the figure which it receives is conveyed ... to ... the 'common' sense ... Third, the 'common' sense functions like a seal, fashioning in the fantasy ... the same figures or ideas which come ... from the external senses ... Fourth, the motive power (i.e. the nerves themselves) has its origin in the brain, where the corporeal imagination is located; and the latter moves the nerves in different ways ... [Lastly], the power through which we know things in the strict sense is purely spiritual, and is no less distinct from the whole body than blood is distinct from bone. (PWDi: 41–2)

But on the crucial question of the last-mentioned transaction across the mind–body divide, he is unusually reticent, and what he does say is uncharacteristically lame:

Metaphysical thoughts, which exercise the pure intellect, help to familiarise us with the notion of the soul; and the study of mathematics, which exercises mainly the imagination in the consideration of shapes and motion, accustoms us to form very distinct notions of bodies. But it is the ordinary course of life and conversation, and abstention from meditation ... that teaches us how to conceive the union of the soul and the body, [since] people who never philosophise and use only their senses have no doubt that the soul moves the body and that the body acts on the soul. They regard both of them as a single thing. (PWDiii: 227)

The problems with this are first, that unreflective people might feel no doubt about something which is in fact problematic; second, that feeling no doubt about something is not the same as clearly understanding it; and third, that these people are not necessarily Cartesian Dualists anyway, so that what they do not doubt need not be what Descartes is trying to ease our minds about. Moreover, if they regard what are in fact two things 'as a single thing', they would actually be at a disadvantage, and would have no thought at all about interactions between mind and body.

The interaction problem has led to a variety of alternatives to Cartesian Dualism. It is not usual nowadays for a philosopher or psychologist to subscribe to the view that minds are immaterial substances. On the contrary, it is usually assumed that the chief task in the philosophy of mind is to show the precise way in which the mind is an aspect of the body it inhabits. For even if one does deny that the mind is an immaterial substance, the second and third questions of section 1 remain: what are mental characteristics, and how do they fit into the general scheme of things? Lots of more or less human-sized material things such as rocks and bushes are incapable of thinking or of having other mental characteristics like feeling pain or anger, so it is natural to ask what needs to be 'added' to a mere material thing if it is to have mental characteristics or a mind. Seen from here, Cartesian Dualism is only one, rather literal, answer to this question. For example, *Behaviourism* is the view that having a mind just amounts to behaving, or being disposed to behave, in appropriate ways. Then rocks and bushes lack minds because they are incapable of the fluid responses to the impact of their environments which are characteristic of humans. On this view, minds are not things, material or otherwise, which people 'have' – in contrast, say, to hearts and livers. Rather, having-a-mind, or *being minded*, is equated with behaving or being disposed to behave in certain ways. In other words, Behaviourism is a theory of mental characteristics which answers 'No sort of thing' to the question 'What sort of thing is a mind?'; which answers 'Capacities to behave' to the question 'What are mental characteristics?'; and which would hand over to, say, the physiologist the question about how these capacities fit into the wider scheme of things.

Another alternative to Cartesian Dualism is the *Mind–Brain Identity Thesis*, according to which the mind just is the brain. Here minds are things – brains – but not immaterial things; and mental characteristics are considered to be aspects of the brain's workings. Versions of this view were developed, in part, as a result of the thought that Behaviourism involves a confusion between *the evidence* usually relied on to tell whether something is minded, and *the fact* for which this is evidence. If we ask *why* humans are capable of the sort of fluid behaviour denied to rocks and bushes, the natural answer is that humans have sophisticated brains and nervous systems, whereas the others do not. Moreover, we know that mental damage and disorder correlate with neural damage and disorder. Arguments based on such thoughts are often taken to demonstrate the superiority of the Mind–Brain Identity Thesis over Behaviourism (see chapter V). Furthermore, there is presumably no general problem about how the brain interacts causally with the rest of the body and the material world, although the details are complicated and partly unknown. So the causal interaction problem that arises for Cartesian Dualism is also sidestepped.

Nevertheless, the Mind–Brain Identity Thesis itself tends to be criticised, at least in its crudest forms, for being chauvinistic. We can imagine aliens, capable of sharing our thoughts and other forms of mentality, which are so physiologically unlike us that they do not have brains at all, but have a mental life on the basis of a completely different kind of internal constitution. Again, it is believed by many that, in the future at least, we shall be able to make computers and other machines capable of sharing at least some of our mental characteristics. Yet it is no part of this claim that such machines will have to be physically the same as human brains. Various forms of *Functionalism* have become fashionable since the 1960s as a result of this objection. Roughly, Functionalism is the view that being minded is having an inner constitution *of some form or another* which makes one capable of the kind of behavioural repertoire characteristic of humans and denied to rocks and bushes. On this view, to have mental characteristics is to have inner structures with the right sort of *functional role*, where the functional role of a structure is defined in terms of its causal relations with inputs (such as perceptual information), outputs (such as behaviour) and other internal structures. A Functionalist is still free to say that, in some loose sense, the (human) mind *is* the brain, so can give the same sort of answer to the interaction problem as is given by the Mind–Brain Identity theorist, and can also adopt broadly the same answer to the question about how the mind fits into the scheme of things. What is denied is that having a brain is *essential* to having a mind, and what is stressed is that mental characteristics should be defined in terms of functional roles.[3]

Various aspects of these three alternatives to Cartesian Dualism will be discussed in subsequent chapters.[4] We shall see that most of the deep issues raised by Cartesian Dualism are also raised by these alternatives. We shall also see that many of the difficulties to be found in Cartesian Dualism, other than the interaction problem, are often carried over to these alternatives. The denial of immaterialism is pretty small beer in the philosophy of mind.

3 Epistemology

So much, for now, for *general* issues about mind–body relations. We turn now to a very *specific* issue in this area, which has been so influential as to have a branch of philosophy all to itself. This is *epistemology*, or the theory of knowledge.[5]

We have perceptual experiences and form beliefs which we take to be generally reliable guides to a material environment which we inhabit. That is, we take ourselves to know things about the material world, where *knowing things about* is a specific relation between minded things and their world. However, Descartes began the *Meditations* by seriously questioning our right to claim such knowledge. His motives were not straightforwardly destructive or sceptical, since he was concerned partly to construct an argument for Cartesian Dualism, and partly to demonstrate that true knowledge could only be attained by following his philosophy. Now it is very doubtful whether one can successfully *derive* Cartesian Dualism from sceptical premises, and few have been convinced by the chain of reasoning from Descartes' sceptical premises to his claim that we can achieve knowledge of the material world. Historically, however, the sceptical issues which Descartes raised have been enormously influential in their own right. Even so, we shall not be directly concerned with the problems of this epistemological tradition. Instead, we shall be focusing on one feature of Descartes' approach which has made them seem so overwhelmingly important.

As regards the supposed argument from sceptical doubt to Cartesian Dualism, Descartes writes

> I saw that while I could pretend that I had no body and that there was no world and no place for me to be in, I could not for all that pretend that I did not exist ... From this I knew that I was a substance whose whole essence is to think, and which does not depend on any place or material thing in order to exist. (PWDi: 127)

He appears to intend something like the following argument:

1 I can pretend that the material human René Descartes does not exist
2 I cannot pretend that I do not exist
3 so, I am not the material human René Descartes.

If we read 'can pretend' as 'can coherently suppose even after reflection', then the argument unpacks as follows. The first premiss is supposed to be given by Descartes' evil demon thought-experiment. Briefly, the idea is that a very powerful demon or hoaxer might cause Descartes to be mistaken about nearly everything, including about whether he has a material body. If this thought is coherent, it shows how the pretence that one has no body could in fact be true, and is thus a thought that one can coherently sustain. This thought-experiment will be discussed in the following section. The second premiss is supposed to come from the thought that if one tries to pretend that one doesn't exist, then reflection reveals that the supposition cannot be true, since how could one pretend without existing?

The problem, though, is that these premisses do not entail Descartes' conclusion. To see this, consider the counter-example

1* I can pretend that Stalin was not a Georgian
2* I cannot pretend that the only Georgian dictator of the Soviet Union was not a Georgian
3* so, Stalin was not the only Georgian dictator of the Soviet Union.

The premisses seem true for the same sorts of reasons as do Descartes': one can imagine a huge OGPU hoax surrounding Stalin's nationality to show how the supposition mentioned in 1* could be coherently sustained, while the supposition clearly could not be coherently sustained that: someone was a Georgian and also not a Georgian. Since this is a flat contradiction, reflection will destroy the attempt to suppose it might be true. Unfortunately, even though the premisses 1* and 2* are true, the conclusion 3* is itself false, showing that the argument-form is invalid. This in turn undermines the Cartesian argument 1–3, since it has the same invalid form. This means we can accept the premisses but have here no reason to accept the conclusion.

As for the line of reasoning by which Descartes tried to escape from his own sceptical starting-point, it is usually agreed that the chief weakness occurs when he tries to prove that a God exists who is good and powerful enough to ensure that we could not be wrong about what we are generally disposed to believe after due care and attention. This is supposed to show that there really is a material world for us to know about, since we cannot really live out the attempt to think otherwise, even after exposure to philosophy. So God would be a deceiver if he allowed us to carry on believing in a non-existent world. But in so far as neither Descartes' own nor any other available proof of the existence of a non-deceiving God carries conviction, Descartes' attempt to lead us out of the scepticism he invites us into does not work.

One very influential Cartesian legacy then, as remarked earlier, has been a strong tendency to become preoccupied with scepticism. And we shall now turn to the aforementioned feature of Cartesianism which underlies it. This will give us our principal theme.

4 Self-containedness and Exteriority

The first key move is to note that even if one cannot derive Cartesian Dualism from sceptical premises, the fact remains that sceptical worries seem inevitable once certain elements of Cartesian Dualism have been accepted, for whatever reason. As intended by Descartes, the idea is that a person's mind is not only distinct from their body, but from *all* bodies. Not only this, but Descartes' intention was also that all mental characteristics are equally separable from, that is could exist just as they are in the absence of, any bodies whatsoever. Descartes not only supposed that mind is separable from all body, but also that individual minds *are self-contained with respect to body*, or capable of having the mental characteristics that they do, independently of the existence of any body. Recall his claim that he is 'a substance whose whole essence is to think, and which does not depend on any place or material thing in order to exist' (PWDi: 127). It might seem that the self-containedness doctrine does not follow immediately from this immaterialist point alone, since immaterialism is compatible with the idea that thinking involves being related in a certain way to, say, structures in the brain. But then one could not contend, as Descartes does, that thinking is essential to the immaterial substance's existence, since if the substance can exist without the brain, it would be able to exist without thinking (without being appropriately related to structures in the brain). So Descartes' view, as already remarked, is that to think

11

is to be aware of non-bodily items called ideas: 'We know for certain that it is the soul which has sensory perceptions, not the body' (PWDi: 164).[6] And it follows from this that the existence of a mental state or happening, such as my now having my present experiences, *is compatible with any possible bodily state of affairs whatsoever, including the state of affairs where there are no bodies at all.* Any mental state could exist just as it is in itself whether or not any bodies exist.

Descartes illustrated some of the consequences of this self-containedness claim with the famous thought-experiment mentioned in the previous section. Suppose we agree that my now having the experiences I am having could occur even if nothing bodily existed. How, then, does my having these experiences give me knowledge about my surroundings? How do my present experiences enable me to know that I am confronting a word-processor? The natural answer is that the word-processor must stand in an appropriate relation to the experiences. For example, we might suggest that the processor *causes* the experiences as the result of incident light reflecting off it and being transmitted through the optic nerve via the eye, and so on (recall Descartes' account of these matters). But, now, what reason could there be for claiming that the experiences are the result of such a process? In general, we know that the existence of a certain effect is compatible with its having one of various (or perhaps even no) causes. Thus a stain on the carpet might be oil or wine. The tickle on my leg might be a mosquito or an inflamed follicle. More dramatically, Descartes suggests, we can imagine that my experiences are caused by an evil demon intent on getting me to think that I have finally made a start on this typescript when I have not. Indeed, we can imagine further that there is no word processor, and moreover no material world at all, so that I do not even have a body, and that instead the entire universe consists of my immaterial mind and the immaterial demon which causes appropriate experiences as input to my mental life. Given the self-containedness of mind with respect to the material world, this situation is at least logically possible. *Scepticism then immediately assumes the first importance since it is natural, to say the least, to want to defend our conviction that this fantastic though logically possible situation is not actual.*

This may seem an easy thing to do. *I* might have problems

checking whether my experiences stand in the right sort of relation to a word-processor, since it seems that all I have to go on are further thoughts and experiences. This applies even if I start to make further empirical enquiries, say by investigating the light in the room or by (no doubt with difficulty) examining my retina and optic system. No matter what investigations into my body and its surroundings I pursue, the end result will always be me having certain experiences and holding certain beliefs: and we have already seen that, given the self-containedness of my mind with respect to everything bodily, such a state of affairs is compatible with any possible bodily state of affairs, including the state of affairs where there are no bodies. A demon could be causing me to have the appropriate experiences and beliefs even though there is no light, are no retinas and optic systems, and so on. However, surely *you* can ascertain that I do indeed have a body, am really confronting a word-processor, and so on? Can't you see that I am not being fooled by a demon? Sadly, not really, if your mind too is self-contained in the way Descartes supposed. For if it is, then the existence of your experiences no more involves the existence of anything bodily than do the existence of mine. Perhaps you are being made to have your experiences by a demon who wishes you to think that I am sitting here, experiencing a word-processor ... when in fact none of these situations obtains.

Another way of putting all this is to say that if minds are self-contained with respect to the material world, then the material world of bodies is *Exterior* to the mind, and the traditional sceptical problem becomes that of trying to secure contact between our self-contained minds and the Exterior material world. (One reason for using 'exterior' rather than the more usual 'external' will be explained shortly. Another will emerge in chapter VIII). As remarked, we are in general convinced that we know things about our material surroundings. But how can this conviction be appropriate if these surroundings are Exterior to our minds? It seems that in order to know things about the world we have to participate in a state of affairs which is in principle beyond the reach of our minds, in the precise sense that our participating in it can make no essential difference *to the state of mind we are in*, to how it is with us. The whole of our mental life could proceed as it does in itself even if there were not one human body or other material thing.[7] Most knowledge thus seems neither attainable nor worth having: Cartesian Dualism seems to make knowledge of a material world irrelevant to anything that can concern us as thinking things, and it is small wonder that Descartes supposed that nothing short of a proof of God's existence could set the matter right.

It is a serious mistake, however, to think that all of this is a problem for Cartesian Dualism alone. First, one can arguably generate sceptical worries without assuming (or concluding) that minds are self-contained with respect to the material world. The existence of dreams, mistakes, hallucinations and illusions might be cited in order to shake our confidence in the reliability of our senses, and hence to undermine our claims to know things on the basis of using them. It is far from obvious that this procedure requires the assumption, or delivers the conclusion, that minds are self-contained in the above way. Second, and much more importantly for our purposes, even if a sceptical argument does presuppose some sort of self-containedness, *it does not also have to presuppose that minds are immaterial substances.* For example, Hilary Putnam's twentieth-century version of Descartes' demon thought-experiment involves imagining that

> [your brain] has been removed from the body and placed in a vat of nutrients which keeps the brain alive. The nerve endings have been connected to a super-scientific computer which causes [you] to have the illusion that everything is perfectly normal. There seem to be people, objects, the sky, etc; but all [you are] experiencing is the result of electronic impulses travelling from the computer to the nerve endings. The computer is so clever that if [you try] to raise [your] hand, the feedback from the computer will cause [you] to 'see' and 'feel' the hand being raised. Moreover, by varying the program, the evil scientist can cause [you] to 'experience' (or hallucinate) any situation or environment the evil scientist wishes. He can also obliterate the memory of the brain operation, so that [you] will seem to [yourself] always to have been in this environment. It can even seem to [you] that [you are] sitting and reading these very words. (RTH: 6)

Putnam himself argues that we are not in fact in this situation.

But the scenario is certainly compatible with at least one version of the Mind–Brain Identity Thesis. If we hold not only that my mind is my brain, but also that all my mental characteristics just are characteristics of my brain considered in itself – patterns of neuron-firing, and so on – then it follows that my material environment and even (the rest of) my body are Exterior to my mind, and the sceptical problem of securing knowledge-links between mind and Exterior material world arises. Since such brain-activity could be the way it is in itself, in principle, even though it has no material surroundings of the usual sort, then my experiences essentially tell me nothing about the nature of these surroundings, if indeed I have any.[8] Putnam's vat-brain thought-experiment is a way of making this position graphic, and is exactly parallel to Descartes' evil demon thought-experiment. This is thus one easy and obvious way in which a problem highly character-istic of Descartes' system can survive the denial of his imma-terialism.

It may seem that even if this version of the Mind–Brain Identity Thesis is true, there is a sense in which mental characteristics are prior to brain characteristics, in that I can know I have a mind before (and without) knowing that I have a brain, so that in this same sense the brain is 'external' to the mind. Now this may well be true. Indeed, this claim introduces the usual concept of what it is for the world or for part of it to be 'external'. But the concept is thoroughly epistemological: the 'externality' of the brain, even when it *is* the mind, is explained in terms of what can be *known* before what. So it is very important to note that the concept of Exteriority introduced above is not epistemological but *ontologi-cal*, that is, concerns the dependence of the *existence* of one thing on another. To say, in this sense, that X is Exterior to Y is to say that Y could in principle exist just as it is in itself, whether or not X did. This shift of focus from 'externality' to Exteriority reflects the fact that our concerns are not the traditional epis-temological ones introduced by Descartes, but their ontological underpinnings: as already remarked, it is because the mind, according to Descartes (and the above version of the Mind–Brain Identity Thesis), is self-contained with respect to the surrounding material world, that sceptical questions immediately seem so urgent. Our concern is to be with the self-containedness doctrine itself, the concept of Exteriority, rather than with the epistemological spin-off.

Note also the equally important point that the doctrine of self-containedness, and the scope of the corresponding ontological concept of Exteriority, are implicitly relative to the theory of mind presupposed. According to the Cartesian Dualist, *all* material happenings are Exterior to any mind. But according to the version of the Mind–Brain Identity Thesis just considered, which entails that my mental activity is activity in my brain, it is not true that all material happenings are Exterior to my mind. Rather, some of these – namely the relevant brain-happenings – just are aspects of my mind, and hence are not Exterior to it in the sense introduced, since my mind could not exist just as it is in itself, even in principle, if these brain-happenings did not exist.[9] Another illustration of the relativity of the concept of Exteriority involves a version of the doctrine of Behaviourism, introduced in section 2. Suppose we say that my present mental characteristics just are my dispositions to behave in certain ways: thus my current state of feeling my feet to be cold just is my current disposition to fetch an extra pair of socks; my current interest in what I am doing just is my disposition to remain here typing. Then we can say that anything inessential to the existence of these dispositions is to that extent Exterior to my mind. Suppose we agree further that these dispositions (and all my other behavioural dispositions) require only that my body and certain of its inner structures exist. Then everything else is Exterior to my mind – everything but my body and the relevant inner structures, so certainly everything beyond my skin. Clearly this form of Behaviourism draws the boundaries of the mind at a different place than does either Cartesian Dualism or our Mind–Brain Identity Thesis. And as we shall see, other theories of mind, including varieties of Functionalism, draw the line in different places. Wherever the line is drawn, minds thereby become self-contained with respect to whatever falls on the far side of the line, and a particularly vicious form of scepticism regarding our claims about this Beyond rears its head. But as remarked, varieties of self-containedness, rather than their attendant scepticisms, are to be our topic. The idea that minds are more or less self-contained with respect to their material surroundings continues to exert a powerful influence in contemporary philosophy, psychology, cognitive science and artificial intelligence design.

5 Mind, consciousness, language

Self-containedness, then, is the great theme we shall be carrying forward from Descartes. But there are two almost equally import- ant ancillary matters which are intertwined with this theme both in Descartes and in our subsequent discussion: and we turn now to these. They are the centrality to the study of the mind of (1) consciousness, and (2) the ability to use language.

Descartes' theory of mind is heavily biased towards conscious- ness. His procedure for establishing the distinction between mind and body is a conscious line of reasoning, which anyone is alleged to be able to think through for themselves, and which is sup- posed to turn solely on the extent of one's consciousness at that time. When he defines thinking, he calls it a form of perception or awareness (of ideas), as we have seen. In so far as one believes that there are aspects of mind which are not conscious – say unconscious drives or subliminal awarenesses – one would thus have to say that even if Descartes' account of mind is correct as far as it goes, it is nevertheless incomplete. But he does not see things this way. In defining a mind as something whose essence is to think, he implies that minds could exist with no other characteristic than that of thinking, or having ideas. In other words, the immaterial mind in itself is just an idea-perceiving entity.

It is not obvious why one should take this line, even as a believer in minds as immaterial substances. Why should not think- ing involve all sorts of immaterial structures not themselves avail- able to consciousness? One might worry that this talk of 'structures' makes the immaterial mind sound just like a special kind of material object:[10] but this is already something of a worry for Descartes, given his view that minds and bodies causally interact. Alternatively, Descartes might argue that just as we can imagine that there is no material world to cause our experiences, so we can imagine that there are no structures to underpin them. But this is not fully convincing. In imagining away the material causes of our experiences, Descartes (and Putnam) imagine instead some other cause for them (demon or scientist). Perhaps

17

the thought that the experiences just appear uncaused makes no sense; Descartes certainly thought so: 'something cannot arise from nothing' (PWDii: 28). Equally, then, perhaps the thought of having ideas without *some* underlying mechanism is also senseless, so that the most we can do is imagine that present experience could have a different kind of underlying mechanism from the one we suppose it to have. In the end, Descartes would probably just reply that he can see clearly and distinctly that no underlying mechanism is required for consciousness, and then appeal to his doctrine that

> the light of nature or faculty of knowledge which God gave us can never encompass any object which is not true in so far as it is indeed encompassed by this faculty, that is, in so far as it is clearly and distinctly perceived. (PWDi: 203)

But even if this doctrine is correct, it remains the case that *I* cannot clearly and distinctly perceive the non-necessity of an underlying mechanism for the having of ideas, and I leave the rest to the reader.

However all this may be, Descartes certainly did acknowledge that much of our distinctive behaviour and activity as human persons does not involve consciousness of ideas. That is, he acknowledged that 'there occur within us ... operations which we perform without any help from reason' (PWDi: 42). But he is emphatic that such operations can be explained solely in terms of the body's mechanisms, and he in various places describes or speculates about the anatomical facts. The sorts of operations he has in mind are those which

> enable us to understand how all the movements of other animals can come about, even though we refuse to allow that they have any awareness of things, but merely grant them a purely corporeal imagination [i.e. sufficiently sophisticated brain or other behaviour-controlling mechanism]. (PWDi: 40)

Humans, he says, have a similar corporeal imagination, and more generally his idea is that animal bodies, including human bodies, are vastly complicated mechanisms which are no more aware or conscious of things than any other 'automaton, or moving machine' (PWDi: 139).

This immediately makes one wonder why he should lay so much emphasis on consciousness and thinking. If we knew enough about natural machines such as human bodies, would we not be able to explain everything they do without mentioning minds at all (cf. chapter IV, section 5, and chapter VIII, section 9)? Descartes might reply that he knows in his own case that he is not merely a non-conscious machine, since 'even if I was dreaming and ... whatever I saw or imagined was false, yet I could not deny that the ideas were truly in my mind' (PWDi: 128). But this raises the thought that even if Descartes knows that *he* has ideas in *his* mind, why should he claim as much about other humans (cf. chapter VI)? After all, he is not aware of their ideas in the way in which he is aware of his own, and it seems very much in the spirit of Cartesian scepticism for him to imagine that he is the only conscious human in existence, and that his fellows are cunningly contrived robots put there by an evil demon set on deceiving him.[11]

Descartes has an answer to this:

> if any [non-conscious] machines bore a resemblance to our bodies and imitated our actions as closely as possible for all practical purposes, we should still have two very certain means of recognising that they were not real men. The first is that they could never use words, or put together signs, as we do in order to declare our thoughts to others ... Secondly, even though such machines might do some things as well as we do them, or perhaps even better, they would inevitably fail in others, which would reveal that they were acting not through understanding but only from the disposition of their organs. (PWDi: 140)

He acknowledges that machines, or animals such as parrots, can produce words, but denies that they 'should produce different arrangements of words so as to give an appropriately meaningful answer to whatever is said in [their] presence' (*ibid.*). Similarly, he holds that 'reason is a universal instrument which can be used in all sorts of situations ... hence it is for all practical purposes impossible for a machine ... to act in all the contingencies of life in the way in which our reason makes us act' (*ibid.*). Descartes thus clearly identifies being conscious, having a mind, with *having the capacity to reason*, and just as emphatically denies that machines could reason. We, on the other hand, clearly can reason, as our meaningful use of language and understanding of what we are doing demonstrate. So we are more than mere natural machines (note that there is an argument here towards Cartesian Dualism which is independent of the epistemological one described in section 3).

Descartes is not saying that the essence of reasoning or thinking is the appropriate use of language. He hardly could consistently say this, since using a language requires substantial bodily involvement, and we have seen he is committed to affirming the Exteriority of anything bodily to the mind and to mental characteristics such as reasoning. For him, then, thought is prior to talk: talk is, at most, a means of 'declaring our thoughts'. So his claim is simply that *having the potential to use language is essential to mindedness*: to have a mind is to be capable of making and understanding meaningful signs if suitably connected to a body with expressive organs, etc., etc. We shall reflect this point by focusing in what follows on what we shall call *the theory of understanding*. This can be interpreted indifferently either as the theory of what goes into having the potential for using language, or as the theory of what goes into the ability to think or reason as we in fact do. Descartes saw no distinction here, and we shall follow him in this throughout.

Now one can agree with him over the importance of language to the mind even if one denies his immaterialism. And this might come about in two ways. Descartes himself would probably accept that a proper theory of reasoning would have to be based on an account of language-like structures. Reasoning, for Descartes, is the correct ordering of ideas, rather than the using of words, but the fact remains that for this to be so ideas would have to stand to one another in logical and other 'linguistic' relations. Thus a study of reasoning processes would be very like the sorts of studies of artificial language gone in for by logicians and theoretical linguists. First, then, one might accept that reasoning is the processing of ideas, but claim that ideas are material or even linguistic structures in brains or similar mechanisms (see chapter V). Here one would accept quite a lot of what Descartes says about the importance of language, but deny his claim that machines, howsoever sophisticated, would not be capable of using language as we do.[12] But second, having come this far, one might

20

drop altogether the talk of ideas, material or otherwise, and instead say that reasoning and thinking have to be understood by way of a study of ordinary, public language and its use. This position, which may, but need not, be a form of Behaviourism (see chapters IV–V), still retains Descartes' sense of the importance of language to thought and reasoning, while dropping most of his other claims: in particular, it reverses his claim that thought is prior to talk. As we shall see, both developments – the positing of linguistic structures in the brain, and the idea that talk is prior to thought – are still alive in contemporary philosophy of mind, and are among the options which philosophers typically choose from (somewhat against the grain, we shall suggest in chapter V that they are perfectly compatible).

A shift to materialism does not obviously force a change from Descartes' views about the centrality of consciousness.[13] But it should also be noted that adopting Descartes' view of the links between linguistic potential and thinking can accompany rejection of his claims about consciousness. For example, one might hold that linguistic structures in the brain need not be objects of conscious awareness, as Descartes' ideas are. Or one might hold that much use of public language is habitual or similarly outside of conscious reflection. Conversely, one might deny Descartes' claim that thinking and reasoning are *essential* to consciousness, and instead suppose that lesser animals and human babies, while incapable of reasoning, thinking and using language, nevertheless have 'raw' or merely sensory forms of consciousness. The English philosopher Locke, who as we shall see in the following chapter accepted many of Descartes' claims, nevertheless said even of cockles and oysters that

> I cannot but think there is some small dull perception whereby they are distinguished from perfect insensibility. (E:II,ix,14)

And he was adamant that more sophisticated non-linguistic animals, and even babies in the womb, experience some ideas derived from their surroundings (E:II,xi,10; E:II,x,5). Some aspects of these issues will be discussed in chapter VI.

21

6 Cartesianism

To sum up, then. In the present chapter we have encountered the elements of Cartesian Dualism: we started with three questions –

Q1: What kind of thing, if anything, is a mind?

Q2: How do minds and the mental fit into the broader scheme of things, and in particular how do minds relate to the material world, especially those bits of the material world which 'have' minds?

Q3: What are mental characteristics – what is it to think, feel, imagine, and so on?

– and in outlining Descartes' answers to them we isolated three important themes to carry forward. They are:

T1: self-containedness and Exteriority;

T2: consciousness;

T3: the theory of understanding (language and reasoning).

T2 and T3 provide the materials for Descartes' answers to Q1 and Q3: according to him, a mind is essentially a thinking and reasoning substance with the potential for using language if connected to a suitable body (T3). Thinking and reasoning is the processing of ideas, and ideas are objects of consciousness or inner perception, that is are *phenomenological objects* (T2). Descartes' answer to Q2 involves T1: any given mind can exist as it is in itself regardless of the nature or even existence of anything bodily or material; material body is Exterior to the mind, the mind is self-contained with respect to body; and minds are thus immaterial, or non-bodily, substances. But this immaterialist aspect of Descartes' view is clearly the most dispensable, least discussable aspect of it. Given the interaction problem (section 2), it is probably better to forget about it. Yet little else need change. One can give exactly the same answers to Q1 and Q3 just by maintaining that the mind is a *material* thinking and reasoning substance, although the purported role of consciousness in the processing of ideas is optional, as recently noted. Moreover, the answer to Q2 can still involve self-containedness to almost the same extent as before: one could still maintain that the material mind is self-contained with respect to its material surroundings, including (the rest of) its own body. In what follows, then, it will be useful to describe various possible positions as *Cartesian*, even when they are avowedly materialistic. Cartesianism is defined by what is common to Descartes and those positions which deny his immaterialism, and perhaps his stress on consciousness, but keep as much else as possible intact. The *Cartesian Tendency*, then, is the strategy of staying as close as possible to Cartesianism in the face of developments or difficulties.

Cartesianism and the Cartesian Tendency are still the broadest currents in the philosophy of mind. My ultimate aim is to champion a radical alternative.

Notes and reading

Works referred to

PWD   Descartes, R., *The Philosophical Writings of Descartes* (3 vols) trans. J. Cottingham, R. Stoothoff, D. Murdoch and (volume 3 only) A. Kenny (Cambridge: Cambridge University Press, 1984-91).

E   Locke, J., *An Essay Concerning Human Understanding*, ed. J. Yolton (London: Everyman, 1961).

RTH   Putnam, H., *Reason, Truth and History* (Cambridge: Cambridge University Press, 1981).

Notes

1 For the purposes that concern us, 'mind' and 'soul' can be regarded as interchangeable.

2 In fact Descartes claimed there to be 'an ambiguity ... in the word "idea". "Idea" can be taken materially, as an operation of the intellect ... [or] objectively, as the thing represented by that operation' (PWDii: 7): thus a Paris-idea would either be the operation that represents Paris, or Paris-as-represented. In what follows we shall normally be discussing ideas in the 'material' sense, although the distinction will come up again briefly in chapter II, sections 3-5.

3 Note that Functionalism is, in itself, compatible with immaterialism, since if there can be immaterial structures which causally interact with material bodies, then such structures could presumably have the appropriate functional roles.

4 For good, complementary introductory texts see Peter Carruthers, *Introducing Persons* (London: Croom Helm, 1986) and Peter Smith and Owen R. Jones, *The Philosophy of Mind: An Introduction* (Cambridge: Cambridge University Press, 1986).

5 See Jonathan Dancy, *Introduction to Contemporary Epistemology* (Oxford: Blackwell, 1985).

6 Descartes does sometimes seem to flirt with the idea that thinking essentially involves structures in the brain: see e.g. PWDi: 139, 166. But in contrast, he also says that 'it is not only the images depicted in the imagination that I call "ideas". Indeed, in so far as these images are in the corporeal imagination, that is, are depicted in some part of the brain, I do not call them "ideas" at all; I call them "ideas" only in so far as they give form to the mind itself, when it is directed towards that part of the brain' (PWDii: 113). For the reasons given in the text, this has to be his considered view.

7 The extremity of the position is memorably captured in a purple passage from Berkeley's *Second Dialogue between Hylas and Philonous*: 'Is there not something in the woods and groves, in the rivers and clear springs that soothes, that delights, that transports the soul? At the prospect of the wide and deep ocean, or some huge mountain whose top is lost in the clouds, or of an old gloomy forest, are not our minds filled with a pleasing horror? Even in rocks and deserts, is there not an agreeable wildness? How sincere a pleasure it is to behold the natural beauties of the earth! . . . Is not the whole system immense, beautiful, glorious beyond expression and beyond thought! What treatment then do those philosophers deserve, who would deprive these noble and delightful scenes of all reality? How should those principles be entertained, that lead us to think all the visible beauty of creation a false imaginary glare?' (*Berkeley: Philosophical Works*, ed. M. Ayers, London: Everyman, 1975: 167). On the other hand, Berkeley's solution to the problem, roughly that of making the material world essentially mind-dependent (see chapter III, section 1), is not as robust as his indignation demands.

8 One thought here, which we shall encounter again in chapter II, is that one's ideas automatically give one knowledge of *whatever happen to be their regular causes*. Thus if the demon (computer) hypothesis is actual, the relevant thinkers are thinking about, and have knowledge of, the demon (computer). This position appears to be implicit in Putnam's argument. But it is unsatisfying in the extreme – we become curiously detached or isolated from the real import of our own thinking, our 'knowledge' is no real use to us at all – and it is based, we shall see, on a profoundly mistaken view of what it is for ideas to represent: see chapter II, section 5; and also chapter VI, and chapter VIII, section 4.

9 Of course, my mind might *seem to me* to be the same even if the brain events were to change. But it does not follow that my mind *would be* the same in itself, since it is a mistake to think that the nature of the mind is exhausted by how it seems, subjectively speaking. See chapters IV–VIII.

10 Compare Gilbert Ryle's caricature of Cartesian Dualism: 'Minds are not bits of clockwork, but bits of not-clockwork . . . not merely ghosts

harnessed to machines [but] themselves . . . spectral machines' *The Concept of Mind* (London: Hutchinson, 1949: 21).

11 This is a form of the traditional Problem of Other Minds: see Carruthers, *Persons*, ch. 1 and Gregory McCulloch, *Using Sartre* (London: Routledge, 1994), ch. 8.

12 Descartes probably in any event overplays the 'universal' power of our reasoning and linguistic abilities: see e.g. Daniel Dennett, *The Intentional Stance* (Cambridge, MA: MIT Press, 1987): 28–33.

13 Thus John R. Searle: 'consciousness . . . is the central mental notion. In one way or another, all other mental notions . . . can only be fully understood as *mental* by way of their relations to consciousness': see *The Rediscovery of the Mind* (Cambridge, MA: MIT Press, 1992): 84. This is in the context of a rejection of immaterialism: 'mental events and processes are as much part of biological natural history as digestion, mitosis, meiosis or enzyme secretion' (*ibid.*: 1; cf. 13–15).

CHAPTER II

Locke and the Theory of Ideas

To understand the development of Cartesianism, we need now to step away somewhat from Descartes and focus on Locke. There are various differences between the two philosophers. First, they come out on different sides of the Rationalism versus Empiricism debate. Locke, the Empiricist, believed that all knowledge is ultimately derived from experience. Descartes, the Rationalist, believed that some knowledge is innate, or built into the structure of our minds, and hence not derived from experience. Locke's attitude to Cartesian Dualism, and especially its bearing on questions of personal identity, is not at all straightforward.[1] He also denied that thinking is the essence of the mind, citing the example of sleep or unconsciousness as a reason, and preferred to say that

> perception of ideas [is] to the soul what motion is to the body: not its essence, but one of its operations. (E:II,i,10)

(This is, however, compatible with belief that the mind is immaterial – something Locke seems ultimately to embrace after first setting it aside; cf. E:I,i,2, and E:II,xxiii,15: but contrast E:IV,iii,6). Further, Locke accepted something very like the atomism of Newton, whereas Descartes argued repeatedly against it. However, this particular disagreement springs from a shared commitment to the new mechanistic science which was at that time replacing established practice which was rooted in the work of Aristotle. Both Descartes and Locke were champions of a new style of philosophising which aimed to replace the scholastic approach that went hand in hand with this Aristotelianism. Moreover, it is undeniable that Locke was heavily influenced by Descartes, and his philosophy of mind is thoroughly Cartesian. He in effect took over many of the key features of Descartes' theory of ideas and developed them, in a way that has been extremely influential in the English-speaking philosophical tradition.

Three features of Locke's theory of ideas are of particular interest to us. The first is that he introduced several important distinctions among them; the second is that he worked the theory explicitly into an account of the understanding, and of how language serves as an instrument of communication; and the third is that he bequeathed a long-lasting bundle of theses concerning what ideas in fact are, and how they represent their objects. We shall take up these three matters in turn.

1 Ideas: some distinctions

Locke divided ideas into two grand categories, depending on their source. Thus he said that there are ideas of *sensation*, which come into our minds by way of our senses, and there are ideas of *reflection*, which form in the mind as a result of its observing its own activity. Examples of ideas of sensation are

> those ideas we have of *yellow, white, heat, cold, soft, hard, bitter, sweet* and all those which we call sensible qualities. (E:II,i,3)

Examples of ideas of reflection are

> *perception, thinking, doubting, believing, reasoning, knowing, willing*, and all the different actings of our own minds. (*Ibid.*)

This distinction is not as innocent as it may look, since on the face of it one could acquire such ideas as *perception, thinking* and *doubting* by observing other people, and this would make them ideas of sensation, at least when so acquired. But Locke's blindness to this point is understandable if we attribute to him the doctrine that the mind is self-contained with respect to the body and the surrounding environment. For then other people's mental characteristics would not show up *as such* in the observable movements of their bodies, and it would seem that a person's only access to the essential nature of mental characteristics would be by reflecting on their own. And Locke certainly did take over this self-containedness doctrine, even if not Descartes' immaterialism (recall that neither entails the other). Some issues raised by ideas of reflection will be considered in chapter VI.

Locke made another grand division, cutting across the one just introduced, between *simple* and *complex* ideas. This distinction ushers in an entire psychology and a theory of knowledge. Simple ideas, such as the ones listed above, are those 'in the reception whereof the mind is only passive' and which are 'received from sensation and reflection' (E:II,xii,1). The intention is that these are basic elements of thought which either come in through the senses or arise as a result of reflection. Locke then proceeds to try to explain all other mental characteristics in terms of operations performed in the first instance on simple ideas. They can be retained, recalled, combined, brought into relation to each other and abstracted from to give general ideas. The results of these operations are (complex) ideas on which these operations can again be performed, and so on apparently indefinitely. In performing such operations the mind is no longer passive, but active and creative. All of this yields Locke's psychology, from which the following claim can then be derived:

> even *the most abstruse ideas*, how remote soever they may seem from sense, or from any operation of our own minds, are yet only such as the understanding frames to itself by repeating and joining together *ideas* that it had either from objects of sense, or from its own operations about them: so that even large *and abstract* ideas *are derived from sensation or reflection*, being no other than what the mind, by the ordinary use of its own faculties, employed about *ideas* received from objects or from the operations it observes in itself about them, may and does attain to. (E:II,xii,8)

And this in turn leads straight to Locke's empiricist epistemology, his view that all knowledge is derived from the senses. Given that ideas of reflection only arise after ideas of sensation have come into the mind, we cannot even *think* anything until the mind has given entry to some ideas of sensation, and all we can think thereafter is the result of repeated operations on this sensory core and on the results of operations. Since we can only *know* something if we can think it, the Empiricism follows:

> the simple *ideas* we receive from sensation and reflection

are the boundaries of our thoughts; beyond which the mind, whatever efforts it may make, is not able to advance one jot; nor can it make any discoveries, when it would pry into the nature and hidden causes of those *ideas*. (E:II,xxiii,29)

This is a very graphic statement of Locke's self-containedness doctrine. And note, relatedly, how stifling it makes our epistemological predicament. If Locke is right, we have it in advance that we can know nothing about the whole material world unless simple sensory ideas are faithful representations of their causes. But given the view that the mind is self-contained with respect to the material world, it is hard to see how we could vindicate our conviction that they are. Not all theorists of ideas are Empiricists, of course: Descartes is not. And this gives him some extra leverage with the sceptical problem, since he can at least claim to know certain things (e.g. that God exists) independently of experience, and try to marshal this knowledge in order to vindicate claims about the fidelity of sensory experience. But as remarked in the previous chapter, few have found this procedure convincing, and it is anyway Locke's stifling Empiricism which has tended to dominate much of the subsequent philosophical tradition.[2]

Among *complex* ideas Locke again distinguishes different types, of which the two that will occupy us are ideas of *substances* and of *(mixed) modes* – I shall henceforward omit the qualification 'mixed'. A substance-idea has two types of component. On the one hand there is a combination of ideas of the familiar sort, such as the 'idea of a dull, whitish colour, with certain degrees of weight, hardness, ductility and fusibility'. Added to this, then, is 'the supposed or confused *idea* of substance', and the result is 'the *idea* of *lead*' (E:II,xii,6). Similarly,

> a combination of the *ideas* of a certain sort of figure, with the powers of motion, thought, and reasoning, joined to substance, make the ordinary *idea* of *a man*. (*Ibid.*)

Mode-ideas are different, in that they 'contain not in them the supposition of subsisting by themselves, but are considered as dependencies on, or affections of substances' (E:II,xii,4). Thus we have 'theft, . . . being the concealed change of the possession of anything, without the consent of the proprietor' (E:II,xii,5). Other examples of modes he gives are beauty, triangle, gratitude, murder. Later, he describes our recognition of modes as partly determined by our interests and general way of life, and the associated need to communicate:

> [people] usually make such collections of *ideas* into complex ideas and affix names to them, as they have frequent use of in their way of living and conversation, leaving others, which they have but seldom an occasion to mention, loose and without names to tie them together ... This shows *how it comes to pass that there are in every language many particular words which cannot be rendered by any one single word or another.* For the several fashions, customs, and manners of one nation making several combinations of *ideas* familiar and necessary in one, which another people have had never any occasion to make... names come of course to be annexed to them. (E:II,xxii,5–6)

Clearly his talk of modes concerns various ways of classifying and subdividing the things around us which are partly determined by facts about our interests, way of life, legal institutions and so on. To adapt one of his own examples, we have special words for mother-killing and father-killing – 'matricide' and 'parricide' – but no special word for woman-killing or man-killing: just the gender-neutral 'murder' and the politically incorrect 'man-slaughter'. This is no doubt because we see a special heinousness in the killing of parents. Now there is a French brand of mouse poison called 'Souricide', and one could imagine a community of French-speakers particularly interested in mice taking this word over and using it as their special word for mouse-killing (French *'souris'* = 'mouse'). Locke's point is that all sorts of systems of classification are possible – all these discriminations are there to be made, and marked by a special word – but that the convenience of life dictates that only some of them are worth attending to.

Although he does not say so, one can also expect there to be another, related phenomenon, where distinctive facts about our ways of classifying are partly determined by special features of our material surroundings. One well-used example concerns Inuits, who are said to have a lot of different words for snow, depending on its type and other features of the context. This is clearly because they spend a lot of time surrounded by the stuff, and so have to take an interest, unlike people who live in more temperate regions. Of course this factor will interact with that mentioned by Locke: special features of our surroundings themselves influence our interests, just as the working-out of our interests makes new features salient or even brings new features into our surroundings. Together, and along with other influences, these things shape our systems of classification.

Such points as these can lead to mischief: someone will say that one system of classification is no better than another, so there is no fact of the matter as to whether there is such a thing as (say) souricide, or whether there is one or fourteen kinds of snow, so there is no such thing as truth, and so on to relativism. But Locke's examples do not support this. Although we do not *recognise* souricide as a feature of our social world, we can nevertheless agree that there is such a thing as mouse-killing (though not as a special legal category, of course). According to Locke, anyway, all these classifications and subclassifications are there to be made, but the ones we actually make will depend first upon our ability to frame ideas, and second upon an interest- and/or environment-driven tendency to fix attention on some combinations of qualities rather than others. Indeed the snow example if anything suggests the opposite of relativism: it suggests that if the world is insistent enough it will force itself upon us. To take the relativistic line would be to say that Western city-dwellers with central heating are as knowledgeable when it comes to snow as Inuits: and this is clearly indefensible.[3]

However this may be, the ideas which are combined into mode-ideas can also be combined with the idea of substance, which for Locke is *not* a partial reflection of our interests and convenience. We may or may not find it important to recognise one or more kinds of lead (lead-from-a-church-roof, lead-mined-by-child-labour), but all substances, says Locke, are 'distinct particular things subsisting by themselves' (E:II,xii,6). In the first instance he is describing what he takes to be our attitude to or beliefs about such things. Although we may be brought to accept that our noticing of some modes rather than others is as much a reflection of our interests as of what is there to be noticed, this is not so where substances are concerned. Rather, he says, we suppose that each particular substance such as lead or gold not only has the sensory qualities that we perceive it to have but also 'some substratum wherein they do exist', a 'supposed, but unknown, support of these qualities, which we imagine cannot subsist . . . without something to support them'. Not only this, but we suppose that these observable qualities 'flow from the particular internal constitution or unknown essence of that substance' (E:II,xxiii,1–3).

This is not immediately pellucid. The mention of unknown substrata brings to mind the distinction between a thing and its properties, and invites us to abstract away the properties and try to consider the propertyless thing itself about which, of course, nothing can be said (for that would be to ascribe a property to it) or, hence, known. This aspect of what Locke says is not worth discussing here: he is, in part, more entangled with scholastic doctrine than his official aims permit. We could also wonder how an Empiricist can talk so breezily about our having such an idea as that of substance, even though he does call it 'obscure and relative' (E:II,xxiii,3). But since our interests are not epistemological, we shall leave this too (the point will resurface briefly in chapter VII). Things get more relevant to our concerns when we note Locke's mention of 'internal constitution' and of the idea that the sensible qualities of a substance 'flow from' it. This, as we shall see in subsequent sections, involves the mechanistic science that Locke was at pains to promote, and also other key doctrines which will be crucial to the argument of Part Two. But before these matters are explained, we first have to consider how they link up with Locke's account of language.

2 Idea, word, object

Descartes, we saw, supposed there to be an essential link between the potential for using language meaningfully, and having any mental characteristics at all. Locke, although willing to allow lesser forms of sensibility, e.g. to cockles and oysters, effectively took over the point as it bears on our own, more sophisticated, minds. In so doing he developed a fairly comprehensive and initially appealing account of language which is central to the history we are concerned with.

Like Descartes, he notes that the mere production of articulate sounds is not itself meaningful use of language, since even parrots can utter words. A further condition is that words should be used to *signify ideas*. More,

> *words, in their primary or immediate signification, stand for nothing but the* ideas *in the mind of him that uses them.* (E:III,ii,2)

Ideas are fundamental, but since a person's ideas are 'within his own breast, invisible and hidden from others', and there is a need to communicate, language has developed. Locke here takes over Descartes' doctrine of the primacy of thought over talk. The undoubted use of language to communicate, however, leads him to make several further important observations. Once an association between a word and an idea has been set up, the word can bring the idea to mind in just the same way as can the idea's original cause. Thus once the word 'cat' has been made to signify the cat-idea, my use of that word can bring a cat-idea into your mind in the same way that your seeing a cat might. This is obviously necessary if language is to serve as an instrument of communication but, Locke continues, two further things are required. The first is that our ideas have to *match*. Locke's view is strongly individualistic, in that the principal move from thought to talk is something which speakers must accomplish for themselves. If I am to utter a word meaningfully, then *I* have to set it up to signify an idea: without this, I simply make a meaningless sound. And the same goes for you. There is thus a substantial assumption made every time we use language to try to communicate: we have to assume that we have both given the same word the same type of idea to signify. If not, we shall simply be at cross purposes:

> unless a man's words excite the same *ideas* in the hearer which he makes them stand for in speaking, he does not speak intelligibly. (E:III,ii,8)

Locke discusses with some relish the various sources and types of misfortune that lurk in this situation, but he does note that the normal assumption is that a word has a 'common acceptation', that is, is used by each person who speaks the language to signify the same type of idea. Call this the Matching assumption. The second component of successful communication mentioned by Locke exploits the fact, noted in chapter I, that ideas can represent things beyond themselves. Thus he remarks that those who use words 'often suppose their words to stand also for the reality of things' (E:III,ii,4). The word 'cat' primarily signifies (for me) my cat-idea and (for you) your cat-idea, but since these ideas represent cats, so, derivatively, does the word. Call this the Representational assumption.

Locke then rather surprisingly says that giving words these extra functions, over and above that of serving for each to signify his or her own ideas, 'is a perverting the use of words, and brings unavoidable obscurity and confusion into their signification' (E:III,ii,5). He presumably has in mind the scope for error and mismatch that these two further functions introduce, but it is nevertheless easy to see that unless the Matching and Representational assumptions hold, language could not facilitate communication at all. Locke himself says that without Representation, 'men would . . . talk barely of their own imaginations' (*ibid.*), his thought no doubt being that unless we make the Representational assumption, my use of 'cat' will at best indicate that I have a cat-idea in mind. However, since the only way it could do this, on Locke's account, is by bringing cat-ideas to the minds of my audience, the reference 'to the reality of things' would thereby be made, for these ideas themselves are representational. As soon as the cat-idea is in mind, cats are in the frame. And this is just as well, since it is hard to see how, on Locke's account, we could gain any confidence in the Matching assumption without first attending to the matters raised by the Representational assumption. Since your ideas are 'invisible, and hidden from others', it seems that the best chance I have of knowing which idea you have made 'cat' signify is by seeing what prompts your use of the word. If (roughly) cats or cat-like things, and nothing else, cause you to say 'cat', then I can have some confidence in the Matching assumption: otherwise, surely, not (we shall discuss a possible alternative in a moment). But unless I can make the Matching assumption, I can have no reason to suppose that we can communicate. And without that there can be no intellectual fellowship, no common stock of knowledge, no real intimacy, no communal projects save the most rudimentary. Thus the Matching assumption, far from merely introducing obscurity and confusion, is essential for human life as we know it; and the Representational assumption, far from perverse, seems to be needed to ground Matching.

It is true that Locke countenances another way of finding out which idea someone's use of a word signifies, namely by asking for a definition. He allows that words signifying complex ideas can be defined, and that to do this one simply spells out the component ideas. Thus if my cat-idea involves the ideas *furry, smallish, smarmy, treacherous, animal*, then I can define 'cat' by uttering the words I use to signify the component ideas. Relatedly, then, he allows two ways in which a word might be learned: one either receives a definition, or suffers exposure to the thing which the word represents. However, if your definition of 'cat' is to indicate to me which idea you use the word to signify, then of course two things have to hold. First, I have to understand the words of the definition (i.e. associate ideas of my own with them), and second, *Matching has to hold with respect to these*. Otherwise the definition will either mean nothing to me, or will put us at cross purposes. But what could justify me in assuming Matching here? Again, there are only two ways: either I check to see what prompts your uses of the words of the definition, or I ask for them to be defined, and then the problem goes on. But it cannot go on for ever, since Locke's view is that all complex ideas can be eventually broken down into simple ones, and that words signifying simple ideas cannot be defined because the ideas cannot be broken down any further. One can only acquire simple ideas by having them in experience (recall Locke's Empiricism), and hence the only way of learning the meaning of a word which signifies a simple idea is by experiencing the idea and associating the word with it. It follows that, ultimately, the only indication I can have that my ideas match yours is by noting the representational character of at least some of your words, that is by seeing what prompts them.

This theory of communication will be considered further in the following chapter. In his related discussion of definitions Locke takes up the matter of *essence*. This is partly because some such notion figures in the scholastic philosophy and Aristotelian science of the day. Locke's talk of essence is thus largely deflationary: his main aim is to urge that the essence of something, say matricide or lead, is simply the complex idea which the definitions of the words 'matricide' or 'lead' would spell out, rather than some special kind of nature in matricide or lead themselves. However, his effort here is compromised by his concession that we do have some dim idea of substance (see the previous section). Hence he comes to distinguish two kinds of essence. One, the *nominal essence*, is

> nothing but that ... *idea* which the general ... name stands for ... *Between the nominal essence and the name* there is so *near a connexion* that the name of any sort of things cannot be attributed to any particular being but what has this *essence*, whereby it answers to the ... *idea* whereof the name is the sign. (E:III,iii,15–16)

Thus assuming that the definitions of 'matricide' and 'lead' respectively are 'mother-killing' and 'soft heavy dull whitish metal', one would give the nominal essence of these things by giving these definitions. 'Essence' is thought appropriate, not for Aristotelian reasons, but because given that these are correct definitions, any matricide is by definition, that is necessarily or essentially, a killing of a mother; and any piece of lead is similarly necessarily metal.

The other kind of essence distinguished by Locke is *real essence*, which is

> the being of anything whereby it is what it is. And thus the real internal, but generally (in substances) unknown, constitution of things, whereon their discoverable qualities depend, may be called their [real] *essence*. (E:III,iii,15)

Locke does not deny that modes have real essence, but he asserts that real essence *just is* nominal essence in these cases. This is on account of his view that modes are partly creatures of the mind, or ways of classifying things which we employ in accordance with our interests, and which are no better (or worse) than certain other available ways of classifying that we do not go in for. All there is to being an example of, say, matricide, is answering to the associated idea, that is, fitting the definition or having the appropriate nominal essence. This also, then, is the real essence of matricide, its 'being ... whereby it is what it is'. The two kinds of essence come apart in the case of substances, however, since there is supposed to be 'more' to being lead than simply answering the definition and thus having the nominal essence.

Being lead also involves having the appropriate inner constitution, but this, being unknown (in Locke's day), is obviously not
specified by the definition, so is not the nominal essence. It is a
distinct real essence. Interestingly, however, Locke still argues
that it is nominal essence which ultimately determines whether
something is a sample of a given substance:

> It is impossible . . . that anything should determine the sorts
> of things which we rank under general names but that *idea*
> which that name is designed as a mark for; which is that,
> as has been shown, which we call the *nominal essence.*
> (E:III,vi,7)

Something is lead if and only if it answers to our definition of
lead, that is, has the nominal essence, regardless of how similar
to or dissimilar from other samples of lead it may be as far as
its internal constitution goes. As we shall see in chapter VII, an
attack on this claim is an intimate component of what is arguably
the most important recent development in the philosophies of
mind and language.

3 Ideas and resemblances

We turn now to Locke's account of what ideas actually are. In
many places, he speaks of ideas as entities, the effects in our
minds of things in our material surroundings. As such, they presumably have some properties or features of their own which
make them what they are: for example, they must have some
feature which the mind notices, since we have seen that ideas
are objects of awareness, or phenomenological objects. But one
property which at least some ideas also have is that they are
representational, that is they purport to be *of* other things: thus
a Paris-idea, whatever it is like in itself, represents, or purports
to be an idea of, Paris. Here Descartes had distinguished between
the 'formal' and the 'objective' reality of an idea, where an idea's
formal reality comprises the intrinsic features it has in itself, and
its objective reality is its representational aspect (PWDii: 28–9;
cf. the alleged ambiguity of 'idea' mentioned in chapter I, section
1, note 2). The most crucial question which any theorist of ideas
has to address is what these two kinds of reality consist in. What
are ideas in themselves, and how do they represent things?

37

There is more than one thread running through Locke's answers to these questions, and they do not seem to make up a coherent whole. But one isolable and immensely influential feature is that he tends to gravitate to the doctrine that ideas in themselves are (mental) *images or pictures*, and that in representing things they purport to *resemble* them. And this view is seductive, not least because we can apparently easily make sense of the distinction between intrinsic and representational properties by thinking of paintings. A painting in itself is (say) a piece of canvas covered with patches of pigment. Someone could appreciate this about a painting without having any clue about pictorial representation. However, someone clued up on representation may also be able to tell that the painting is a cat-painting, that is, purports to represent a cat. And one explanation of this might be that the shapes and colours on the canvas bear a resemblance to those of cats. (Note too that one might see something as a cat-representation without having much clue as to its nature in itself.) As just mentioned, there are other strands in Locke's account of representation which are inimical to this imagist interpretation: but we shall see good, independent reasons for rejecting them as claims about representation.

Locke calls the view that ideas are images 'as ... in a mirror' a view that 'it would by most men be judged very extravagant if one should say otherwise' (E:II,viii,16). Descartes, more cautiously, attributes the view to (scholastic) 'philosophers', acknowledging that it is encouraged by appreciating 'how easily a picture can stimulate our mind to conceive the objects depicted in it' (PWDi: 165). They then both proceed to attack the view with strong arguments. First, *words* such as 'cat' also represent cats, but while one can make sense of the idea of (a use of a) word as having intrinsic properties (e.g. it is a straggle of ink, or a sound), it is not true that words usually resemble the things they represent (PWDi: 81, 165; E:II,i,7). 'Cuckoo' perhaps sounds (but does not look) like the corresponding bird, and at a pinch one might say the same about 'duck' (imagine saying it with a heavy cold). But these are unusual exceptions. Second, even where images are concerned, talk of resemblance is less straightforward than it might seem. Here are Descartes' excellent observations:

You can see this in the case of engravings: consisting simply

38

of a little ink placed here and there on a piece of paper, they represent to us forests, towns, people and even battles and storms; and although they make us think of countless different qualities in those objects, it is only in respect of shape that there is any real resemblance. And even this resemblance is very imperfect, since engravings represent to us bodies of varying relief and depth on a surface which is entirely flat. Moreover, in accordance with the rules of perspective, they often represent circles by ovals . . . squares by rhombuses . . . and similarly for other shapes. (PWDi: 165)

These objections are strong (for replies of sorts see section 5), and one would expect their appearance to presage alternative accounts of the nature of ideas and of their representational powers. But this is not quite what happens. Descartes acknowledges that he is left with the problem of explaining how inputs to the senses can put us in mind 'of all the various qualities of the objects to which they correspond' (PWDi: 166), but goes no further. Moreover, he occasionally seems to suggest that he is only meaning to attack the claim that ideas *must* resemble what they are ideas of, rather than the claim that they *can* (PWDi: 82). Locke, on the other hand, *as well as* offering an alternative (for which, see below), is soon found claiming that the ideas of 'solidity, extension, figure, motion or rest, and number' (E:II,vii,9)

> *are resemblances* of them, and their patterns do really exist in the bodies themselves . . . a circle or square are the same, whether in *idea* or existence, in the mind or in the [material world]. (E:II,vii,16–18)

So what is going on? Why introduce an attractive claim, attack it cogently, then rather than simply produce an alternative go on apparently to embrace the principle of it?

4 Primary and secondary

A large part of the answer is that both philosophers are striving to accommodate the science of their day, and in more than one way. One thing this involves them in doing, as we have already noted, is opposing various traditional scholastic doctrines and elements of Aristotelian science. One such is an account of representation which derives from Aristotle. On this view, roughly, an individual is, say, a cat because it participates in the form *Cathood*, which is supposed to be what all cats have in common as cats. Analogously, when an individual thinks about cats, this is because his or her mind takes on that same form of *Cathood*. The claim is not that in thinking about a cat one becomes a cat, of course. Rather, there are supposed to be two different ways of taking on the form of a cat – one is by *being a cat*, the other is by *representing a cat* – and this gives an obvious sense in which what is represented resembles what is doing the representing. Now one of the themes of the new science promoted by Descartes and Locke was that such doctrines explain nothing, and are to be replaced by mechanistic accounts. So to some extent, their hostility to accounting for representation in terms of resemblance reflects this anti-scholastic orientation.

But this is not the end of the matter. For as we shall see, they need something like the resemblance doctrine, in a suitably non-Aristotelian version, if the theory of ideas is going to look even passingly plausible: and this explains why Locke, at least, tended to persist with it. And here lies a further difficulty, since they both considered that mechanistic science had shown that not *all* ideas resemble the things they are ideas of, even in the non-Aristotelian version. Hence, independently of their opposition to Aristotelian science, they need to show that ideas do not *have to* resemble their objects without necessarily abandoning the claim that they *can*.

In his account, Locke distinguishes qualities, which are had by material objects, from our ideas of these qualities, which are in our minds (E:II,viii,8). Thus there is the roundness of the plate and there is my idea of the plate's roundness. He is very sloppy in observing this official distinction, often speaking of an idea as being both in the mind and in the object represented: and no doubt this is due to some residual influence of the Aristotelian doctrine of forms which he officially rejected.[4] He also distinguishes between qualities that are really 'in' objects, that is intrinsic qualities, from those which are not. Neutrally, the distinction can be illustrated by the distinction between *having two legs* and *being a spouse*. Both might be true of some individual X. But being a spouse, unlike having two legs, involves someone other than X, namely the person to whom X is married. Thus although X could in principle have two legs even if nothing else existed, X could not be a spouse under those circumstances: someone can only be a spouse if someone else who they are married to also exists. Thus *having two legs* is an intrinsic quality, whereas *being a spouse* is not.

Locke's claim that our ideas of qualities such as shape do resemble the qualities themselves is made in the context of a claim that some ideas do not so resemble any quality in an object. This is his way of making the celebrated distinction between primary and secondary qualities:

> These I call *original* or *primary* qualities of body; which I think we may observe to produce simple ideas in us, viz. solidity, extension, figure, motion or rest, and number ... Secondly, qualities which in truth are nothing in the objects themselves but powers to produce various sensations in us, ... as colours, sounds, tastes etc ... I call *secondary qualities*. (E:II,viii,9–10: cf. Descartes at PWDi: 216–19)

Here we shall not be concerned with this distinction, nor with the different sorts of arguments which may be provided for it.[5] The main aim is to see the light which Locke's handling of the doctrine sheds on the theory of ideas. As Locke himself points out, his making of the distinction comes in the midst of a 'little excursion into natural philosophy [i.e. mechanistic science]' (E:II,viii,22). What is driving him is the (then) new idea that everything about a material object can be explained in mechanistic terms: for Locke, this meant that an object's being able to cause the effects it has on other things, including human minds, is entirely explainable in terms of (a) its primary qualities and (b) the 'bulk, texture and figure of [its] minute parts ... on which [its] real constitution ... depend[s]' (E:II,xxii,8). Thus the squareness of the peg explains why it will not fit into the round hole. The collisions between (as we would say) the molecules of a gas and the walls of its container explain why the gas exerts pressure. Similarly, according to Locke, the squareness of the peg explains why we see it as square, since it causes in us an idea of squareness which resembles that quality. But, he goes on, there is no reason to suppose that resemblance always obtains between mechanistic causes and their effects; (1) not in general, and (2) *not even when the effects are ideas in minds.*

He illustrates the general point with the example of the sun's power to melt a piece of wax. He says that

> when we consider the sun in reference to wax, which it melts . . . , we look upon the . . . softness produced in the wax not as [a quality] in the sun but [an effect] produced by *powers* in it. (E:II,vii,24)

The sun does not need to be soft in order to make the wax soft. The stone may shatter the vase without itself being shattered. So there is obviously no general requirement for effects to resemble their causes. Locke calls things like the sun's power to melt wax secondary qualities, implying that they are not straightforwardly intrinsic to the things which have them, but can only be understood in terms of the things upon which the powers are exercised.

What of the particular point about *ideas* not having to resemble their causes? Again, this can be established relatively easily, as both Locke and Descartes are aware (E:II,viii,16; PWDi: 82). A nettle may sting me, but there is no reason to suppose that the sting I feel resembles anything in the nettle. In particular, the cause of the sting – some transfer of a substance from spines on the nettle to the surface of my skin – does not at all resemble the stinging feeling: indeed, it hardly makes sense to suppose such a thing. Given that the stinging feeling is an idea, then, it follows that ideas do not have to resemble their causes.

Armed with these points, Locke then makes the crucial move in his argument for the primary–secondary quality distinction. He claims that ideas of colours, tastes, smells, etc. *are like stinging feelings in precisely this respect*: they do not resemble their causes in the objects. Rather, these causes are best regarded as powers to produce the appropriate ideas in us, powers in the objects which derive from the primary qualities of their parts, and not from their having anything in them which, for example, our colour-ideas resemble. This is the most debated aspect of his way of making the distinction, and in particular three questions immediately suggest themselves:

1 Why suppose that ideas of primary qualities *do* resemble the qualities?
2 Why suppose that the ideas of secondary qualities do not?
3 What precise role in the argument is the example of stinging feelings supposed to play?

In considering these questions we shall see that there is a major tension in Locke's position whose only real relief can come from the doctrine that at least some ideas are images in the mind, and that representation is to be linked to the notion of resemblance.

5 Resemblance, representation, sensation

The first question might look like Cartesian scepticism: why suppose that there are any objects *at all* causing our ideas, rather than Descartes' demon? But although Locke does face that question, this is not the present point. Suppose we grant him that there are material objects with primary qualities in our surroundings. Why say that our ideas of these qualities *resemble* them? It is not as though Locke has been able to put an idea of squareness and a square object side by side, and note the resemblance. So why claim resemblance? One thought now is to suppose that he does not need to mean 'resemblance' literally: all he needs to mean is that our square-ideas represent things as being square, and things *really can be square*. Taken this way, his talk of resemblance is just quaint or metaphorical talk of representational fidelity, and ideas do not have to be thought of as images. Indeed, some commentators go so far as to claim that Locke did not altogether consider ideas to be entities of any kind, and that when he spoke of *having a square-idea*, he often merely meant *being in a square-representing state of mind*, with no intended suggestion that any idea was literally in or before the mind. We shall return to this claim: for now, we should note that if Locke's talk of resemblance is not taken literally, then it is so far left completely unexplained what it is to represent something faithfully as being square (or anything else).

This construal of his talk of resemblance as metaphorical certainly fits some of what Locke says about secondary qualities. His official view is that objects do have secondary qualities, but because these qualities are best regarded as powers rather than intrinsic qualities, there is an element of error in our common-sense view of them. We generally suppose that our ideas of them are caused by intrinsic qualities rather than powers:

> We are apt to imagine that our *ideas* [of secondary qualities] are resemblances of something in the objects, and not the effects of certain powers placed in the modification of their primary qualities, with which primary qualities the *ideas* produced in us have no resemblance. (E:II,viii,25)

Here he draws a distinction between such things as the sun's power to melt the wax, and the tomato's redness. Our experience of the former does not, according to Locke, represent it as intrinsic to the sun; but our experience of the latter does represent it as intrinsic to the tomato. And he is absolutely right as far as this second point is concerned: in our experience, the redness is as much 'in' the tomato as is the shape it colours in. For this reason, Locke calls things like the sun's power *secondary qualities mediately perceivable*, and things like the tomato's redness *secondary qualities immediately perceivable* (E:II,viii,26). And if he is right that colour is really a power, then he is right that our ordinary colour-ideas do not absolutely faithfully represent their causes. Then his talk of their failing to resemble their causes can be construed, in accordance with the suggestion of the previous paragraph, merely as metaphorical talk of this lack of representational fidelity. Ideas of immediately perceivable secondary qualities represent them as intrinsic, but they are not intrinsic (I shall henceforth omit the qualification 'immediately perceivable'). And we can suppose him to base this last claim, in answer to the second question at the end of the previous section, on the thought that the best *mechanistic explanation* of how objects act on us delivers the conclusion that colour, sound, taste, etc. are powers which objects have, derived from the primary qualities of their parts, and not intrinsic qualities as our experience represents them to be.

So far so good, it may seem. But what we have said is already at odds with what Locke elsewhere says about representation and resemblance. For example:

> Our *simple* ideas ... all agree to the reality of things, not that they are all of them the images ... of what does

exist; ... though whiteness and coldness are no more in snow than pain is, yet those *ideas* of whiteness and coldness, pain, etc, being in us the effects of powers in things without us ... are real *ideas* in us whereby we distinguish the qualities ... in things themselves. (E:II,xxx,2)

Here representing or 'agreeing to the reality of things' is carefully *distinguished* from resembling, which is said not be be necessary for such agreement. So in saying that ideas of primary qualities do resemble things, whereas ideas of secondary qualities do not, Locke cannot simply be construed as speaking quaintly or metaphorically about representational fidelity. Worse, the talk of images and resemblance in the above passage seems to be intended quite literally. So what does Locke take representational fidelity to consist in? He continues the above passage thus, giving an unequivocal answer:

these several appearances being designed to be the marks whereby we are to know and distinguish things which we have to do with, our *ideas* do as well serve us to that purpose and are as real distinguishing characters, whether they be only constant effects or else exact resemblances of something in the things themselves: the reality lying in that steady correspondence they have with the distinct constitutions of real beings ... it suffices that they are constantly produced by them. (*Ibid.*)

This is a causal theory of representation: an idea serves to represent a quality of something if it is 'steadily' or 'constantly' produced by it. Thus even ideas of secondary qualities 'agree to the reality of things', that is faithfully or truly represent the powers that cause them, and a literal interpretation of Locke's claim that they simply do not *resemble* the qualities seems unavoidable. On this way of taking him, Locke's account goes as follows. An idea of a round, red object is an image which depicts it as round and red, as a painting might. But the object is in fact a dense colourless circular mass of particles (this thought is quite coherent: recall that there actually are such things, for example panes of glass). Light reflected by the object ultimately transmits the roundness to the eye, and the nerves take it on to the brain and into the mind, where it is faithfully depicted. At the same time, the disturbance in the reflected light caused by the surface distribution of the colourless particles causes a certain disturbance in the messages transmitted through the brain, which leads to the surface being depicted as red in the mind. But this, although constituting a reliable sign of a power in the object, is unfaithful depiction, an artefact of the whole system of transmission, rather than a simulacrum of the object's surface. In case this sounds unlikely, recall that not all effects resemble their causes (e.g. the softness in the wax and the sun), not even when the effects are in the mind and can serve as signs of their causes (e.g. the stinging feeling and the nettle).

Seeing the matter thus helps us to appreciate why Locke should say this without apology:

> For, methinks, the *understanding* is not so much unlike a closet wholly shut from light, with only some little opening left, to let in external visible resemblances, or *ideas* of things without; would the pictures coming into such a dark room but stay there, and lie so orderly as to be found upon occasion, it would very much resemble the understanding of a man in reference to all objects of sight and the *ideas* of them. (E:II,xi,17)

Note here the comparison between ideas and pictures. Note too the apparent commitment to the doctrine that the mind is self-contained with respect to the material world. This of course raises the epistemological question whether Locke is entitled to say that our ideas faithfully represent their causes, either by resembling them or otherwise: but that is another matter. Still, we mentioned earlier that some commentators deny that Locke thought of ideas as entities of any kind. This is very hard to square with the aspects of his view adduced in the foregoing. But one motivation for the claim seems to be that otherwise Locke is condemned to Cartesian scepticism, since the mind has to be thought of as separated from the material world by a 'screen' of ideas. Thus the editor of an influential collection of essays on Locke suggests that

> [although, perhaps] Locke never wholly freed himself from the notion that ideas of sense might be ... entities, ... he was certainly not concerned to promote this view and never

seriously doubted that sensation does provide us with every assurance we could wish of the existence of outward things. (LHU: 6–7)

This seems to deconstruct as follows: although there are places where Locke regards ideas as entities, and thus invites scepticism, his overall view contains a different conception of ideas which makes the sceptical threat less pressing. But this is a confusion. What condemns Locke to Cartesian scepticism is not the doctrine that ideas are pictures or even entities, but the background suggestion that the mind is self-contained with respect to the material world. If my experience now can be the way it is in itself no matter what state the material world may be in (if, indeed, there is a material world), then it matters not to the sceptical point whether we think of the experience as literally an awareness of a picture of a word-processor, or whether we think of it as a word-processor-representing-type experience. Either way, if someone claims that one can have such experiences independently of the nature or even existence of one's surroundings, then they are already on the high road to Cartesian scepticism. Argument over whether Lockean ideas are entities is completely irrelevant to this, and what is already a somewhat forced reading of Locke in fact requires him to be prey to this confusion also.

It is worth noting that there are further, phenomenological reasons why the theory of ideas proceeds more smoothly if representational ideas are construed as images. Both Descartes and Locke treat the mind as a predominantly conscious arena: mental operations are explained as manipulations of ideas, and the basic relation between a mind and an idea is perception or awareness. Thus Locke:

> it is altogether as intelligible to say that a body is extended without parts, as that anything *thinks without being conscious of it* or perceiving that it does so ... Consciousness is the perception of what passes in a man's own mind. (E:II,i,19)

It is true that he is using 'thinks' broadly, to cover any kind of mental operation at all, but the fact remains that this also embraces the making of judgements, the framing of opinions about this or that. And, first, it is right that one should make room for this: thoughts and opinions can run through the mind and be as accessible to consciousness as, say, the sting of a nettle or the look of a tomato. It is highly debatable whether all mental characteristics can be explained in terms of consciousness, but still, room has to be left for conscious judging and opining. Now if making a judgement is construed as performing a certain operation on an idea; and if an idea is construed as an image available to awareness; then there is a model here of how judging can be a conscious event. Similarly, there is a model of how understanding, which is a prerequisite of judging, can feature in consciousness. To understand the elements of a judgement just is to contemplate the relevant aspects of the image involved.

Second, similar points can be made about communication, as we shall see in much more detail in chapter VI. Using language as a method of communication is itself a predominantly conscious enterprise. I am normally conscious of what I am saying to you as I speak, and when you understand what I have said to you that is because you were conscious of the same thing. Communicated meaning has, in this sense, a phenomenological dimension. Locke's account of this, mentioned in section 2 above, involves the claim that words can come to excite ideas in the mind just as the things the words apply to can: your saying 'cat' can make a cat-idea appear in my mind just as a perceptual encounter with a cat might. An obvious merit of this account is that since the ideas excited in my mind by your words are phenomenological objects, our grasp of what you say comes out as a conscious episode, as it should.

Third, recall the objection that words and engravings can represent things without resembling them, or at least (in the case of engravings) without resembling them all that much. Locke touches on this problem as it afflicts words, when he acknowledges that the connection between words and ideas is entirely arbitrary. For we might add that much the same goes for the connection between words and things: 'carpet' is no better or worse fitted to pick out types of floor-covering than is *'alfombra'*. English speakers do it one way, Spanish speakers another, and that is all there is to it, notwithstanding exceptions such as 'cuckoo' which were noted in section 3. Still, this leaves it unexplained how these arbitrary associations between words and things can amount to meaning, that is make the use of words an expression of understanding and a way of representing the world. Locke's implicit reply is that the nature of ideas yields the necessary explanation: both 'carpet' and '*alfombra*' signify the same idea, and these words pick out the things they do because of this association. Now this clearly would be no explanation at all if the association between idea and object were just as mysterious and arbitrary. On the other hand, if it is assumed that the ideas unproblematically represent the things by resembling them, then an explanation of sorts is in sight: words (indirectly) represent by signifying ideas which (directly) represent by resembling. Note too that a similar treatment might be offered of Descartes' sketchy engravings if it is supposed that ideas are very detailed images. And given the richness of experience, surely this supposition could be justified.

It may be replied that this last matter could be explained in terms of Locke's causal theory of representation: and similarly, that the previous phenomenological points only require ideas to be sensations like pains, rather than images. However, this actually serves to highlight a grave weakness in Locke's overall theory of representation. He is quite wrong to assimilate ideas to sensations, and/or explain representation simply in terms of causal correlation (here we take up the third question raised at the end of the previous section). For ideas of primary and of secondary qualities have representational properties, as well as intrinsic properties of their own. But stinging feelings and other bodily sensations do not have representational properties. They have intrinsic properties, such as feeling a certain way, which the mind is able to notice. But they do not in their nature represent things beyond themselves. Locke partly registers this by calling things like stinging feelings 'bare effects of power' – they are *merely* effects in us caused by something beyond. In this they are no different from, say, ulcers caused by acid, except that ulcers need not feel like anything whereas feelings, presumably, always will (and feelings would have an immaterial aspect according to Cartesian Dualism). But neither feelings nor ulcers intrinsically represent something beyond themselves. Against this, an idea of redness cannot be regarded as a 'bare effect of power', since even if we accept that secondary qualities are powers rather than intrinsic qualities, this does not change the idea of redness into something more like a feeling or an ulcer. It still (misleadingly) represents its cause by *purporting* to resemble it; a stinging feeling, on the other hand, does not even *purport* to represent or resemble its cause.

The seriousness of the problem here can be missed because of loose talk about representation. Thus Descartes speaks of the tendency of words and (ordinary) pictures to 'stimulate our minds to conceive [of] objects' (PWDi: 165): either occurrences of the word 'cat' or a few lines in an engraving can put us in mind of cats. Talk like this is dangerous because the next thought is that, obviously, feelings and ulcers can also put us in mind of what we suppose to be their causes. Feeling the sting I think 'Nettles'; feeling the ulcer I think 'Too much acid'. But this should not obscure the fact that ideas of redness are representational in themselves, whereas any association between feelings or ulcers and what they put us in mind of is thoroughly incidental. When one is having an experience of a red, round object, the object is 'there' in the experience, and both shape and colour figure as 'in' the object. The sting, on the other hand, does not figure in experience as a quality 'in' a nettle, partly because the nettle itself is not represented as being 'there' in the experienced sting. To repeat, it is no part of an ulcer's or a feeling's nature to represent its cause, whereas it is part of an idea of redness's nature that it should represent. It is true that one finds it extremely difficult to separate the stinging feeling from the thought 'Nettles', and in this sense the stinging feeling is, for us, something like a dim sign of nettles. Nevertheless, we can imagine having (or other creatures having) a sensation like that without there being any thought attached that it came from some cause beyond the skin, let alone from a nettle. But try to imagine your state of seeing something red being experienced not as a (possibly delusory) presentation of a coloured object. This makes no sense. As remarked above, the redness of the tomato figures in experience as as much an aspect of the tomato as does the tomato's shape: neither shape nor colour is experienced as an effect in us. But the sting we get from the nettle really does figure in experience as an effect in us.[6]

This crucial difference is captured within the theory of ideas if instead of simply defining representation in terms of cause, one links it to the notion of resemblance. Then the present difference between an idea of red and a stinging feeling would be explained in terms of the fact that the former, but not the latter, figures in an image-like depiction. In this way, we get some kind of grip on the fact that whereas the idea of red at least *purports* to represent a quality of an object, just like an idea of shape, the stinging feeling does not.[7]

To reinforce the differences, note that I might (blindfolded) bite an apple and, feeling a jarring sensation in my teeth, think 'Green'. Here the sensation in my teeth gives me a certain thought about the apple, a thought involving (according to Locke) an idea which represents it as green. Having this thought may or may not make me think about something else: but either way, the idea of greenness is here already figuring in thought, and not just as a stimulus to thought. Still, this example suggests a possible way forward for one out to defend Locke's causal theory. Perhaps in seeing something as red the following happens: there occurs in my mind a 'bare effect of power' which we may as well call a sensation of red; and I then swiftly, and without noticing, form the judgement that the thing is red. This suggestion might seem promising with regard to certain other secondary qualities. In learning by touch that a thing is cool, I certainly do feel sensations in the surface of my body, and these feelings contribute to my judging as I do. Similarly, in tasting beer I enjoy exquisite sensations on my tongue and on the sides of my mouth. Moreover, the mooted pattern of explanation might seem to be suggested by the following claim made by Locke:

> the *ideas we receive by sensation are often* in grown people *altered by the judgement*, without our taking notice of it. When we set before our eyes a round globe of any uniform colour ... it is certain that the *idea* thereby imprinted in the mind is of a flat circle, variously shadowed, with several degrees of light and brightness coming to our eyes. But we having, by use, been accustomed to perceive what kind of appearance convex bodies are wont to make in us, ... the judgement presently, by an habitual custom, alters the appearances into their causes. (E:II,ix,8)

But in fact, there is no way forward here: the previous paragraph is a hopeless tangle. First, this passage from Locke describes how judgement might somehow eclipse the incoming idea of a flat circle with that of a globe. But the incoming circle-idea is itself representational, not a 'bare effect of power', not a sensation. To suppose it is would be plainly absurd: try to imagine a (visual) circle-idea which, like a pain, is experienced merely as an effect in the body.[8] Second, if the alleged incoming sensation of red produces the judgement that the object is red, then this judgement itself embraces a representational idea of redness, whose intrinsic representational nature thus still needs to be explained. The positing of the sensation of red achieves nothing. (And in fact the same goes with respect to touch and taste. Even if I experience 'bare effects of power' on my skin and in my mouth, these episodes also lead me to make judgements – 'It's cool', 'That's hoppy' – which embrace representational secondary-quality ideas.) Third, the posit is anyway just as absurd as that of a sensation of circularity. Look at a round, red object. Try to make sense of the suggestion that this experience contains a component associated with the redness which is like a feeling, a bare effect of power, but no such component associated with the roundness. Finally, it may well be the case that when something causes me to see it as red, it has all kinds of effects on my body (e.g. in my optic nerve and my brain) which do not themselves represent the object as red, but which are causally responsible for my ultimately so representing it. Even Descartes, as we have seen, accepted that the nature of the ideas caused in the mind depends on what happens in the brain and nerves. Call these non-representational effects 'sensations of red' if you like. But note that an exactly parallel line of reasoning will give you sensations of circularity too, and take care not to call these sensations 'ideas'. For ideas are objects of the mind's immediate awareness, whereas these bodily goings-on are not.

In sum, then, there are weighty reasons, both points of interpretation and points of independent substance, for keeping the imagist elements of Locke's theory in full view. The main point here should not be misunderstood. It is not that the imagist theory of ideas is *correct*: on the contrary, as we shall see in chapters IV and VI, it is wholly mistaken, not just in detail but in practically all fundamentals. The point, rather, is twofold: first, that Locke's overall account hangs together much more coherently if his talk of resemblance is taken literally (and his causal conception of representation enriched with the notion of resemblance); and second, that the theory of ideas has tended – rightly – to be most influential when it has been so construed.

6 Mind and language

That, then, was Locke's theory of ideas and his account of language and representation. Two final comments are in order. The first is that although these views are intended to interlock in the ways explained, with the theory of ideas underpinning the ability to understand and communicate with language, there is a curious conceptual gap. Locke's expansive talk of representational links between words and things, the matching of ideas had by different speakers, and so on, seems hollow when one recalls his stifling conception of the mind. Even the conviction that there are other people to talk to (indeed, the conviction that I have a mouth to talk with) is vulnerable given the doctrine that the mind is self-contained with respect to the surrounding world. On the one hand, as soon as language comes up for discussion, the need is to talk of public mechanisms, shared knowledge, common surroundings. On the other, the talk of the mind by both Descartes and Locke has been unreservedly first-personal and individualistic. Yet the two issues can hardly be prised apart, given, as both philosophers rightly stress, the tight connection between our mental capacities and our potential for using language. Nor is the problem simply the epistemological one – how can Descartes and Locke know all this about other people and the world, given their claim that it is all Exterior? The problem is essentially a matter of the kind of resources which seem to be needed to deal with two such apparently different, yet intimately related, matters as thought and talk. As we shall see, this severe problem has gone on resonating through philosophy long after the breaking of the Descartes-induced preoccupation with epistemology.

The second comment is that even if Locke's official view is a form of Cartesian Dualism, the immaterialist aspect of it is inessential. Much of what he says about ideas, concerning the distinctions among them and their connections with linguistic ability, can still be said by someone who believes them to be material structures in the brain. It is true that this makes it difficult to go on thinking of them as (coloured) images, particularly if Locke is right that material things are really colourless in themselves.

But the imagistic conception of ideas, despite the attractions we have noted, has anyway to be abandoned. Besides, immaterialism is no real help here: how could a non-spatial substance contain images, which occupy space? What this means is that the Lockean linkage between representation and *resemblance* has to be replaced by something else.[9] But this still leaves much else intact: Locke's distinctions among ideas; the essentials of his self-containedness doctrine; the claims that thought is the processing of ideas, that words represent by being associated with ideas, and that thought is prior to talk. As we shall see in chapter V, a closely related form of materialistic Cartesianism, which construes ideas not as images-in-the-brain but as *words*-in-the-brain, is very common in contemporary circles influenced by scientific psychology.

Notes and reading

Works referred to

PWD   Descartes, R., *The Philosophical Writings of Descartes* (3 vols) trans. J. Cottingham, R. Stoothoff, D. Murdoch and (vol. 3 only) A. Kenny (Cambridge: Cambridge University Press, 1984-91).

E   Locke, J., *An Essay Concerning Human Understanding*, ed. J. Yolton (London: Everyman, 1961).

LHU   Tipton, I. (ed.) *Locke on Human Understanding* (Oxford: Oxford University Press, 1977).

Notes

1 For a very helpful account, see Harold Noonan, *Personal Identity* (London: Routledge, 1989), ch. 2.

2 Locke's chief weapon against Cartesian scepticism seems to involve his causal theory of representation, described in section 5 below. Roughly, the view seems to be that since ideas are the effects in us of their 'external' causes, brought about by regular processes, they *thereby* count as faithful representations of these causes and give us knowledge of them: 'Our simple ideas being barely such perceptions as God has fitted us to receive and given power to external objects to produce in us by established laws and ways, suitable to his wisdom and goodness, though incomprehensible to us, their truth consists in nothing else but in such appearances as are produced in us and must be suitable to those powers he has placed in external objects, or else they could not be produced in us' (E:II,xxxii,14). The obvious objec-

tion is that these ideas could be the regular effects of Descartes' demon, or of the computer attached to the vat-brain, rather than the objects we take ourselves to be surrounded by. (Note that Locke may here be relying on Descartes' point that God is no deceiver.) As remarked in chapter I, note 8, one might counter this objection with the suggestion that in such an event, our thoughts would in fact be thoughts about the demon or the computer, and so would still count as knowledge. The implausibility of this, we shall ultimately see, is linked to the weakness of Locke's causal theory discussed in section 5.

3 However, in so far as one supposes that legal and ethical systems succeed in tracking legal or ethical reality, there may be a slightly respectable source of limited relativism in the fact that people indifferent to mice could find themselves arguing that although there is such a thing as killing a mouse, *there is no such thing as souricide.* For moral facts by their nature demand attention: they cannot simply be ignored for convenience as if they were uninteresting brands of snow. Still, if rejection of souricide is combined with a certain kind of tolerance towards the imagined French community with a special interest in mice, then it could lead ultimately to relativism about legal and ethical reality. But it is not obvious that the point could be generalised.

4 This tendency also seems to interact in complex ways with the ambiguity of 'idea' claimed by Descartes (PWDii: 7): for a helpful account see Michael Ayers, *Locke* (London: Routledge, 1991), vol. I, chs 6 and 7.

5 See e.g. John Mackie, *Problems from Locke* (Oxford: Clarendon Press, 1976), ch. 1.

6 Failure to address this point seems to me to undermine the argument in the strikingly Lockean treatment in Robert Kirk, 'The trouble with ultra-externalism', *Proceedings of the Aristotelian Society* 94 (1994): see especially pp. 294–5 and 304–5; cf G. McCulloch, 'Not much trouble for ultra externalism', *Analysis* 54: 265–9. It should be remarked here that at least some sensations are representational after a fashion in that they are experienced as having a location in the body: thus a *pain in the neck*, a *sting in the foot.* One can (but need not) claim on this basis that sensations are thus experienced as qualities of the relevant parts of the body. Even so, this is not the same as representing, or purporting to represent, their 'external' cause. Arguably some experiences involve both kinds of representation (the hoppiness is experienced as *in the mouth* as well as *in the beer*). But when I experience the red as *in the tomato* I do not also experience it as, say, *in my eyes.*

7 This naturally raises the worry that on this approach, ideas of red would not after all be representations of their causes (because they do not resemble them). But this worry is unfounded: once the distinction has been made between genuine representations, like images, and mere bare effects, like sensations, there is no harm in

re-introducing the notion of cause as an ingredient of representation. This could then give a fairly satisfying sense in which ideas of colours do represent their causes, but somewhat misleadingly.

8 Coming into a shaded place from the bright sunlight can cause one to have after-images: there are coloured patches 'before the eyes'. Such things are often adduced as visual sensations; and it may seem true that in experiencing after-images we do not take ourselves to be in a state which purports to represent the surface of an object. However, it does not follow from this that we experience after-images as effects in ourselves of 'external' objects. And in fact we do not: we take ourselves to be suffering from a familiar kind of illusion. Moreover, this kind of experience *does* in itself purport to represent a surface, in that one can mistake blotches on the wall for after-images *and vice versa*. The thought that after-images are 'in us' is a feature not of their intrinsic character, as it is in the case of a stinging feeling, but a consequence of the familiarity of this kind of illusion.

9 Much recent work involves an approach similar to Locke's causal theory: thus see Jerry Fodor, *A Theory of Content* (Cambridge, MA: MIT Press, 1990), chs 1–4. We shall see that just as the bare causal element of Locke's theory misses out what is essentially representational about, say, *seeing something as red*, so approaches like Fodor's fail to accommodate the given character of representational states: chapters VI and VIII (especially section 4) below.

CHAPTER III

Frege and the Theory of Understanding

The next part of our story involves happenings from around two centuries later, and the work of the German Gottlob Frege. Frege started out as a mathematician, but his dissatisfaction with the standards of proof prevalent among the mathematicians of his day led him, by and by, to work out the elements of what has since been developed as symbolic or mathematical logic. In so doing he made by far the greatest single advance in logic since Aristotle's invention of the subject, and opened the way for later developments in artificial intelligence. His work laid the foundations for modern philosophy of language and, indeed, helped to change the direction of philosophy in the mainstream of the English-speaking tradition. He is by far the most important nineteenth-century philosopher as far as this tradition is concerned, and it is absolutely impossible to make any worthwhile contribution to it without first having mastered his basic ideas. Our chief interest in Frege concerns the bearing of his views about *language and how it is understood* on those of Descartes and Locke. Frege helped to make possible some radical criticisms of the Cartesian account of how thought and talk are related, and we shall see in later chapters that these ultimately necessitate a root-and-branch rejection of the Cartesian conception of the mind.

1 Idealism and realism

Such was the impact of Cartesian doctrines that the focus in philosophy remained largely epistemological until well into the present century. Descartes passed on his sceptical challenge, chiefly on account of a general acceptance, even if only implicit, of the idea that the mind is self-contained with respect to the material world, i.e. capable of being the way it is in itself even if there is no material world. If anything, Locke's 'dark room' came to assume an even greater prominence. This is especially apparent in the various forms of *idealism* which entered philosophy after Locke, starting with Berkeley. Berkeley accepted the basic principle of Locke's theory of ideas, but argued that there was no hope of establishing contact with an Exterior world in such a system. Rather than treating this as an occasion for sceptical despair, however, Berkeley saw it as a form of liberation since, he argued, the very idea of an Exterior world which our ideas represent but to which our minds have no epistemologically significant access is incoherent.[1] If the supposed material world really is Exterior, then it is literally nothing to us, and no account of how we live and think can have any place for it. Hence, for Berkeley, the essential philosophical task became one of explaining what we are doing when we talk and think of rocks, bushes and so on, if we cannot be talking and thinking of Exterior things. Idealism is, in a nutshell, the view that material things are in some way part of the mind (and so not Exterior to it): according to Berkeley, things such as rocks and bushes are *collections of ideas*. And others who came after also saw this as the general way to proceed, although there are different versions of idealism (one more recent version, positivism, will occupy us here and there in later chapters). It is one of the great paradoxes of philosophy that approaches which developed alongside and in support of the beginnings of mechanistic science, which has furnished the most comprehensive understanding of the material world available to date, should have transmuted into various forms of the view that there is no material world beyond ourselves.

Frege proceeded by denying idealism and affirming *realism*. Just as idealists claim that the material world is somehow part of the mind, realists deny this, and claim that the material world exists independently of the mind. The easiest way to fix on the difference for present purposes is to imagine what could exist in a universe with no minds in it. For the idealist, the answer is 'nothing', or, at least, 'no material thing'. Thus if there were no minds there would be no rocks and bushes and other material objects. For there cannot be ideas without minds to have them, and there cannot be collections of ideas without ideas. According to the realist, on the other hand, the absence of minds would not prevent there being material things. Thus one can imagine a world much like ours existing on its own without ever having had any minds in it. Frege put his realism thus:

> The field and the frogs in it, the sun which shines on them are there no matter whether I look at them or not, but the sense-impression I have of green exists only because of me, I am its bearer . . . ideas need a bearer. Things of the outer world are however independent. (T: 26–7)

Now it is *very important indeed to realise that this realism is not the same as the claim that the material world is Exterior to the mind*. It is one thing to say that the material world could exist without any minds in it (realism), and quite another to say that any minds there are would be self-contained with respect to the material world (Exteriority). Of course, these views can sit happily alongside one another, so snugly in fact that they can be conflated. Both Descartes and Locke were realists, and they also believed the material world to be Exterior to the mind. But as we have already seen (chapter I, section 4), *self-containedness is thoroughly relative to the theory of mind assumed*, and so this leaves it open that there should be theories of mind which embrace realism but which reject self-containedness with respect to the material world. Such theories of mind will concern us a great deal below. So be clear:

> *realism* entails that the world could exist unaltered in itself without any minds,

whereas

> *Exteriority* entails that minds could exist unaltered in themselves without the world.

These are wholly different suggestions: the Cheshire cat can exist without the smile, but the smile cannot exist without the Cheshire cat.[2]

2 Idea, sense, meaning

Frege was primarily interested in developing artificial languages for the adequate formalisation of logic and mathematics, and was scornful of natural languages. But his writings are full of hints as to how to theorise about natural language, and others have not been slow in developing them. In what follows we shall be concerned exclusively with these applications.

His account takes as basic simple sentences like 'Istanbul is a city', in which a predicate ('is a city') is attached to a name ('Istanbul'). And looked at from a great height, what he says about such expressions resembles what Locke would have said. Thus Frege held that the name 'Istanbul' represents the city Istanbul, that is the place to be found on the Bosporus, and that the predicate 'is a city' represents cities. Locke would have said these things. Moreover, Frege held that the expressions, both name and predicate, are associated with something else, in addition to what they represent, which can be present before, or grasped by, the mind or the understanding. Locke said something close to this too. When we get a little closer and the details start to emerge, however, enormous differences become apparent. By far the most important of these is that whereas Locke put great weight on the claim that words signify ideas, Frege argued strongly against the relevance of this. Although he accepted that words do conjure up ideas in people's minds, he saw this as a mere psychological fact, of no interest at all to the philosopher of language and understanding. What words express and what minds grasp, he said, are *senses*, which unlike ideas are not in anyone's mind but are objective, so that a single sense is capable of being grasped by different minds:

> This constitutes an essential distinction between the idea and the sign's sense, which may be common property of many and therefore is not a part or mode of the individual mind. For one can hardly deny that mankind has a common store of thoughts which is transmitted from one generation to another. (S&M: 59)

There is also a difference in the way Frege took 'is a city' to represent cities. He considered all expressions to express a sense and also to have a *Meaning*.[3] In the case of a name like 'Istanbul', this Meaning is the object represented, the city. But in the case of a predicate, what is Meant is an abstract item called a *function*, which is responsible for the logical powers attributed to the expression. However, this involves the function in determining the class of things of which the predicate is true. And in this case, of course, that would be the class of cities: the class whose members are London, Istanbul, Paris, Sunderland... So the predicate does represent cities after all, albeit somewhat indirectly. For the purposes of what follows we shall not need to mention functions again.[4]

Where words are concerned, then, Locke made an essentially *twofold* distinction, between idea signified and objects represented, and took the signification of the idea to be *language's principal function*. Against this, Frege made a *threefold* distinction: 'the Meaning and sense of a sign are to be distinguished from the associated idea' (S&M: 59). And he took the association between word and idea to be *quite irrelevant to the functioning of language*, which is to be taken care of largely[5] by the theories of sense and of Meaning.

Frege's theory of Meaning contains his seminal contributions to logic. It is, as already noted, concerned with the relations between words and things in the world. He took it as unproblematic that we do have material surroundings which we can use language to talk about, and can know that we are doing this:

> when we say 'the Moon', we do not intend to speak of our
> idea of the Moon, nor are we satisfied with the sense alone,
> but we presuppose a Meaning. (S&M: 61)

Whether this was because he rejected the idea that the material world is Exterior to the mind, or because he simply ignored the sceptical problems that this view brings, is not entirely clear since he did not write at length about the philosophy of mind or epistemology specifically. But he was quite adamant that no adequate theory of language and logic can proceed without assuming a real, mind-independent world. And whether or not there are alternatives to this claim, it is a natural one to make, especially when the subject is logic. Consider the connection between logic and *truth*. A logically valid argument is one whose conclusion must be true if its premisses are. Logic, then, can be regarded as the study of *truth-preserving* moves from one set of sentences or propositions to another. But this means that truth is a property of a sentence or proposition in which a logician has to take a special interest:

> To discover truths is the task of all sciences; it falls to logic to discern the laws of truth. (T: 17)

Now a very natural way of understanding what it is for, say, 'Istanbul is a city' to be true is to think of it as involving relations between the component expressions and distinct, real-worldly things. Certainly this was the way, very broadly speaking, in which Frege proceeded in his theory of Meaning. Indeed, he was remarkably unconcerned about positing objective, mind-independent entities. This is most apparent in his approach to abstract entities such as numbers (and senses, as we shall see). He was at bottom untroubled[6] by the thought that things like the number one really do exist, not as material objects, but as abstract objects. Frege believed that abstract objects are as real as material ones. To say that something is abstract, for Frege, is simply to say that it is not material (or, better, does not have any causal powers: see F, section 26). It is not to say that it does not really exist, or only exists 'in our thoughts'. Thus just as the word 'Istanbul' stands in a representational relation to the city on the Bosporus, so the numeral '1' stands in the same representational relation to the smallest odd natural number. 'Istanbul' and '1' alike are names, and both things named are equally part of the furniture of the universe: although only the city can cause anything to happen.

The (impressive) technical details will not concern us, but what Frege aimed for was a comprehensive account of a large part of language (and others have since extended this), based on the idea that the workings of expressions of increasing complexity should be explained in terms of how they are constructed out of simpler elements. Each element – each name, each simple predicate, and so on – is to be assigned both a sense and a Meaning, and the senses and Meanings of more complex expressions are then derived from the senses and Meanings of their component parts (and the way in which these parts are combined). Thus once 'Istanbul' and 'is a city' have been assigned a sense and a Meaning each, the nature of Frege's system is such that the sense and Meaning of 'Istanbul is a city' are also determined. Nothing more needs to be added. Note a *very* distant echo here of Locke's thought that complex ideas are built up in systematic ways from simple ones. Both philosophers are responding, in their very different ways, to the almost irresistible idea that language and reason are compositional, or build in a regular, orderly way from a simple base.

Frege's theory of sense is much less well worked out than his theory of Meaning. But whereas the latter concerns the representational links between language and world, the former concerns the links between language and *mind*. Language is not a free-floating phenomenon, but is something whose essence is to be used, principally by creatures with minds. And as mentioned already, the most crucial language–mind relation is that of *understanding*, since one cannot do much with a stretch of language considered as language unless one understands it. So the theory of sense concerns, above all, what is involved in being able to understand language. Indeed, as will become increasingly apparent, to theorise about the senses of words just is to theorise about what it is to be able to understand them (and vice versa). The theory of sense sits at the point at which Frege's views bear most directly on issues which we have seen to be of critical interest to both Descartes and Locke. But the approach is very different indeed, and it will be helpful now to have the elements of Frege's view before us. That done, we can then turn to his arguments against the theory of ideas.

3 The theory of sense

Why does an account of understanding require an extra notion over and above that of Meaning? Why are not representational relations between language and world enough? Here are two Fregean reasons for adding a theory of sense to the theory of Meaning.

The first is that a piece of language might be perfectly understandable, that is say something, without the matter of truth and hence Meaning being involved at all. Thus stories or fiction are perfectly understandable, but according to Frege we are not concerned with truth when telling them: 'Then Superman whacked the baddie on the chin and they all lived happily ever after' is neither true nor false, according to Frege, although it is perfectly understandable (see S&M: 62). Such uses of language thus have sense but do not have Meaning. The second reason is that pieces of language might have the same Meaning but not say the same thing. Thus the two sentences

Istanbul is a city

and

Constantinople is a city

match Meaning for Meaning, since they are put together in the same way out of components which themselves have the same Meanings (the only difference is that 'Constantinople' is put for 'Istanbul', and these both Mean the same city on the Bosporus). But clearly someone might understand one of them without understanding the other (e.g. if they had never heard of a place called 'Constantinople'), and even if they did understand them both, they might suppose one to be true and the other to be false, for example if they did not realise that Istanbul *is* Constantinople, and instead were under the impression that Constantinople is a small Greek holiday resort. Again, then, it seems that the theory of what it is to understand these pieces of language must go beyond what is provided by the theory of Meaning.

So what are senses? We have already seen that they are supposed to be distinct from Lockean ideas; that the senses of complex expressions such as sentences are determined by the senses of their components; that senses can be grasped by the mind; and that grasping a sense is understanding the word which expresses it. Frege also considered senses to be perfectly real, though abstract, entities. Moreover, senses exist eternally, and whether or not they are ever grasped by a mind:

> the thought, for example, which we express in the Pythagorean theorem is timelessly true, true independently of whether anyone takes it to be true. It needs no bearer. It is not true for the first time when it is discovered, but is like a planet which, already before anyone has seen it, has been in interaction with other planets. (T: 29; by 'thought' Frege here means the sense of a sentence. His comparison between undiscovered thoughts and planets should not be

64

taken too literally, given his official view that thoughts cannot interact *causally*.)

Frege also makes several claims about the relationships between sense and his other principal notion, Meaning. The theory of Meaning, we have said, is concerned with the representational relations between language and world: thus it will have to pronounce on the relation between a name like 'Istanbul' and the world. Frege's view, we saw, is that the name Means the city of Istanbul. But the notion of sense figures here in three crucial ways. First, Frege holds that strictly speaking it is senses which represent the world, so that the representational relation between language and world is indirect. Words express senses which represent the world:

> to the sign there corresponds a definite sense and to that in turn a definite Meaning. (S&M: 58)

> when we call a sentence true we really mean its sense is. (T: 19)

(Note a distant echo of Locke, who held that words primarily signify ideas, and only represent things thanks to the fact that the signified ideas do.) Second, in the case of names, at any rate, Frege glosses this representational power of a sense by saying that the sense of a name contains 'the mode of presentation' of the Meaning (S&M: 57). In grasping a sense someone thereby understands the expression whose sense it is. And Frege claims that when one grasps a sense, its Meaning is presented to the understanding *in a certain way or mode*. Perhaps the clearest quick explication of this is in terms of thinking about something *as* one thing rather than another. I can think about Istanbul *as Istanbul*, or *as that place over there*, or *as the city athwart the Bosporus*. These are different ways of thinking about Istanbul, and so correspond to three different modes of presentation of it, and hence three senses. Similarly I can think of water *as water*, or *as H_2O* or *as the stuff I wash in*. There are clearly in general indefinitely many senses corresponding to the one Meaning, that is indefinitely many ways of regarding or thinking about an object. Each

> serves to illuminate only a single aspect of the Meaning . . .

Comprehensive knowledge of the Meaning would require us to be able to say immediately whether any given sense belongs to it. To such knowledge we never attain. (S&M: 58)

Hence the permanent possibility that expressions which do not differ in Meaning, such as 'Istanbul' and 'Constantinople', should figure in the understanding as though they were names of distinct things. Third, however, this leads to an important feature of sense–Meaning relations which will figure in Part Two. Although many senses can present the one Meaning, any particular sense always presents at most one and the same Meaning: there cannot be many Meanings presented by one sense. This we can express by saying that *sense determines Meaning*. It is easy to see why one should say this. For to suppose otherwise is to suppose that one could grasp a sense and it still not be settled what one was thinking about. In consequence, one would be able to understand a word like 'Istanbul' yet it still be left open what one was using the word to talk about. Yet this seems absurd: learning the name just is a way of coming to be able to talk about the city. The two stages seem to be inseparably rolled into one. However, we shall see that many vexing issues are raised here.

Some of these issues connect with another aspect of sense–Meaning relations which we have already mentioned. This is Frege's claim that an expression might have sense but lack a Meaning. We saw above that he makes this claim about the case of fiction, but it is tempting to extend it to non-fictional uses of language, and Frege seems content to do this too:

It may perhaps be granted that every well-formed . . . proper name always has a sense. But this is not to say that to the sense there also corresponds a Meaning . . . In grasping a sense, one is not certainly assured of a Meaning. (S&M: 62)

And perhaps lots of the words we use in fact do not represent anything at all: it is at least logically possible that, say, 'Aristotle', 'electron', 'the largest number', 'the centre of gravity of the universe' do not pick out anything at all. If so, then these expressions have no Meaning. Nevertheless, it certainly seems that they have sense, that is are understandable, *whether or not they have Meaning*. And this immediately seems to make room for a form of self-containedness for the mind or understanding. In so far as there can be sense without Meaning, the understanding will be self-contained with respect to Meaning, that is Meaning will be Exterior to the mind. Since Meanings are often worldly things like Istanbul or water, it thus seems that sense-without-Meaning implies a corresponding self-containedness with respect to the world as far as the understanding is concerned: these parts of the world are Exterior to the understanding. Thus my understanding of the word 'Istanbul' could be the same as it is in itself, *qua* understanding, even in situations where Istanbul did not exist. We shall see in chapter VII that this possible self-containedness of sense with respect to Meaning leads Frege into grave difficulties, and we shall ultimately see that it is best either abandoned or very severely restricted.[7]

Although Frege rejected Locke's theory of ideas as a theory of understanding, we should note that quite a few of Locke's doctrines about words can be more or less smoothly transplanted into Frege's system. Just as his view that simple ideas combine to form complex ones is echoed by Frege's view that the senses of simple expressions combine to form the senses of complex expressions, so aspects of Locke's corresponding claims about definition could be retained by the Fregean. There is nothing obvious to stop a Fregean from claiming, in the spirit of Locke, that a word like 'lead' should have its sense spelled out by a definition involving more primitive words ('whitish', 'heavy', 'metal': but see chapter IV, section 3, and chapter VII). Such a move would simplify the theory of understanding enormously, since all one would need to do then would be to specify in some other way the senses of primitive words, and let definition (and modes of sentence-construction) take care of the rest. And perhaps the primitive words could be handled as Locke suggests, by noting the things which prompt their use. Of course, simple thing–word correlations would not be enough, since the notion of sense demands that we accommodate different modes of presentation of the same thing. Nevertheless, setting up thing–word correlations would be a start, and it is not easy to see how else one might proceed at the primitive level. Note too that a Fregean could accept much of what Locke says about words which represent substances and modes, since this is primarily a matter of whether we think a kind of classification is in some way arbitrary and influenced by our interests, or whether we think it simply reflects the structure of nature itself. There is no obvious reason to suppose that this distinction cannot be adopted in the theory of sense. In short, even if the theory of ideas can be overturned as a theory of understanding, many of its component claims seem capable of being carried over into similar possible claims within the theory of sense.

But *can* the theory of ideas be overturned as a theory of understanding? To begin to answer this we urgently need to see why Frege replaced Locke's twofold distinction with his own threefold one.

4 Frege against ideas

Note first that Locke could accept Frege's theory of Meaning, of language–world relations, and could also accept Frege's claims about how the Meanings of complex expressions are built up systematically on the basis of the Meanings of their parts. And, of course, Locke *did* think that there is something over and above language–world relations, to do with what it is to understand language: and he *did* think that this too is systematic. So we can imagine a twentieth-century Lockean who claims to accept the broad principle of Frege's distinction between sense and Meaning, but who *identifies senses with ideas*! Such a theorist could then say, for example, that my image/idea of Istanbul presents the city in one mode or manner; that my 'Constantinople' image does so in another, and so on.[8] In proceeding like this, the modern Lockean would both gain all the benefits of Frege's great advances in systematic logic, and maintain the elements of the theory of ideas, while evidently dispensing with the need to posit a distinct realm of abstract senses. To this there are two obvious objections. One is that ideas as posited by Locke (images in the mind) simply do not exist, so that the work of senses has to be done in some other way (see the following chapter). The other is that although ideas as posited by Locke do exist, they cannot play the appropriate role in the account of understanding. Frege took the second line: he accepted ideas, but rejected their relevance to understanding. So what are his arguments?

His first is that people can share senses, that is more than one person can grasp the same sense, whereas, of course, people cannot share ideas. My ideas are in my mind, yours are in yours, and it makes no sense to suppose that we could move them from mind to mind. Frege appears to have two related considerations in view here. One is that we can communicate, and that when we do we share the same thoughts. And the other is that when our minds meet in this way there is real scope for logical and other objective forms of disagreement or agreement. I may think something ('All swans are white') and you may think something else which contradicts it ('There are black swans'). Frege's view is that when this happens we have moved into the objective arena of logic. There is an objective logical clash between us, and not merely, say, a difference in taste or preference, as there would be if I thought 'I like bananas' and you thought 'I don't'. In this second case we could both be right, agree to differ and pass on. But in the first case, even if we do 'agree to differ' we cannot both be right, and the clash survives our passing on. Frege's claim is that were thinking just a matter of having our own ideas, there could be no such thing as real contradiction:

> If every thought requires a bearer, to the contents of whose consciousness it belongs, then it would be a thought of this bearer only and there would be no science common to many, on which many could work. But I, perhaps, have my own science, namely a whole of thought whose bearer I am and another person has his[?] ... No contradiction between the two sciences would then be possible and it would really be idle to dispute about truth, as idle, indeed almost ludicrous, as it would be for two people to dispute whether a hundred-mark note were genuine, where each meant the the one he himself had in his pocket and understood the word 'genuine' in his own particular sense. (T: 29)

One can imagine Locke replying as follows. It is true that ideas cannot pass from mind to mind, so that we cannot share ideas. But it seems perfectly possible for our ideas to match one another, as remarked in the previous chapter. And surely this is all that is required for us to be able to communicate. Moreover, our ideas can stand in other structural relations to each other – my idea represents the world as being one way, yours represents it as being another – and why cannot these sorts of relations allow our minds to meet appropriately and engage in logical disputes?

A picture of Napoleon can represent him as ginger-haired and be contradicted by another which represents him as bald.

Frege might reply, first, that if it is the structural relations among ideas which logic is concerned with, then it is right to say that ideas themselves are irrelevant to logic. What matter are the things that people have in common – objective relations among ideas – and not the ideas themselves. But Locke could reply that this still requires people to have ideas, and that it is not clear why one should have to talk of senses as anything additional.

Frege has another, more telling line of argument (F: 35–6), which exploits a possible objection to Locke's theory of communication actually foreseen by Locke. Why should we suppose that matching between ideas ever occurs? In the previous chapter, we noted that the ultimate reason for claiming a match between the ideas of different persons would be to note the representational relations had by the words used to signify simple ideas. But Locke himself suggests that even this may not be enough to assure exact matching:

> *the same object [might] produce in several men's minds different* ideas at the same time: e.g. if the idea that violet produced in one man's mind by his eyes were the same that a marigold produced in another man's, and *vice versa*. (E:II,xxxii,15)

He has in mind here systematic switching of the ideas of the colours blue and yellow. Since it is systematic, the switch would not show up in the behaviour, linguistic or otherwise, of the two men. Both would learn to use 'yellow' by being shown bananas, egg-yolks, daffodils. Both would learn 'blue' by being shown the sky, Leicester City shirts, forget-me-nots. Both would thus call all the same things 'blue' and 'yellow' (in the same circumstances). Both would respond in the same way (other things being equal) to the orders 'Fetch me something blue', 'Paint this wall yellow' and so on. The difference between them would be entirely subjective, would be simply a matter of how their respective ideas struck them.

Locke is strangely insouciant about this possibility. He continues the above passage with since this could never be known, because one man's mind could not pass into another man's body ..., neither the ideas hereby, nor the names, would be at all confounded, or any falsehood be in either ... whatever [the] appearances were in his mind, he would be able regularly to distinguish things for his use by those appearances, *and understand and signify those distinctions marked by the names 'blue' and 'yellow', as if the appearances or ideas in his mind ... were exactly the same with the ideas in other men's minds.* (*Ibid.,* emphasis added)

As it happens, he goes on, it is likely that such a situation does not arise, but even if it did, it would be 'of little use either for the improvement of our knowledge or conveniency of life' to find this out (*ibid.*). However, in conceding the switching possibility Locke looks to be throwing away his account of communication. For if there is an unknowable possibility that the Matching assumption does not generally hold, then there is a parallel unknowable possibility that we are all permanently and irretrievably at cross purposes. And this answers to nothing in our conception of what it is to communicate successfully. Thus Locke could try to bite the bullet and simply accept that maybe we are all unknowably at cross purposes. But he has too much good sense to do this: he disregards the possibility as irrelevant to the question of knowledge and to the 'conveniency of life'. And this just is to concede that *subjective matching is irrelevant to the main purpose of communication*, which is to enable us to co-operate and to share thoughts and knowledge. Language functions perfectly well, whatever relations hold between our ideas (if we have any), just so long as we rub along in the normal pursuits which involve or require it. Of course, we do get at cross purposes, and this shows up eventually in various kinds of frustration that our projects can suffer. But if there is no potential for such frustrations, then there is no question about it: language is working properly and we are successfully communicating. Any thought that we might yet be at a kind of cross purpose introduces a notion of success in communication which simply does not engage with our experience of language.

Nor is there any future for Locke in his claim that the switching situation in reality does not arise. The fact that it appears to describe a possible situation is enough to ruin an account of communication based on subjective matching. In any case, short of a Descartes-style appeal to God's good offices to assure us that our ideas do match appropriately, all Locke could appeal to are various kinds of experiment that might be conducted. But even if I could open up your head and see coloured pictures inside – surely the best possible scenario – this would not help. For my seeing your ideas would be mediated by my having my own ideas of them, and the crucial question of whether they match would be left open. Perhaps your idea is yellow but I see it as blue! As Frege says, to compare our ideas we should need to 'bring [them] together in one consciousness' (T: 27), and this is impossible, as Locke also acknowledges in the passage above. Frege continues 'even if it were possible to make an idea disappear from one consciousness and, at the same time, to make an idea appear in another consciousness, the question whether it were the same idea in both would still remain unanswerable' (*ibid.*). So it is hard to see how Locke could justify his confidence that subjective matching normally holds. And to repeat, his admission even of the possibility of systematic switching seems to ruin his account of communication anyway.

At one place Frege goes so far as to say that the question whether our ideas match is 'nonsensical' (T: 27), since the notion of making a comparison makes no sense. If this is right, then of course any view based on subjective matching is obviously doomed, since one cannot base an account of communication on a nonsensical notion. If there is no fact of the matter as to whether our ideas match, then there could be no fact of the matter about whether we communicate. However, this claim of Frege's is very strong, and seems to involve the contentious argument that because we cannot do anything to find out whether matching obtains, there is nothing to find out. This is contentious because it seems to make sense to suppose that some objective relation might hold between two things even though we could never find this out. But perhaps ideas are a special case, since their only reality *as ideas* is exhausted by how they appear. Since, then, my idea can never appear the same as or different from yours (for there is no one to whom it could so appear), it cannot be the same as or different from yours.[9] This seems to be the burden of when the word 'red' does not state a property of things but is supposed to characterize sense-impressions belonging to my consciousness, it is only applicable within the sphere of my consciousness. (T: 27)

But however this may be, Frege does not need this strong claim. He even seems at one point to entertain the thought that 'two men ... may have similar sense-impressions' (T: 36): but in any case, we have seen that unknowable, subjective matching has no place in the theory of communication. This completely idle alleged fact about our ideas has no bearing on the matter of success with language. Either way, then, whether or not we have ideas, and whether or not they do or even can match, an adequate theory of communication needs to make a fresh start.

The crucial question now is: how damaging is this to Locke in particular and Cartesianism in general? The first thing to note is that Frege's objections do not turn at all on whether ideas are immaterial or material, so any attempt to explain communication in terms of isomorphisms between the brains of speakers is equally undermined. If we rub along successfully in the normal way when using language, then it does not matter whether our brains match or, indeed, whether we are at all similar physiologically (recall Functionalism from chapter I, section 2). But it is possible for a Cartesian to accept all this yet reply that *everything else is left intact*. For example, it could still be claimed that hosting ideas/brain structures is part of a mechanism which, in humans anyway, needs to be in place if language is to be understood at all. And on the basis of this thought, the following counter-attack against Frege's positive claims is possible.

Granted that mere subjective or internal relations between individuals can have no bearing on the way language functions in communication, it needs more argument to get to Frege's favoured position, that successful communication requires a *sharing of senses*. First, why should not the same word express different senses to different people? Even though these differences would have to be discoverable in principle, in order to protect Frege's view from his own argument against Locke, one could argue that they need not impede successful communication and the 'conveniency of life'. As long as our uses of 'Istanbul' all represent the same city, what does it matter if mine express one sense and yours another? So even if sense is required to supplement the theory of Meaning, as argued in the previous section, in order to explain how understanding is possible, it is still not clear why equivalence at the level of Meaning should not suffice for communication to succeed for the practical purposes which seem to matter most of all. Indeed Frege envisages just such a possibility, and goes on that such interpersonal differences in sense would not matter in practice, although they should be avoided in a perfect language (S&M: 58n; T: 24–5). We might wonder what notion of perfection is in play here.

But second, and worse, we can go on to claim that the case for sense being required to explain how understanding is possible has not been made anyway. Why shouldn't the theory of Meaning be used for an account of communication, and the theory of *ideas* (material or otherwise) be used for an account of understanding? Once Cartesians have conceded that subjective matching is irrelevant in the theory of communication, why should they make any more concessions *at all*?[10]

This is a powerful reply, and it will take us some time (more or less the rest of the book) to show what is wrong with it. As regards the first, easier point, a Fregean could reply that interpersonal differences in sense are a snare, in that they contain within them the potential for misunderstanding and confusion. If you understand a word one way, and I understand it another, then even if we happen to Mean the same thing by it, there could well be room for doubt or confusion over this fact. So the notion of shared sense is not redundant where communication is concerned. Why should I expect you to go where I tell you to go if I cannot suppose that you understand 'Go to Istanbul' in the same way that I do? But the problem with this reply, besides its sketchiness, is that it assumes that the second, more challenging point above has been answered. Why theorise in terms of sense *at all*, rather than in terms of Meaning and ideas? How is it supposed to have emerged that understanding and successful communication could not be ultimately explained satisfactorily with just these resources?

In short, we have not yet seen a decisive argument against the position mentioned at the beginning of the present section: a view which takes over the bulk of Frege's theories of sense and Meaning, but which *uses Lockean ideas to do the jobs earmarked for sense.* This position would be a blend of Lockean and Fregean elements, but in rejecting Frege's realm of objective senses it would be a lot more Lockean than Fregean, even without the claim that successful communication requires subjective matching. In the following chapter we shall begin to see why this suggestion must be rejected.

Notes and reading

Works referred to

F   Frege, G., *The Foundations of Arithmetic*, trans. J.L. Austin (Oxford: Blackwell, 1950).

S&M   Frege, G., 'On sense and Meaning' in *Translations from the Philosophical Writings of Gottlob Frege*, 3rd edn, eds P. Geach and M. Black (Oxford: Blackwell, 1980).

T   Frege, G., 'The thought: a logical enquiry', trans. A. and M. Quinton in *Philosophical Logic*, ed. P. Strawson (Oxford: Oxford University Press, 1967).

E   Locke, J., *An Essay Concerning Human Understanding*, ed. J. Yolton (London: Everyman, 1961).

PI   Wittgenstein, L., *Philosophical Investigations*, trans. G.E.M. Anscombe (Oxford: Blackwell, 1953).

Notes

1 Thus see Berkeley, *Of the Principles of Human Knowledge* §5: 'can there be a nicer strain of abstraction than to distinguish the existence of sensible objects from their being perceived, so as to conceive them existing unperceived? Light and colours, heat and cold, extension and figures, in a word the things we see and feel, what are they but so many sensations, notions, ideas or impressions on the sense; and is it possible to separate, even in thought, any of these from perception?' *Berkeley: Philosophical Works*, ed. M. Ayers, (London: Everyman, 1975) 78.

2 See Gregory McCulloch, *Using Sartre* (London: Routledge, 1994), chs 6–7.

3 The capitalisation indicates that this is the translation of Frege's word *Bedeutung*. Although this would ordinarily be translated simply by the English 'meaning', two reasons necessitate the capitalisation. First, Frege used his word with a decidedly technical edge (hence it was initially usually translated as 'reference'); and second, writers in English often use 'meaning' where Frege would have used his word *Sinn*, normally translated as 'sense'. Thus see chapter IV below.

4 See 'Function and concept' in P. Geach and M. Black, eds, *Translations from the Philosophical Writings of Gottlob Frege*, 3rd edn, (Oxford: Blackwell, 1980), and Gregory McCulloch, *The Game of the Name* (Oxford: Oxford University Press, 1989), ch. 1.

5 Frege also distinguished in passing between sense and *tone*, and in much more depth between sense and the *force* of different kinds of speech-act, such as asserting and questioning. See Michael Dummett, *Frege: Philosophy of Language* (London: Duckworth, 1975) chs 1 and 10.

6 Thus Wittgenstein: 'The last time I saw Frege, as we were waiting at the station for my train, I said to him "Don't you ever find *any* difficulty in your theory that numbers are objects?" He replied "Sometimes I *seem* to see a difficulty – but then again I *don't* see it." ' Reported in Peter Geach and Elizabeth Anscombe, *Three Philosophers* (Oxford: Blackwell, 1962): 130.

7 Predictably enough, this possible self-containedness of sense and understanding with respect to Meaning has spawned a modern variant of idealism. This is *anti-realism* in the philosophy of language, a view invented more or less single-handedly by the important contemporary Oxford philosopher Michael Dummett and developed quite extensively by his former student Crispin Wright: see e.g. Dummett's *Truth and Other Enigmas* (London: Duckworth, 1978), chs 10 and 21, and Wright's *Realism, Meaning and Truth*, 2nd edn (Oxford: Blackwell, 1993). Just as Berkeley argued that Descartes' and Locke's Exterior things are nothing to us, and so can have no place in any account of how we think and live; so Dummett and later Wright have urged that in so far as the purported elements of Frege's theory of Meaning are Exterior, they too can have no place in any account of our life and our use of language. It is beyond the scope of the present work to pursue the question of idealism, either as propounded by Berkeley or by these Oxonians, although the matter will come up again in chapter V and in chapter VII, section 3.

8 This identification seems especially attractive if we think of ideas not 'materially' but 'objectively', so that a Paris-idea would then be Paris-as-represented: see chapter I, note 2.

9 Wittgenstein arguably takes this a step further in the Private Language Argument (PI: §§243ff.). If there is not really any difference between how an idea appears (to me) and how it is in itself, then there is no content to the thought that I might misidentify one of my ideas when claiming it to be the same as one I had earlier: if it seems right to me now to say this, it *is* right. But far from this showing that knowledge of ideas is an especially secure, error-free form of knowledge, all this shows, says Wittgenstein, is that there are no such things as similarities or differences among ideas, and hence no such things as ideas. If there were such relations among ideas, then it ought to be possible to go wrong about them at least in principle, since surely the ideas and their relations to one another would have

to be one thing, and my judgements about them another. If this separation cannot be maintained, so that I might go wrong in principle, then talk of my always being right is perfectly empty.

10 I have been assuming that Locke intended the matching required for a word to have a 'common acceptation' to be subjective matching. But it may be suggested that all Locke intends is that ideas match in the appropriate way if they have the same representational properties, as defined in terms of his causal theory of representation (see chapter II, section 5). Ideas could obviously match in this way without matching subjectively: and this would explain Locke's cavalier attitude towards the switching possibility. This does not seem to me, however, to be the most sensitive interpretation of Locke hereabouts. First, it would be very misleading to introduce this rather special sense of 'same idea' without flagging it explicitly. So when Locke just says that the primary function of a word is to signify ideas, and that a secondary feature is that we generally assume that others signify the same idea with the same word, that does rather strongly suggest the reading in the text. Moreover, since he also at the same point says that a further function of ideas is to represent the reality of things, it would have been especially easy for him to do the flagging (common acceptation = same reference to the reality). Second, Locke's account of secondary qualities would run into severe trouble. Thus: which are the blue things? The ones with the power to cause ideas-of-blue in us. Which are the ideas-of-blue? The ones apt to be caused by blue things! One way out of this circle would be to assume that most/typical humans have ideas of subjective character BLUE caused in them by blue things, so that blue things would be defined as things with the power to cause BLUE-type ideas in such humans, and ideas-of-blue would be *any* ideas caused by blue things so defined (and some of them could be YELLOW-type ideas, as in the switching case). This would certainly explain Locke's assurance that switching cases probably do not occur (but on what basis can he say this?). However, all of this seems to me to introduce a measure of the third-personal which is very alien to Locke's approach. On his view, each of us is a little dark room of ideas, and one's understanding cannot reach beyond one's room in any respect. If our minds are to meet at all in genuine communication, then, it can only be in virtue of common patterns in the contents of the rooms. Given his resolutely first-personal approach, it is hard not to suppose that these have to be subjectively perceived patterns. This then gives a simpler, more phenomenological definition of idea-of-blue: an idea-of-blue is a BLUE-type idea (think again here of the desirability of linking representation with the notion of purporting to resemble: chapter II, section 5). Given this, his admission of the possibility of switching does wreck his theory of communication (if blue things cause YELLOW-type ideas in me, then my word 'blue' signifies an idea-of-yellow). Perhaps the truth is, as often, that no single coherent

CHAPTER IV

Wittgenstein: Use and Understanding

The next place to look is in Wittgenstein. Wittgenstein was heavily influenced by what he called 'Frege's great works', and was part of the first wave of logicians, which included his teacher in Cambridge, Russell, who brought Frege's logical advances to the wider philosophical public. His early work *Tractatus Logico-Philosophicus* is an application of Fregean ideas to the analysis of language and thought (the above quote is taken from its Preface). But Wittgenstein later became dissatisfied with this project, not merely in detail but in principle, and his other major work, *Philosophical Investigations*, contains a sustained critique of it and associated projects. Among these is the Lockean theory of ideas, which had continued to exert a large influence in the philosophy of mind and language. Wittgenstein finally laid it to rest, at least in its imagist version. But variants of his criticisms apply just as much to Frege's conception of what it is to grasp a sense. Wittgenstein thus became, up to a point, anti-Fregean. However, we shall see that many of his positive views about understanding can be fitted into a broadly Fregean account with little strain (just as aspects of Locke's theory can carry over to Frege's): and seen in this light, Wittgenstein is the one who fully liberated Fregean accounts of sense and understanding from the influence of the theory of ideas, and showed why they are to be preferred.

Wittgenstein is not an easy philosopher to write about. Mostly this is due to his style of composition, which involves writing short, sometimes loosely connected paragraphs and aphorisms rather than continuous prose divided up into chapters and orchestrated by the usual forms of authorial direction. This makes him difficult to read at first, and invites wildly varying interpretations of what he really meant. The problems are compounded by his predilection for portentous claims about the futility of philosophy, itself part of a general tendency to lofty, oracular pronouncement. At the same time, many of the ideas about language and understanding which criss-cross through the works are clearly of immense power and profundity. The net result is that Wittgenstein scholarship is overburdened by a vast, contradictory and sometimes unpleasantly sanctimonious secondary literature. In what follows we shall mostly steer clear of all this, and concentrate on those aspects of the *Philosophical Investigations* which bear most directly on our main theme. In particular, as remarked, our interest is in what Wittgenstein can bring to the Fregean account of understanding, and thus in what contribution he can make to our discussion of Cartesianism, the theory of ideas and the self-containedness of the mind.

1 Understanding as static

Quite early on in *Philosophical Investigations* Wittgenstein says that

> For a *large* class of cases – though not for all – in which we employ the word 'meaning' it can be defined thus: the meaning of a word is its use in the language. (PI: §43)

Here and elsewhere he is using the word 'meaning' not in Frege's technical way, which we indicated by capitalisation, but rather to advert to the theory of understanding: to know the meaning of a word is to understand it. In other words, where Wittgenstein talks of meaning, Frege would talk of *sense*. The claim in the above passage is thus that understanding a word, that is grasping its sense, is using it as part of language. This theme runs through the work and is illustrated in a variety of ways and contexts. For example, Wittgenstein introduces the notion of a language-game, by which he means, in part, a very primitive or simplified language. But he also means the 'game' part of it literally: 'Think of much of the use of words in games like ring-a-ring-a-roses', and his intention is to call 'the whole, consisting of language and the actions into which it is woven, the "language-game" ' (PI: §7). In the same connection he frequently draws attention to the role that the use of language plays in our day to day living: 'to imagine a language is to imagine a form of life' (PI: §19);

> the term 'language-game' is meant to bring into prominence the fact that the *speaking* of language is part of an activity, or of a form of life. (PI: §23)

Elsewhere he exhorts us to forget about philosophical theorising and simply 'look and see' what happens when words are used (PI: §66). The philosophy of language (and indeed all philosophy)

> simply puts everything before us, and neither explains nor deduces anything. – Since everything lies open to view there is nothing to explain. (PI: §126)

These last remarks look defeatist and unsatisfying. Equally, the repeated observations about what happens when language is used can look like crashing platitudes:

> Suppose someone points to a vase and says 'Look at that marvellous blue – the shape isn't the point.' – Or: 'Look at the marvellous shape – the colour doesn't matter.' Without doubt you will do something *different* when you act upon these two invitations. But do you always do the *same* thing when you direct your attention to the colour? . . . You sometimes attend to the colour by putting your hand up to keep the outline from view; or by not looking at the outline of the thing; sometimes by staring at the object and trying to remember where you saw that colour before. (PI: §33)

Well, yes, the initiate too often says, but why bother to say this? What's he getting at? The answer is that these remarks are part of a sustained and somewhat revolutionary criticism of what were (and in some quarters still are) virtually orthodox tenets in the philosophy of mind and language. For our purposes, chief among these are the views that understanding is (a) static, and (b) something additional to the use of language, 'hidden behind those coarser and therefore more readily visible accompaniments' (PI: §153). The first matter will be dealt with in the present chapter, and we shall return to the second in the next, and throughout Part II.

To say that understanding is static is to say that one can explain what is involved in understanding words by describing a momentary, simple state of affairs, a sort of snapshot, involving the understander. One version of this approach with which we are already familiar is the claim made by both Descartes and Locke that understanding is a matter of being aware of an idea. The underlying thought is that in so being aware of an idea one is thereby put into the position of understanding the word which signifies it. Such awareness therefore is supposed to explain one's ability to use the word in question: and Wittgenstein argues with finality that *it can do no such thing*. His main point is that an idea cannot in itself compel the understanding to take it one way rather than another. Therefore the bare awareness of the idea does not explain the actual way in which it *is* taken, and hence does not explain the use of the associated word. The snapshot of the understander explains nothing.

This is easy to see if we suppose that ideas are images, which as we saw in chapter II is very much in the spirit of the theory. It is very tempting to think that an image's representational properties are simply 'drawn in', in that what it is supposed to be an image of can just be read off the way it looks. But this is the first mistake:

> I see a picture; it represents an old man walking up a steep path leaning on a stick. – How? Might it not have looked just the same if he had been sliding downhill in that position? Perhaps a Martian would describe the picture so. (PI: §139n)

In other words, we still need an account of what it is to take a picture one way rather than another – this, after all, is what understanding *it* consists in. But describing the form of the picture does not explain this. Wittgenstein goes on that *no* sign or image can in itself compel a particular way of taking it. Thus there would be no point in adding arrows or other indications to the drawing of the old man in order to make it clearer how to take it. Each of these additions can also be taken in different ways, so their mere presence does not explain what it is to take them one way rather than another.

Wittgenstein is not here denying, of course, that there are usually all sorts of conscious accompaniments of understanding: his thought is not at all that our minds are blank and empty when we exercise our understanding (for more on this, see chapter VI). His point is merely that these conscious accompaniments are not *themselves* what understanding, or meaning one thing rather than another, consists in:

> There are, of course, what can be called 'characteristic experiences' of pointing to (e.g.) the shape [of something]. For example, following the outline with one's finger or one's eyes as one points. – But *this* does not happen in all cases in which I 'mean the shape', and no more does any other one characteristic process occur in all these cases. Besides, even if something of the sort did recur in all cases, it would still depend on the circumstances – that is, on what happened before and after the pointing – whether we should say 'he pointed to the shape and not to the colour'. (PI: §35)

The next move is to think of an idea not as an image, then, but as something else which *can* compel the understanding in the appropriate way. But what could this be? 'You have no model of this superlative fact...' (PI: §192). The problem is that if understanding a word is to explain one's ability to use it, then the state of affairs which understanding is alleged to consist in must itself determine exercises of the ability. But how could *any* static state of affairs do this? As Wittgenstein says:

> When someone says the word 'cube' to me, for example, I know what it means. But can the whole *use* of the word come before my mind, when I *understand* it in this way? ... Can what we grasp *in a flash* accord with a use, fit or fail to fit it? And how can what is present to us in an instant, what comes before our mind in an instant, fit a *use*? (PI: §139)

So much for this part of his attack on the theory of ideas (for another see the following section). The argument is most obviously successful against imagist versions of the theory and/or immaterialist versions (which would involve 'superlative facts'). But it remains to be seen whether it also works against non-imagist, materialistic versions (see chapters V and VI).

Wittgenstein also attacks the thought that one can explain understanding in terms of simple correlations between words and the things they represent. Such a view might include the claim that to understand 'cat' to mean cats is to use it to refer to cats.

He first observes that this would be, at best, an incomplete account of language, since many words are not used to refer to things in this straightforward way:

> Think of exclamations alone, with their completely different functions.
>
> Water!
> Away!
> Ow!
> Help!
> Fine!
> No!
>
> Are you inclined still to call these words 'names of objects'? (PI: §27)

We might also mention examples such as 'and', 'if', 'maybe', 'altogether' and 'did' in the same spirit. But even in cases where the naming account seems appropriate, as with 'nouns like "table", "chair", "bread" and... people's names' (PI: §1), Wittgenstein argues persuasively that fixing *simply* on a snapshot of the word–thing relation explains very little about the understanding:

> One thinks that learning language consists in giving names to objects. Viz, to human beings, to shapes, to colours, to pains, to moods, to numbers, etc. To repeat – naming is something like attaching a label to a thing. One can say that this is preparatory to the use of a word. But *what* is it a preparation *for*? (PI: §26)

The point of the question is to introduce the thought that the future uses of a word can no more be contained in the bare act of attaching a label to a thing than they can be contained in the bare act of contemplating a picture, or in any other static state of affairs, 'as if what we did next were given with the mere act of naming' (PI: §27). For in fact the ability to name already presupposes sophisticated linguistic and conceptual abilities, and so cannot itself be used to *explain* what having these abilities amounts to. To be sure, someone who already knows how to use words to talk about things can be introduced to a new word 'ostensively', that is by being shown the sort of thing it applies to. And, of course, there is room for getting at cross purposes, as when I show someone a fat cat, intending to teach them what 'cat' means, and they think I'm telling them the word for being fat. But this illustrates that when things do go smoothly, and the new word is learned, 'the ostensive definition explains the use – the meaning – of the word *when the overall role of the word in language is clear*' (PI: §30, emphases added). That is, rather than our capacity to learn ostensively explaining the ability to name, the ability to name is part of an explanation of how ostensive definition can succeed.

One can accept all this without altogether giving up the claim, common to Descartes, Locke, Frege and many others, that words represent things in the world. Wittgenstein himself is happy to allow that 'the *meaning* of a name is sometimes explained by pointing to its *bearer*' (PI: §43), and he thus accepts that his claims leave some room for word–thing relations to play a role in the explanation of language:

> Think ... how singular is the use of a person's name to *call* him! (PI: §27)

> I mean, how does he call HIM to mind?
> *How does he call him?* (PI: §691)

Moreover, consider the simple language-game he describes in which

> A is building with building-stones: there are blocks, pillars, slabs and beams. B has to pass the stones, and that in the order in which A needs them. For this purpose they use a language consisting of the words 'block', 'pillar', 'slab', 'beam'. A calls them out; – B brings the stone which he has learnt to bring at such-and-such a call. – Conceive this as a complete primitive language. (PI: §2)

Although Wittgenstein is right that merely fastening on a snap-shot of the naming-relation between, say, 'slab' and the slabs on the site will not by itself tell us much about what it is for our builders to understand the word, he could hardly deny that such understanding has *something to do with* relations that hold between A, B, the word and the slabs (and nor does he: see section 3). The only obviously obligatory point in the foregoing is that fixating on static word–thing relations explains very little about the understanding. Just as an act of contemplating an idea which could in itself compel future uses of a word would be 'a superlative fact', so a simple act of naming which did this would be 'an occult process' (PI: §38). It thus seems that one could accept Wittgenstein's criticisms of naming without opposing Frege's theory of Meaning as such. If so, then to this extent anyway, Frege's theory of Meaning could still figure as a *component* of a Wittgensteinian view (just as it could figure as a component of a Lockean view: chapter III, section 4).

It is very hard to quarrel with the Wittgensteinian attack on these snapshot accounts of understanding. Their point in a nutshell is that taking an image one way or another, or fixing a label to a thing for future use, are merely *examples* of the kind of thing we are trying to explain – what it is to understand a sign as a sign – and so help themselves to what they are supposed to be explaining: a fact which is obscured by a tendency to give them a sort of magical status (hence 'occult' and 'superlative'). Up to a point, then, we can take all this as bolstering views that we have been offered already by Frege. The attack on the superlative fact supplies a reason for rejecting the (imagist) theory of ideas as an account of understanding, and the attack on the occult process can support Frege's claim that the theory of Meaning alone is not sufficient to deal with understanding, and so must be supplemented: the existence of word–thing relations presupposes dynamic linguistic abilities which still need to be explained. However, it is still not clear whether this supplementation has to come from the theory of sense or from (say) a materialistic, non-imagist theory of ideas. And as if matters were not already complicated enough, there is anyway a further moral to draw, since Frege's own account of understanding, such as it is, is vulnerable to an extension of these Wittgensteinian attacks.

Fregean senses are supposed to be abstract, objective things which can be 'grasped' by the mind. But what *is* it to grasp a sense? Frege says that

> the sense of a proper name is grasped by everyone who is sufficiently familiar with the language or totality of designations to which it belongs. (S&M: 57–8)

But this tells us nothing about what grasping *is*: rather, it simply adverts to the linguistic abilities which grasping sense is supposed to illuminate (since grasping the sense of a word is supposed to be what understanding it amounts to: talk of grasping sense and talk of understanding are two sides of the same coin). Elsewhere, he says that senses belong to a 'third realm', distinct from both the contents of the individual mind (ideas) and from material things (T: 29). But he recognises that this makes senses rather remote from our linguistic practice and thinking:

> And yet! What value could there be for us in the eternally unchangeable which could neither undergo effects nor have an effect on us? Something entirely and in every respect inactive would be unreal and non-existent for us ... What would a thought be for me that was never apprehended by me? (T: 37)

He concludes that a thought 'acts' (i.e. has causal effect)

> by being apprehended and taken to be true. This is a process in the inner world of a thinker which can have further consequences in this inner world and which, encroaching on the sphere of the will, can also make itself noticeable in the outer world. (T: 38)

But this piles mystery on mystery. In so far as thoughts are abstract, it is self-contradictory to suppose them to have causal effects. Worse, if being acausal makes thoughts 'non-existent for us', then the same would have to be said of the mathematical and logical entities on which Frege's entire philosophy of logic rests. Perhaps, instead, we could take seriously the idea that when he describes thoughts as not belonging to the perceptible material world, he means that they are immaterial in something like Descartes' sense.[1] But this would hardly help, for now we have, in effect, Descartes' interaction problem (chapter I, section 2): how can something in an immaterial 'third realm' causally interact with things in the material realm? It is hard not to conclude that to succeed in grasping a sense would be to participate in a superlative fact; that the relation of grasping itself would be occult. What bearing can these mysterious things have on our ordinary linguistic understanding?

In short, even if Frege's theory of Meaning is substantially correct as far as it goes; and even if he is right to argue that the theory of understanding needs to add something extra in some way; indeed, even though Wittgenstein's criticisms have shown that adding the (imagist) theory of ideas will not help; even so, Frege's own suggestions on what this 'something extra' should be are unappealing. In effect his view is faced by this dilemma: either his talk of grasping senses explains nothing about understanding because it is just another way of saying that understanding occurs; or it explains nothing because it appeals to occult ways of gaining contact with a realm of superlative facts. Either way it explains nothing.

To repeat, this is not to say that Wittgenstein rejects Frege's contentions in this area altogether. In attacking the thought that understanding can be accounted for solely in terms of naming, Wittgenstein at least agrees with Frege that the theory of Meaning would not be enough on its own to account for understanding. In attacking the theory of ideas, and offering a radically alternative account of understanding (see section 3), Wittgenstein agrees too that it would be incorrect to supplement the theory of Meaning with the theory of ideas. Given that, as we have already seen, Wittgensteinian views *could* incorporate Frege's theory of Meaning, it follows that we are free to interpret Wittgenstein's positive theory of understanding as an attempt to provide a theory of *sense* immune to the objections levelled at Frege's own version, and thus to interpret his overall position as a version of a broadly Fregean approach to mind and language. This is how we shall construe Wittgensteinian views henceforth. Meanwhile, his attitude towards snapshot conceptions of understanding is nicely summed up by him as follows:

> When we say 'Every word in language signifies something' we have so far said *nothing whatever* ... Imagine someone saying: '*All* tools serve to modify something' ... – Would anything be gained by this assimilation of expressions? (PI: §§13–14)

2 Definitions and family resemblance

Another influential feature of Wittgenstein's attack on the theory of ideas concerns the claim that one's understanding of certain words can be spelled out in definitions which use simpler words. This claim, as we saw in chapter II, section 2, is integral to Locke's theory of ideas and of how words signify them: and we also saw that a Fregean may, but need not, adopt a similar view (chapter III, section 3). Wittgenstein argues that the linguistic facts simply will not support this proposal. The example he uses is that of 'game':

> What is common to them all? – Don't say: 'There *must* be something common, or they would not all be called "games" ' – but *look and see* whether there is anything common to all... Look for example at board-games... Now pass to card-games; here, you find many correspondences with the first group, but many common features drop out, and others appear. When we pass next to ball-games, much that is common is retained, but much is lost... And the result of this examination is: we see a complicated network of similarities overlapping and criss-crossing: sometimes overall similarities, sometimes similarities of detail. (PI: §66)

Something falls into the class of Xs not, in general, because it satisfies the definition of 'X' and thus shares the features with all other Xs which Locke would have said make up the nominal essence of Xs. Rather, Xs fall into this class because they exhibit various overlapping similarities to one another. Wittgenstein uses two metaphors to make this plainer. One is that we should imagine that the Xs are all bonded together like a rope, that is by way of a lot of overlapping threads each of which is shorter than the whole, so that no one thread runs from one end to the other. As long as the overlaps are tight and numerous enough, this does not threaten the integrity of the rope: no continuous thread is required. Similarly, as long as the pattern of overlapping similarities is stable enough, Xs need not have one or more essential features in common. The other metaphor is that of 'family resemblance'. There may be a definite 'Smith' face, in that all of the extended family Smith look alike and can be easily seen to belong to that family. But a closer look need not reveal there to be one or more specific features which all those with the 'Smith' face share. Rather, there might be a pool of features – large ears, square chin, piercing eyes, high cheek-bones – of which all of the Smiths have one or more, although there is no one of these features which all with the Smith face have. This enables them to resemble each other without sharing an essential Smith-feature.

This claim of Wittgenstein's is compatible with some of what Locke says about words for modes: indeed, in a sense, Wittgenstein takes the spirit of Locke's account rather further. Modes, recall, are more or less arbitrary classifications of things which reflect our interests in some rather than others of the real differences among the things themselves: hence mouse-killing is as distinct a thing in itself as mother-killing, but we (and others with our sense of priorities) notice the latter to the point of having a special word for it, whereas the former has no special salience. This much of what Locke says is quite congenial to Wittgenstein's family-resemblance view, especially the invocation of our interests. For in rejecting Locke's thought that a mode is held together by a definition or nominal essence, Wittgenstein leaves even more work to be done by our sense of what is natural and worth fastening on to. If Xs are not held together as Xs by a nominal essence, then it can only be that X-noticers find it natural to pick up on certain networks of overlapping features rather than others. This is just a fact about their 'form of life'.

It may seem that for Wittgenstein's point to apply, there has to be an original stock of features which we just can notice things as having, and out of which we spin our ropes of overlapping threads, so that if there is a pool of Smith-features, these cannot be subject to the same anti-Lockean point. But why should not Mr Smith's eyes be piercing because they are blue and clear, while the younger Ms Smith's are piercing because they are pale green and slightly prominent? Similar points could then be made about 'prominent', 'clear' and so on. But a Lockean might reply that this will have to stop somewhere, with (say) a basic stock of simple sensory qualities out of which all the other threads are spun. This would at least salvage an aspect of Locke's distinction between simple and complex ideas, and his claim that the latter are built up in regular ways out of the former. True, he would no longer be able to speak of images or of definitions, but he could apparently hang on to the notion of a basic sensory core of indefinable similarities between things. But Wittgenstein would take away even this small crumb. He attacks the notion of simplicity, arguing that it is thoroughly relative to context (as is, then, the co-ordinate notion of complexity: see PI: §§47ff.). And he points out that even apparently primitive sensory similarities such as shared colours are relative to culture, interest and other factors.[2]

As far as the main point about definition and nominal essence is concerned, reflection does seem largely to bear out Wittgenstein's claims, and hence to hammer another nail into the coffin of Locke's theory of ideas. There are a few words whose definitions spring easily to mind – 'bachelor', 'widow', 'oculist' – and it is true that scientists, lawyers, mathematicians and others sometimes provide explicit definitions for terms. But in these latter cases the providing of the definition is often simply relative to a specific, local purpose. Rather than reflecting the common understanding of the terms, moreover, such definitions often involve self-conscious departure from usage, as in the development of a new theoretical concept. Not only that, but such ordinary definitions as there are do not form the kind of hierarchy required by Locke, according to whom complex ideas are broken down by definitions into increasingly simple ones until we arrive at words for indefinable simple ideas of sensation. Even if 'bachelor' is correctly defined as 'unmarried man', and even if 'man' can go into 'male featherless animal with two legs' (and would that be right? – see chapter VII), it is not clear where to go next. Looking in the dictionary, which ought to help if anything could, will not. Dictionaries often do not provide definitions in the sense intended by Locke: and they do not show how it is possible to define all terms, ultimately, in primitive sensory vocabulary. Rather, they supply such hints and examples as are best likely to inform the reader about the ways in which the word is used, for example by listing words with similar meaning, describing characteristic contexts in which the word concerned is appropriate, giving sample sentences containing it. So either lexicographers are falling down on their job, or Wittgenstein is right about definitions, and Locke's theory of ideas has suffered another blow (note too that any attempt by Fregeans to spell out the senses of words in terms of definitions would be similarly compromised). The matter of definitions will be taken up again in chapter VII, when we revisit Locke's theory of substance.

These, then, are Wittgenstein's powerful, destructive arguments against Locke's theory of ideas in particular and snapshot conceptions of the understanding in general. We now face an obvious question: so what, then, is Wittgenstein's positive view?

3 Dynamism in the theory of understanding

If understanding is not static, how might dynamism be injected into the theory of understanding? We shall consider Wittgenstein's own suggestions first, and return later to the question whether others, such as materialistic Cartesians, could do as well, or better.

We saw earlier that Wittgenstein is wont to make rather defeatist-looking claims about the methods and possibilities of philosophy, which is supposed to try and explain nothing and simply to describe things as they are, since everything that might interest us is 'open to view'. But these claims take on a new complexion, at least where the philosophy of understanding is concerned, once his attacks on snapshot conceptions have been absorbed. The aim is to avoid positing superlative facts and occult processes in the description of what it is to understand words. And for Wittgenstein, this means that such a description can only take the form of exhibiting our linguistic practices themselves. In so doing one will indeed say what it is to understand, or (if you like) grasp the sense of, this or that expression. But rather than trying to say what this is in terms of a philosopher's pseudo-scientific theories or static abstractions, one will simply be describing the dynamic facts as they present themselves. Given the centrality of the use of language to our whole way of living, getting hold of such an account could stop at nothing short of a getting hold, howsoever sketchily and incompletely, of a 'form of life'.

Within a form of life, understanding a word is just a matter of exhibiting a pattern of use, that is having an ability, which involves an habitual way of applying the word, a 'custom': 'To understand a language is to be master of a technique' (PI: §199). To be such a master involves such things as applying the word to its proper objects in suitable situations; making appropriate judgements; drawing appropriate inferences. This may seem hopelessly bland, but in fact it is the reverse of that, since the idea is that such ways of acting and judging are *themselves* the medium, as it were, of the logical complexity of language. To get some idea of the force of this claim, recall that for Frege, the logical powers of language are explained in terms of the theory of Meaning, but the bearers of Meaning, strictly speaking, are senses rather than words. This means that, for Frege, *senses are the medium of logic.*

92

But he claimed that a logically adequate language would be able to stand proxy for this medium in our theorising about logical relations:

> The thought, in itself non-sensible, clothes itself in the material garment of a sentence and thereby becomes comprehensible to us. (T: 20)

This is of course convenient, given the mysteriousness of our alleged relations to senses in Frege's own account, and it supplied one reason why Frege concentrated on formal languages rather than natural language.[3] Natural languages are messy, redundant and constantly changing in response to our needs (and confusions), rather than designed expressly to exhibit the logical structure of the thoughts their sentences are used to express. Frege's formal language, on the other hand, is designed to be *logically perspicuous*, in that the grammatical type of an expression is to correspond to its logical type. The best brief illustration of this is in his theory of generality. In English, the sentences

1 Sally smokes

and

2 Everyone smokes

look to have much the same sort of grammatical form, namely a subject ('Sally' or 'everyone') joined on to a predicate ('smokes'). This similarity is reflected in traditional approaches to logic, which mirror and are mirrored by ordinary grammatical classifications. However, at the very heart of Frege's revolution in logic was a clear appreciation that the grammatical similarity between our two sentences conceals a drastic logical difference: and this difference is made plain by the new grammatical forms assigned when the sentences are translated into a logically perspicuous language. In standard modern systems, derived from the one invented by Frege, our two sentences would come out as

1* Fa

and

2* ;x(Fx)

respectively, (where 'a' translates 'Sally', 'F' translates 'smokes' and '; x . . . x' translates 'everyone'): and these very different grammatical forms reflect the differences in the logical properties of 'Sally' and 'everyone' which Frege set out to explicate.[4]

For Wittgenstein, however, this Fregean way of explicating logical complexity is at best a double abstraction. First, people do not speak artificial languages, so an account is needed of the relationship between the perspicuous representations used by logicians, and the actual linguistic practices of natural-language speakers. That would remove the first abstraction. Sense is meant to do this where Frege is concerned, of course, since he was happy that the same sense might be expressed by sentences of different languages (S&M: 58). But we have seen that *simply* positing a 'third realm' of senses explains nothing. So, second, Wittgenstein's view is that the necessary source of the logical complexity of natural language would come from *its use*. That would remove the second abstraction. In this precise manner, the use itself, our practice with the words, is the medium of logic. This point is illustrated in the simple language-game involving builders A and B which we encountered in section 1. Recall that 'B has to pass the stones, and that in the order in which A needs them. For this purpose they use a language consisting of the words "block", "pillar", "slab", "beam" ' (PI: §2). Wittgenstein considers the order 'Slab!' which A might issue from time to time, and raises the natural thought that this has to be understood as 'only a shortened form of the sentence "Bring me a slab" '. He replies, memorably,

> But why should I not on the contrary have called the sentence 'Bring me a slab' a *lengthening* of the sentence 'Slab!'? – Because if you shout 'Slab!' you really mean: 'Bring me a slab.' – But how do you do this: how do you *mean that* while you *say* 'Slab!'? Do you say the unshortened sentence to yourself? And why should I translate the call 'Slab!' into a different expression in order to say what someone means by it? And if they mean the same thing – why should I not say: 'When he says "Slab!" he means "Slab!" '? Again, if you can mean 'Bring me a slab', why should you not be able to mean 'Slab!'? – But when I call 'Slab!', then what I want is, *that he should bring me a slab!* – Certainly, but does

'wanting this' consist in thinking in some form or other a different sentence from the one you utter? – (PI: §19)

His point, of course, is that the logical complexity of 'Slab!', as articulated in the phrase *what I want is, that he should bring me a slab*, is due to the place that the sentence has in the builders' 'form of life'. It is natural for us to translate it as 'Bring me a slab', because our language contains more words and hence the possibilities of forming related sentences about slabs: '*our language* contains the possibility of those other sentences' (PI: §20). But what underlies the correctness of this translation is neither the fact that A thinks to himself 'I want him to bring me a slab' before or during speaking, nor the fact that A's sentence and our translation both stand in a mysterious relation to the same abstract sense. Rather, *the translation's correctness is grounded in the similarities between what they do with 'Slab!' and what we do with 'Bring me a slab'*:

> doesn't the fact that sentences have the same sense consist in their having the same *use*? (PI: §20)

These actions and abilities are the bedrock of understanding or, as we put it earlier, are the medium of logic. These are the mundane facts to which Wittgenstein appeals in order to avoid the superlative and the occult. And this is the way that he hopes to inject dynamism into the theory of understanding, to counteract the weaknesses from which we have seen snapshot conceptions, Frege's as well as Locke's, to suffer.

To object in this way to Frege's double abstraction is not necessarily to be hostile to formal languages, or to be anti-logic, or to strike any other sort of know-nothing pose. All of the above is compatible with the thought that Frege's developments in logic were a genuine advance in our conception of what correct reasoning requires. The only point that has to be carried away is that the actuality from which formal logicians quite properly abstract is constituted by our deeds and linguistic practices. It is true that Wittgenstein himself might want to draw more than this out of it:

> logic does not treat of language – or of thought – in the sense in which a natural science treats of a natural phenomenon, and the most that can be said is that we *construct* ideal languages. But here the word "ideal" is liable to mislead, for

it sounds as if these languages were better, or more perfect, than our everyday language; and as if it took the logician to shew people at last what a proper sentence looked like. (PI: §81)

But the fact is that formal languages *are* better than natural ones *in some respects*, including that of logical perspicuity. To say this is not, however, to imply that non-logicians do not know what proper sentences look like. Of course the sentences of natural language are 'proper sentences': only this does not mean that they cannot be improved upon for certain formal purposes. And if all this is right, then there is no objection in the foregoing to our continuing to regard Wittgensteinian views as formulable within a broadly Fregean framework.

Note the appearance in the discussion of the slab-language of Wittgenstein's rejection, already mentioned, of the thought that understanding is a 'hidden' process which accompanies our use of words. Some such thought can survive his attack on the claim that understanding is static, since this leaves intact the idea of a dynamic 'hidden' process. But Wittgenstein is adamant. We saw above that he denies that we need to think to ourselves something other than we say. Elsewhere, he denies that *any other* form of accompanying process can be the essence of understanding, of which our actual uses of words are merely the visible products. As we shall see in the following chapter, this puts him at odds with a great deal of contemporary Cartesian orthodoxy in the philosophy of mind, as well as in related disciplines such as artificial intelligence, theoretical linguistics and psychology.

4 Thought, talk, self-containedness

So where does all this leave us? We have been seeing that Frege and Wittgenstein continue the tradition of Locke and Descartes of regarding the understanding of language as a key feature of our minds. As we saw, Descartes supposed that having the potential to use language (if suitably embodied) is a necessary condition of having any mind at all; and although Locke allowed some glimmer of awareness even to cockles and oysters, he was adamant that linguistic potential is what makes our minds so superior to those of languageless beasts. Wittgenstein too seems happy to allow non-linguistic forms of mindedness, while emphasising the great advance that language brings:

> One can imagine an animal angry, frightened, unhappy, happy, startled. But hopeful? And why not? A dog believes his master is at the door. But can he also believe his master will come the day after tomorrow? – And *what* can he not do here? – How do I do it? Can only those hope who can talk? Only those who have mastered the use of a language. That is to say, the phenomena of hope are modes of this complicated form of life. (PI: §IIi)

But of course, the huge change that has occurred by the time we get to Wittgenstein is that having these linguistic abilities is not to be explained in terms of contemplating ideas or of grasping senses: rather, the abilities themselves are the bedrock of understanding. At least as far as these more sophisticated forms of mentality are concerned, then, *Wittgenstein reverses the Cartesian priority of thought over talk*. Understanding words, hoping, having beliefs about the day after tomorrow, and being able to do all the things that mark us out from languageless beasts – these are aspects of mind to which *using* language is essential, according to Wittgenstein. Similarly, then, on the Wittgensteinian approach, we should not think of the mind as a thing, material or not, in the head of the minded subject:

> The human body is the best picture of the human soul. (PI: §IIiv)

This in turn is incompatible with one kind of self-containedness found in Descartes and Locke. Wittgenstein at least cannot say that the (typical, human) mind is *self-contained with respect to the human body*. Rather, the description or 'picture' of this mind is a description or 'picture' of the body. Whether or not Wittgenstein is right about this, of course, depends on (among other things) whether other, Cartesian 'pictures' of the mind are compatible with what is right in his rejection of snapshot conceptions of understanding. This we have still to investigate. But this unfinished business should not blind us to the huge change in philosophy of mind that occurs if we accept Wittgenstein's positive account of understanding. If understanding is an aspect of mind, as all the philosophers we have considered agree it is; and if understanding is constituted by our linguistic practices and related activities or 'forms of life'; then these activities and practices are *themselves* aspects of mind, and not merely contingent bodily effects of the mind's workings. This is what it means to accept Wittgenstein's point that understanding is not a 'hidden accompaniment' of use.

What of self-containedness with respect to the body's material surroundings? On the one hand, it might seem that this too is ruled out by Wittgenstein. How can we give any description of 'the weave of our life' (PI: §IIi) without describing how we move among and interact with the things around us? And recall that if we regard Wittgenstein's account of understanding as a candidate for the theory of sense in a broadly Fregean context, then we anyway have to take descriptions of our interactions with things as introducing the modes in which elements from the theory of Meaning are presented to us. It is hard to see how a person's use of the word 'cat' could be conceived without voluminous and essential references to their dealings with cats. In describing these dealings one would be, in effect, describing the way(s) in which that person thinks about cats, and hence describing the mode in which cats are presented.

However, even here things are less simple than one might suppose, as we shall see in chapters VII and VIII. And in any case, recall that Frege supposed that expressions can have sense without Meaning, and that this seems to open up the prospect of a form of Exteriority for the realm of Meaning with respect to the understanding: facts about the latter could be as they are in themselves even if there were no realm of Meaning. Then if we consider examples more remote from the speaker's everyday world than cats are likely to be, it is not so clear that Wittgenstein can rule out self-containedness with respect to our material world altogether. Think of the use of 'Istanbul' of a person who has never left the USA. Perhaps the complete story here would have to make reference to links which ultimately hold between even such a person and the city, via mention of books, photographs, other persons and so on. But it is not obvious how the story would have to be filled out, and how essential *Istanbul itself* would be to the story.[5] And what of names for persons who may not have existed ('Robin Hood') or of things which certainly have never existed ('unicorn')? And surely the uses of words typical of cosmologists or ancient historians do not involve interaction worthy of the name with their 'official' subject-matter, but rather are included in a form of life based on measuring instruments, books, relics? Similarly, if there is a general problem about relating the grasp of Fregean senses to linguistic practice, there will be a parallel problem when trying to construe the activities of mathematicians and logicians as involving dealings with abstract entities.

Examples like these suggest that some form of self-containedness with respect to the surrounding world can survive even Wittgensteinian conclusions. Indeed we can imagine a spectrum of possible views, starting with what we shall call *in-the-skin Wittgensteinianism*. On this view, understanding is indeed mastery of a technique, but our descriptions of these techniques must not refer to anything in the surroundings of the individual concerned – nothing beyond the skin – which would all be deemed Exterior. It is very unlikely that the historical Wittgenstein would have recognised this as a version of his own view, and perhaps we could not get very far with the proposed descriptions (see chapter V, sections 2 and 4). But it does seem a theoretical possibility, or, perhaps better, an imaginary limit. Then moving away from it, in any case, will be varieties of what we shall call *in-the-world Wittgensteinianism*. On this approach, descriptions of techniques are allowed to make essential mention of aspects of the individual's surroundings, and the more inclusive and specific these descriptions are allowed to be, and the more they mention comparatively remote aspects of the world (recall the ancient historians), the more extreme will be our form of in-the-world Wittgensteinianism, and correspondingly less of the world will count as Exterior. The issues raised by this will run throughout Part Two, and we shall eventually recommend a strong form of in-the-world Wittgensteinianism.

5 Naturalism and normativity

We need to round off our picture of Wittgenstein by noting one further important feature of his position. On the one hand there are strong naturalistic tendencies. *Naturalism* is normally understood in the present context as the view that persons, and in particular their minds and associated linguistic and other capacities, are part of the natural order as investigated by sciences like physics, chemistry and biology. Thus of activities which constitute 'forms of life' Wittgenstein says

> commanding, questioning, recounting, chatting, are as much a part of our natural history as walking, eating, drinking, playing. (PI: §25)

In addition, we have seen the weight he puts on our natural tendencies to classify and see indefinable 'family' resemblances among things: and we have seen how, overall, his idea is that our ordinary ways with words, and the manner in which these involve our day-to-day practices, underpin the logical complexity of language and constitute our understanding of it. We can contrast naturalism with *supernaturalism*. Cartesian Dualism is probably best seen as a form of supernaturalism, since it is unlikely that immaterial thinking substances can be regarded as part of the natural order just mentioned, that is as things whose operations can be investigated by the physical sciences, things which just evolved along with mouths and prehensile hands. Rather, it is more in tune with the immaterialist form in which Descartes presented Cartesianism, to imagine God inserting the immaterial mind into the body-machine at the appropriate time, thereby creating a human person with the ability to think, reason and understand language.

It may now seem obvious that superlative facts and occult processes go with supernaturalism, and that Wittgenstein's opposition to them is a further, salutary reflection of his naturalism. But here there is a problem. This arises because our ordinary uses of words are rule-governed. This means that in using a word we are guided by norms, or standards of correctness and incorrectness. The word 'cat' as we understand it applies to feline animals but not to canines. Thus one goes right in applying 'cat' to Felix, but wrong in applying it to Fido. This is a point which had been emphasised by Frege:

> The word 'law' is used in two senses. When we speak of the laws of morals ... we mean regulations which ought to be obeyed but with which actual happenings are not always in conformity. Laws of nature [on the other hand] are the

generalisations of natural occurrences with which the occurrences are always in accordance. (T: 17)

Just as, then, we must distinguish, in the realm of conduct, *anthropological* accounts of what people actually do from *prescriptive* accounts of what people ought to do, so too in logic. There are *psychological* laws about how people do reason and there are *logical* laws about how they ought to reason:

> The assertion both of what is false and of what is true takes place in accordance with psychological laws. A derivation from these and an explanation of a mental process that terminates in an assertion can never take the place of a proof of what is asserted. (*Ibid.*)

Similarly, psychology might explain why X called Felix a cat and why Y called Fido a cat. But this is not yet to touch the point that X was right and Y was wrong (assuming they both meant to be speaking English words with their customary meanings, of course).

Now it is a platitude of modern times that the natural world as treated by the physical sciences is in itself valueless, that there is no right and wrong or good and bad in the world itself. In the field of morals this has resulted mostly in attempts either to deny any meaning or point to moral talk, or to explain its point in terms of the 'privileging' or enforcement, either nice or nasty, of the wishes and desires of some individuals or groups over those of others. In so far as naturalism is true and persons are thus part of the natural world, one would expect a similar kind of problem about how to find room for the norms of reasoning. So recall that Descartes cited the linguistic creativity and reasoning powers of persons as what distinguished them from mere natural machines (chapter I, section 5): and it is perhaps no accident that Frege resorted to talk of a 'third realm' of senses, even while he was trying to secure logic and language the objectivity which the possibility of shared science seemed to require. Contrariwise, it is not uncommon to find people who regard logic, like morals, as the result of enforcement, a 'privileging' of one particular style of perhaps phallocentric discourse, the outcome of powerful white men telling everyone else how to think. Given the prevalence of naturalism and the problem of reconciling it with the reality of values and norms, this despairing reaction is only to be expected.

However all this may be, the tension between naturalism and normativity finds a very powerful expression in Wittgenstein's thought. His view is that understanding, the medium of logic, is constituted by our ordinary practices with words. It follows, then, that normativity must also figure somehow at this level: something about our practices must make it the case that rules are enshrined which dictate the difference between right and wrong in our use of words. The problem starts to emerge when we realise that any particular stretch of linguistic activity is finite, that is, contains a limited number of applications of the words involved. However, the rules involved are supposed to stretch beyond these finite applications and to dictate what would be right and wrong in an unlimited number of other cases too. To say that 'cat' is understood by us in the way in which it is understood is not simply to say that it has been applied to x,y,z, . . . : it is also to say that it *will be* applied to u,v,w, . . . (assuming our understanding of the word does not change); and that it *would have been* applied to r,s,t, . . . had circumstances been different (and our understanding of it had remained constant). And how can a finite practice have such implications? What is it about a practice which makes it the case that one rule is enshrined rather than another? How can what we do determine what we will and would have done? For example, every cat is also either a cat, or-a-dog-born-in-the-21st-century, so that every time up to now that we have applied 'cat' to a cat, we have also applied it to a cat, or-a-dog-born-in-the-21st-century. Thus it seems that everything we have done with the word 'cat' so far is compatible with our meaning *cat, or dog-born-in-the-21st-century* by it. So what is it about us that determines that we do not mean this?

A simple answer is that we understand 'cat' to have one particular sense rather than another. But this gets the cart before the horse in a Wittgensteinian setting: understanding a word to have a particular sense, after all, is supposed to be explained in terms of our practice with it, rather than the other way around. More, the resort to senses, if it is taken in the way Frege intended, looks like a straight move to supernaturalism. Nor will it help to point out that, if asked, we will reply that 'cat' means *cat* and not, say, *cat, or dog-born-in-the-21st-century*. Our uses of the words in this explanation are just as subject to the problem as any other uses of words we might produce. Perhaps 'cat, or dog-born-in-the-21st-century' means *cat, or dog-born-in-the-21st-century, or pig-with-twelve-legs*!

A more promising answer is that our understanding of a word is not to be accounted for just in terms of our actual, finite uses, but rather in terms of our dispositions or tendencies to do other things. To see the shape of this suggestion, note first that the claim

we understand 'cat' to mean *cat*

has certain affinities with the claim

these pieces of sugar are soluble in water.

To say this second thing is not to say that the pieces have dissolved in water nor even that they will dissolve in water: they might never have, and might be destroyed before they ever can, but this does not make them insoluble. It is nearer the mark to say that they *would* dissolve if they were to be placed in (unsaturated) water. In other words, *being soluble in water* is a disposition which sugar has, the disposition-to-dissolve-in-water-in-appropriate-circumstances. Similarly, we might say that understanding 'cat' to mean *cat* is a disposition which we have, a disposition-to-apply-'cat' to certain things but not to others. We are not disposed to apply 'cat' to dogs born in the 21st century, and that is why our practice does not enshrine the rule that we should. Given this, the normativity of rule-following would come out as no more inherently mysterious or supernatural than dispositions such as solubility

It is rather sobering to face the fact that this promising-looking answer faces a very serious objection. First, sugar's solubility in water is a matter of natural law: when a piece of sugar dissolves, then, it is not following a norm. It is not acting in accordance with a rule which it might well have gone against. If a piece of sugar failed to dissolve in an appropriate sample of water, that would simply show that the alleged natural law 'sugar is soluble in water' is false as it stands. We could not say that the law is true, but this piece of sugar made a mistake in not obeying it. On the other hand, if someone in bad light or whatever applies 'cat' to a dog then there is room to say that they are making a mistake, and not acting as they should. Of course, the putative natural law

people who mean *cat* by 'cat' never apply it to dogs

would be falsified by such an occurrence. But the claim

this person means *cat* by 'cat'

would not thereby be falsified: *that is what allowing for mistakes leaves room for.* In sum, dispositions to apply words do not in themselves appear to carry the normativity to be found in our practices.

How, then, should one respond to the problem of normativity? Given that a retreat to supernaturalism looks distinctly unpromising, there appear to be three types of response. The first, which is becoming more common, is to derive a sceptical (or more properly nihilistic) conclusion. If Wittgenstein really has demonstrated that understanding cannot be explained in terms of inner processes, the contemplation of ideas, the grasping of senses and so on, then all we are left with are dispositions to use words. So if they cannot deliver an account of meaning and understanding, *there are simply no such things.* This is obviously an example of naturalism about a domain leading on to a denial that there can be any norms, any rightness or wrongness, in that domain. But the outcome here is spectacular: there is no such thing as meaning, and there is no such thing as correct understanding of language. Such claims are quite fashionable on the basis of overgeneralised theses in the theory of literary criticism, but their roots are in the analytical philosophy of the first half of the present century, and ultimately in naturalism. We shall return to this sort of view briefly in chapter VIII, section 9.

Some interpret Wittgenstein as having embraced such a nihilistic response.[6] But it is perhaps nearer the mark to see him as offering a second way out, namely that understanding words is a basic, given fact about us which cannot be explained or analysed in more primitive terms. Certainly such a construal of him squares with repeated claims like:

This was our paradox: no course of action could be determined by a rule, because every course of action can be made out to accord with a rule ... What this shews is that there is a way of grasping a rule which is *not an interpretation*, but which is exhibited in what we call 'obeying the rule' and 'going against it' in actual cases. (PI: §201)

Philosophy may in no way interfere with the actual use of language; it can in the end only describe it. For it cannot give it any foundation either. It leaves everything as it is. (PI: §124)

It also accords well with his arguments against things having essences in common which informative definitions might disclose. Moreover, if linguistic practice *just is* the medium of logic, then how could there be anything more basic about our understanding than the very practices we engage in?[7] However, whether or not Wittgenstein favoured this response, it faces a nasty-looking dilemma. First, how can this claim about understanding being a primitive unanalysable fact about us avoid being a retreat to supernaturalism? For it can look as though this alleged primitive fact is simply stuck on to the body's natural behaviour in a way analogous to that in which Descartes' immaterial mind is inserted into the body-machine. But second, once we have all the facts about a person's dispositions to use words, what else is there? And if this account of dispositions does not cover the matter of understanding, why worry?[8] Why not simply drop all talk of the alleged unanalysable facts? In other words, this second response is in danger either of smuggling in supernaturalism by the back door, or of collapsing into nihilism.

We shall ultimately try to save this second response from the dilemma by suggesting that it is not really naturalism that is threatened by normativity, but scientism: the view that all there is to be known can be expressed or explained in the terms of the natural sciences. But before coming to that we need to consider at greater length a third response to the normativity problem. This is that we should try to make the story about dispositions more sophisticated, and e.g. try to explain what it is to make a mistake in terms of dispositions to correct oneself, accept the corrections of others, and so on. One obvious danger here is that there may well be no real illumination to be had of what it is to understand: rather, the account will simply help itself to what we are already given about the understanding of words and simply tinker relentlessly with the story about dispositions in order to make it fit. In other words, there is a danger here of once more getting the cart before the horse. It is because we mean *cat* by 'cat' that we are disposed to apply the word to cats and not dogs, and similarly disposed to withdraw mistaken applications of it to dogs, accept the corrections of others and so on. Claims about what we understand words to mean serve to organise and make sense of the pattern of our dispositions to use them.

Be this as it may, one could still argue that a properly worked-out account of the kinds of dispositions that constitute this pattern would at least have shown how the normativity present in our practices is grounded in perfectly natural bodily dispositions, and would thus be worth having just for that reason. And this connects, rather conveniently, with lingering dissent from Wittgenstein's positive approach that can survive the arguments of the present chapter. This emanates from the materialistic Cartesianism which, as far as we have been able to tell, is not refuted by Wittgenstein's arguments against the imagist theory of ideas and other views which present understanding as static. Up to a point, then, the suggestion that we try to refine the dispositional account of normativity can join forces somewhat with the suggestion that we go back to the beginning. If Wittgenstein leads us to where we blankly confront the problem of how practices, the alleged bedrock of our understanding, could possibly incorporate norms, then the thought is that we are better not to follow. If this is what seeing linguistic behaviour as the medium of logic delivers, then we had better look for something else. This is connected with the thought that Wittgensteinian views are, at bottom, forms of Behaviourism, and that Behaviourism overlooks entirely the *explanatory* dimension of the mind. Once we see this matter aright, the thought goes, everything else will fall into place. The obvious anti-Behaviouristic suggestion is that the way forward here is to talk about the brain. This is a pefectly natural phenomenon; why should not its perfectly natural activities be the medium of logic and understanding, and its perfectly natural dispositions the source of normativity in our practices? We shall now turn to this very common contemporary position.

Notes and reading

Works referred to

S&M   Frege, G., 'On sense and Meaning' in *Translations from the Philosophical Writings of Gottlob Frege*, 3rd edn, eds P. Geach and M. Black (Oxford: Blackwell, 1980).

T   Frege, G., 'The thought: a logical enquiry', trans. A. and M. Quinton in *Philosophical Logic*, ed. P. Strawson (Oxford: Oxford University Press, 1967).

PI   Wittgenstein, L., *Philosophical Investigations*, trans. G.E.M. Anscombe (Oxford: Blackwell, 1953).

Notes

1 Thus in the Quinton translation of 'The thought', Frege is at one point represented as describing a thought as 'in itself immaterial' (T: 20). But the German word actually used, *unsinnlich*, simply means imperceptible by the senses, and carries no suggestion of the mental or spiritual, or any other Cartesian connotation. Thanks here to Robert Black.

2 Locke could reply that this at least leaves some such notion as *exact matching shade*, but the problem here is that it seems to have no application in our experience. For A may look to be the same shade as B, and B may look to be the same shade as C, while A does not look to be the same shade as C. So how can *exact matching shade* be a primitive sensory similarity?

3 As Michael Dummett explains very clearly, Frege is not very faithful in practice to his doctrine that strictly speaking it is senses rather than words which have Meaning: *Origins of Analytical Philosophy* (London: Duckworth, 1993), chs 10 and 12.

4 See Michael Dummett, *Frege: Philosophy of Language* (London: Duckworth, 1975), chs 2 and 15, and Peter Geach, *Reference and Generality* (Ithaca, NY: Cornell University Press, 1962).

5 See Saul Kripke, *Naming and Necessity* (Oxford: Blackwell, 1980), and Gregory McCulloch, *The Game of the Name* (Oxford: Oxford University Press, 1989), ch. 8.

6 See Saul Kripke, *Wittgenstein on Rules and Private Language* (Oxford: Blackwell, 1982). Despite its generally acknowledged faults as an interpretation of Wittgenstein, this excellent book is the best introduction available to the normativity problems raised in the present section.

7 See e.g. Colin McGinn, *Wittgenstein on Meaning* (Oxford: Blackwell, 1984): 150–64, and John McDowell, 'Meaning and Intentionality in Wittgenstein's later philosophy', in P.A. French, T. Uehling and H. Wettstein, eds, *Midwest Studies in Philosophy Vol. XVII* (Notre Dame, IN: University of Notre Dame, 1992).

8 This is one natural way of seeing the arguments for the indeterminacy of translation in chapter 2 of W.V.O. Quine's *Word and Object* (Cambridge, MA: MIT Press, 1960). Thus see the later claim that 'Brentano's thesis of the irreducibility of intentional idioms [i.e. talk about meanings] is of a piece with the thesis of the indeterminacy of translation. One may accept the Brentano thesis either as showing the indispensability of intentional idioms and the importance of an autonomous science of intention, or as showing the baselessness of intentional idioms and the emptiness of a science of intention. My attitude . . . is the second' (221). The question of whether there is a *science* of intention is one thing, left open in what follows: but the question of whether intentional idioms are *baseless* is surely something else – see chapter VI; and chapter VIII, section 9.

CHAPTER V

Behaviourism and Mentalism

Wittgenstein's emphasis on linguistic practices in the theory of understanding is part of a general anti-Cartesian tendency in the first half of the twentieth century. In particular, Cartesianism was for a time eclipsed by Behaviourism in both psychology and analytical philosophy (not that Wittgenstein was a Behaviourist, as we shall see); and *Existentialism*, another roughly contemporaneous anti-Cartesian tradition, emphasised embodiment in a manner strikingly like Wittgenstein's (it will be discussed briefly in the following chapter). However, all of this was very swiftly countered by a great resurgence of Cartesianism, and in this sense, philosophy of mind somersaulted in the space of half a century. Initiated partly by various developments in psychology, linguistics, computer science and artificial intelligence, and accompanying a great ideological shift in analytical philosophy, the contemporary form of Cartesianism is resolutely materialistic and naturalistic: the study of the mind is equated with the study, at a certain level of abstraction, of the brain. What makes it Cartesian is, partly, its concentration on such functions as perception, information processing, reasoning and linguistic potential. But even more, it is that its enquiries are usually pursued under the overriding assumption that the human mind, being at bottom the brain, is self-contained with respect to its material surroundings, including, often, the (rest of the) human body. The present chapter is concerned with this development, and its exact bearing on the arguments we have surveyed in the preceding chapters.

1 Behaviourism

Behaviourism started as an attempt to inject scientific objectivity into psychology. This was in reaction to *introspectionist* methods which involved the idea, presumably deriving from the Cartesian tradition, that the way to investigate the mind is for individuals to introspect and report what is turned up. It is hard to see how this could produce an objective science, however, since there is no obvious way of systematising the results of such subjective enquiries. Worse, the idea that people are influenced by unconscious beliefs and desires, unavailable to introspection, hardly supports the programme. So what is objective about persons? What is it about me that can be observed by you and anyone else suitably situated, and compared to the equivalent observable aspect of others, and hence perhaps systematised under scientific law? My behaviour. Thus it was proposed that psychology should explain complex mental accomplishments such as seeking, feeding and, ultimately, writing books and learning about Exteriority, in terms of the environment's impacts on individuals, especially its tendency to reinforce some reactions and extinguish others. Individuals, driven initially by biological needs for e.g. food and sexual gratification, gradually become minded by being pressed by the environment into the shape we call 'having a mind'.

This drive to base psychology on observable matters had a more distant philosophical underpinning, related to themes we have already encountered. As remarked at the beginning of chapter III, the development of science paradoxically went hand in hand with a new style of Empiricist philosophising which encouraged the view that there is no world beyond ourselves. In the philosophy of science this leads to a deep suspicion of unobservable entities. How can we know things about electrons, charge, magnetism, when they are beyond our powers of observation? What can result is *Instrumentalism*, a kind of idealism about unobservable entities, according to which they are merely fictions posited to help organise and predict observable occurrences. Science is seen as a mechanism for discovering statistical and other regularities in the observable realm, for which purpose it is fruitful to *pretend* that there are entities beyond in an unobservable realm. Now what counts as observable obviously depends on how strict the theorists are being about the Lockean 'dark

110

room' conception of the observer, and also depends on the science in question. But it is clear that when applied to psychology this approach would deliver the result that the regularities to seek are those exhibited in behaviour, and that 'inner' mental states are mere fictions.

It remains, for philosophers anyway, to worry about what we are saying when we say things like 'X is intelligent', 'X believes it is raining', 'X wants a bicycle for Christmas'. If Behaviourism is true, then surely these descriptions of X have to be construed as somehow all about behaviour? In so far as they are not so construed, there is a suspicion that they contain suspect references to unknowable spiritual mechanisms, say. This led to proposals to *translate* them into talk of actual and possible behaviour. Thus 'X believes it is raining' might go into 'X is putting on her raincoat, glancing at the sky and making clucking noises, and if offered an umbrella she would probably take it . . .'. Such an approach – *Reductive Behaviourism* – clearly has some superficial affinities with Wittgenstein's position, with its emphasis on doing and its antipathy to hidden processes, although the similarities here, as we shall see, are greatly outweighed by the differences. Be that as it may, Reductive Behaviourism is a philosopher's linguistic proposal, and belongs with well-known views motivated for parallel reasons (*Phenomenalism*: the proposal to translate talk of material objects into talk of ideas or sense data; *Operationalism*: the proposal to translate talk of unobservable physical entities into talk of measuring instruments). Such proposals, fuelled jointly by the exploitation of Frege's logical advances, which provided new techniques for sophisticated translation, and by the epistemological concerns taken from Descartes, Locke, Berkeley, Hume . . . , these were the *raison d'etre* of *Logical Positivism*. This movement developed initially in Vienna in the 1920s and 1930s around Schlick, Carnap, Neurath and others, before transplanting itself to the USA, where it became a very dominant philosophical ideology.[1]

2 Mentalism

The only real problem with Behaviourism is that it does not work. In psychology, it perhaps yields some advances in the understanding of salivating dogs and rats in mazes, but as regards explaining more complex forms of behaviour, it rarely advanced much beyond the mere sketch of a possible explanation: and when it did, this was often because it surreptitiously helped itself to non-behaviouristic elements. One severe problem here is that of describing environmental inputs or 'stimuli' without presupposing them to be conceptually organised by the subject. This is crucial, since to make such a presupposition is to import ineliminable reference to the subject's powers of mental organisation into an account which is supposed to explain them in other terms. One illustration of the severity of this problem, given by the influential anti-Behaviourist Jerry Fodor, starts from the point that

> While foreign languages strike the ear as an almost continuous flow of sound, one's own language appears to be segmented in some quite definite way. Moreover, speakers exhibit considerable interjudge reliability when they are asked to describe the segmentation of particular [spoken] sentences in their language. (PE: 80)

Fodor goes on that this situation is 'somewhat puzzling', since if the perceived segmentation were an objective feature of the stimuli, then there is no reason why pauses should not be heard in a foreign language: whereas if they are somehow subjectively projected by listeners, then why should there be so much interjudge agreement? In fact, Fodor reports, the perceived pauses do not correlate with energy drops in the acoustic signals but with the grammatical structure of the uttered sentence:

> Almost everyone who speaks English will locate a pause in the juncture of the phrase 'Bob#Lees', though one can certify by spectrographic analysis ... that the acoustic pattern is closer to Bo#bLees. (PE: 81–2)

Perception of segmentation seems to depend, then, on understanding the utterance, at least as far as its grammar: and that is why a language not understood sounds like a continuous flow. But *understanding* seems to presuppose the agent's mentality. And what of the interjudge agreement? Fodor says here that if we posit internal processing of the incoming information, involving in this case 'unconscious' application of shared grammatical rules (PE: 84), then both the perception of segmentation and the interjudge agreement are immediately explained. In other words, *understanding*, of grammar anyway, is here equated with the internal processing of incoming information. This positing of internal psychological structures in order to explain observable behaviour or ability is called *Mentalism*. The details of this particular case are not important: what is important is that Mentalism has become very common in psychological theories of such things as perception and linguistic competence.

Now practising Behaviourists did not assert that human bodies are empty. Everyone acknowledged that they are full of interesting stuff, much of it responsible for the way they behave. But the innards had their own sciences already – anatomy, physiology, neurology – so unless psychology set itself up as the study of the immaterial soul, it was not clear what it was meant to be about. The idea that it should seek regularities in behaviour, and try to explain these in terms of conditioning and reinforcement, was thus a tremendous liberation: particularly in the light of the positivistic ideology. However, this ideology, at bottom idealistic, itself came under pressure and was gradually abandoned and replaced by various kinds of realism (chapter III, section 1). Given the importance of Frege's logical revolution to the philosophy of the present century, his influence must eventually have told (he also had an influence on psychology by a more roundabout route, as we shall see shortly). But a perhaps more decisive factor was the creeping scientism that came to dominate analytical philosophy. It is hard to treat science as the only source of knowledge while also insisting that its voluminous talk of unobservable entities cannot be taken at face value, that is as an attempt to say what the world is really like in itself, regardless of how it impinges on our awareness. As a result, *Scientific Realism* has superseded Logical Positivism as the dominant ideology of analytical philosophy.[2] It takes over the scientism and the concern with language and logic of Logical Positivism, but expunges its idealistic tendency and replaces it with forthright realism, at least where the entities sanctioned by physical science are concerned. According to the Scientific Realist, talk of electrons and the like is not talk of useful fictions, but talk of real but unobservable things which we have every reason to suppose exist.

Once positivism is replaced by realism, that is, the ideological objection to taking an official interest in what goes on behind the data among which regularities are being sought disappears. More, it comes to be seen as a confusion not to take such an official interest: given realism, the scientist's job includes developing explanatory theories about unobservable entities which are held to cause the data to come out as they do. But this creates a *prima facie* difficulty for psychologists: as already remarked, the innards already have their own sciences. The way out here involved the rise of computer science and the project of creating artificial intelligence (AI). A central aim of this project is to produce machines capable of the sort of task which, if performed by a human, would count as intelligent behaviour. An organising factor was the AI hypothesis that

> any system that exhibits general intelligence will prove upon analysis to be a physical-symbol system . . . [and] any physical-symbol system of sufficient size can . . . exhibit general intelligence. (CSE: 111)

A physical-symbol system 'is a machine that produces through time an evolving collection of symbol structures' (CSE 110–11). These authors go on that 'the roots of the hypothesis go back to the program of Frege . . . for formalizing logic' (CSE: 112). The point is not that Frege himself proposed the AI hypothesis, but that his great advances in formalisation led to viable suggestions about how powerful logical languages might be realised in mechanical systems. Such systems would then be able to perform calculations, logical manipulations and other activities associated with reasoning. The next step, crucial in the development of Mentalism in psychology, is to note that, since the human brain is at least involved in 'exhibiting general intelligence', the above quote implies that it too will turn out to be a physical-symbol system. And in fact this concept had already been applied directly to the brain in a seminal attempt to

> record the behaviour of complicated [neural] nets in the notation of the symbolic logic of propositions. (LNA: 23)

Thus the upshot of the move from positivism to realism, as far as psychology is concerned, is the conception of it as a study of certain of the functions of the brain, *to be carried out at a higher level of abstraction* than that employed in neurology and related body-sciences. Given the developments in computer science and

AI, Mentalism, the successor to Behaviourism, tends towards the view that the mind is to be understood as a sort of computer, and the hypothesis that all mental computation is the manipulation of symbols is usually interpreted as the doctrine that there is a *Language of Thought* instantiated in the brain. The same parallels with AI and computer science encourage the idea that *anything* with the right sort of internal organisation underlying appropriate performance can count as minded, regardless of what it is made of. Then we can still say, if we like, that the mind is the brain (among humans), but our account of mental characteristics will be couched at a level which ignores the actual material implementation, and allows that other physical arrangements which are not brains may yet be (e.g. alien or artificial) minds. Functionalism, the idea that to be minded is to have inner states with the right causal relations among themselves and with inputs and outputs, is one (but not the only) way of trying to spell this out further.

All of this is the background to the modern hypothesis, mentioned briefly in chapter I, sections 5 and 6, that the mind works by processing language-like elements. And it clearly has much in common with the Cartesian doctrine that the mind works by processing ideas, so providing an obvious affinity between traditional Cartesianism and contemporary Mentalism. Indeed, it only requires one final step to turn Mentalism into a forthright version of materialistic Cartesianism. For Cartesian Dualism itself *can easily* be regarded as a form of Mentalism. On this view of it, the operations of the immaterial mind are the unobservable (to the public) psychological mechanisms, and certain of the activities of the body are the observable (to the public) data, caused to be the way they are because of the operations of the psychological mechanisms. This gives, if you like, a quasi-scientific version of the mind's self-containedness with respect to the body. Just as electrons could be the way they are in themselves even if there were no cloud-chambers in which they could have effects; and just as rocks and bushes could be the way they are in themselves even if there were no perceivers on whom they could have effects; so immaterial minds could be the way they are in themselves even if there were no bodies for them to cause to behave. Moreover, it is apparent that very little need change here, except for the better, if the Mind–Brain Identity Thesis is adopted instead of immaterialism. One loses the problem of how the immaterial mind could cause the body to behave: but the natural response here is 'Good riddance!' Otherwise, the essential shape of the Mentalism is retained. The brain, or perhaps more accurately the brain and the nervous system together, constitute the inner psychological mechanisms which cause the overt behaviour of the body, the data which the psychologist needs to systematise and then explain. One more natural adjustment can then take us to Functionalism, and it thus seems that the Mentalism described above is the proper, contemporary, scientifically respectable organ of Cartesian doctrine: and, conversely, that Descartes, his immaterialism and stress on consciousness notwithstanding, is the true precursor of the scientific approach to the mind.

We now have to see, however, that this last, obvious-looking synthesis overlooks a simple, but fundamental, point, and so sows the seeds of a fatal mistake.

3 Scientific psychology and 'folk psychology'

The first crucial point to keep sight of is that the development from Behaviourism to Mentalism belongs in the first instance to scientific psychology, that is to the attempt to provide explanatory mechanisms for underpinning intelligent performance and the like. Hence despite the described affinities with Cartesian Dualism, there is at least a difference of emphasis. This is most clearly seen in Descartes' claim that ideas are phenomenological objects or items of awareness, and his concomitant stress on the centrality of consciousness. This is to be contrasted with Fodor's talk of unconscious psychological structures underlying our use of language: and more generally, one should not suppose that the central claim of this Mentalism is that the brain *consciously* computes elements of the Language of Thought. Now one might suppose that this merely reflects the fact that Descartes put too much stress on consciousness: a thought which is somewhat reinforced by the Fregean and Wittgensteinian attacks on the theory of ideas which were described in chapters III and IV. However, there is a much deeper point in the offing.

One can distinguish things as they are given to us in everyday life, and things as they are given to us through science: thus the familiar solid brown table in the kitchen, and the cloud of buzzing particles. It is natural to say that this is but one thing given in two quite different ways. But they certainly are different ways. One can obviously regard the table in the familiar way without thinking of it as, or even suspecting that it might be thought of as, a cloud of buzzing particles. Conversely, one can imagine creatures with different kinds of sense organs and a very different culture who can conceive of the table as a scientific object but have no grip on our familiar view of it (though they will presumably have their own everyday way of encountering it). This talk of the everyday view of things concerns how they appear to us, that is, figure in our conscious life. To say that the familiar table is coloured and solid is to say that we are aware of it as coloured and encounter it as solid: hard and resisting and not full of space. Even if we come to believe that *really* it is mostly colourless empty space, we do not thereby cease to encounter it as coloured and solid: our visual field does not black out; we do not find ourselves able to wade through the table. All of this is, in a perfectly ordinary sense, an aspect of the *phenomenology* of our existence, of what it is like[3] to be us, and the familiar everyday table is in this same ordinary sense a phenomenological object.

The distinction between how things are given to us in ordinary life and how they are given to us through science can also be made in the case of the *mind*: there is the everyday or *folk psychological* view of the mind, and there is the scientific psychological view. Now it may be that there is reason to take a computational, Mentalistic approach in the scientific case, that is to think of the mind as the brain (at least among humans) and the brain as a kind of computer. But even if this is correct, it is clear that this sort of scientific story does not, and is not intended to, ring true from the folk psychological point of view. Even if minds *are* computational mechanisms, they do not strike us that way in everyday life. They are not presented to us like that in so far as we are folk psychologists, and even if we come to believe that that is what they are. Consequently, it is possible that Descartes' emphasis on the conscious aspects of mind, and his treatment of ideas as phenomenological objects, indicate that he was at least partly interested in the everyday mind, that is, the mind as it strikes us in folk psychology. And whether or not Descartes was, it is certainly possible to take such an interest: for example, Wittgenstein with his emphasis on our ordinary practices, the

117

'weave of our life', can hardly be seen as doing anything else – recall 'the human body is the best picture of the human soul' (PI: §IIiv).

Given all this, there is actually a need for connecting argument to take us from the Mentalism we have described, which is a view that belongs to scientific psychology, to any particular claim about the status of the folk psychological mind. And this need is thoroughly buried beneath the line of thought that treats Descartes as a precursor, albeit immaterialist, of Mentalism. To the extent that Descartes' phenomenological claims can be interpreted as descriptions of the mind as recorded in folk psychology, it is an oversimplification to see him merely as positing 'unobservable' psychic mechanisms in order to explain behavioural regularities. This is not a point about Descartes' actual intentions, but a point about the options which exist in the space between scientific psychology and folk psychology.

The clearest way to illustrate this very important point is to consider the relations between Mentalism and the Wittgensteinian approach described in the preceding chapter. From the perspective of Mentalism, the natural and often expressed thought is that Wittgenstein's view, in so far as it can be made coherent, has to be a (perhaps obscure) form of Behaviourism. And given the failures of Behaviourism, recently described, it then seems equally natural that his views about the understanding are better replaced by some version of the idea that understanding is constituted by computations in the brain. So the move to realism might seem itself to rule out the Wittgensteinian position. But this is a travesty. Despite his hostility to the thought that understanding is really a hidden process which accompanies behavioural manifestations, and despite the appearance of behaviouristic sympathies, there is no need to take Wittgenstein's view as behaviouristic. First, much of his hostility to hidden processes is either hostility to the theory of ideas as such, or hostility to the claim that e.g. in order to mean *fetch me a brick* by 'Brick!' one has to think to oneself 'Fetch me a brick'. In other words, much of this attack is directed at claims that the hidden process of understanding is some *conscious* accompaniment of using words:

> What is essential is to see that the same thing can come before our minds when we hear the word and the appli-

cation still be different. Has it the *same* meaning both times?
I think we shall say not. (PI: §140)

But this much of the attack is usually accepted to have worked,
and to be compatible with Mentalism. As remarked, the words
of the Language of Thought are not supposed generally to be
available to consciousness.

Furthermore, Wittgenstein's view is, rather obviously, *compatible* with the idea that abilities to use words are causally grounded
in the structures of the brain. Indeed, to deny this would simply
be foolish, and would invite empirical refutation: of course the
movements of throat, larynx, head, eyes, arms and so on which
are involved in the use of words are brought about by structures
in the brain. Who can seriously imagine otherwise these days?
Surely not even the most reactionary of Wittgensteinians or,
indeed, hold-outs who still subscribe to Behaviourism. True, it is
a further step from here to the claim that these brain structures
can be described, at a suitable level of abstraction, in the kind of
psychological and computational vocabulary envisaged by Mentalists, and another step or more again to the Language of
Thought hypothesis. But although Wittgenstein makes occasional
remarks which indicate a lack of sympathy with such approaches,[4]
we do not have to follow him here. On the whole, the proof of
the pudding has to be in the eating. If psychologists and workers
in AI can develop concepts and methods which enhance our
understanding of how we manage to be capable of the very
complex abilities of which we are capable, then that would be
enough to vindicate their claims on behalf of their enterprise. Of
course a lot of different issues are involved here, among them
the question whether such internal processing as goes on in my
brain is something I *do*, albeit 'unconsciously', rather than simply
something that happens in me, like the secretion of acid in the
stomach. But the important point to get hold of is that this is not
the ground on which to fight for Wittgenstein's claims about
our abilities being the medium of logic, or what constitutes our
understanding.

*For conceding Mentalism in scientific psychology is not the same
thing as conceding the mind's self-containedness with respect to
the body. Conceding the computational approach in scientific psychology is not the same thing as conceding that this delivers an*

adequate conception of the folk psychological mind. This is the crucial thing. Of course, there is a clear sense in which *the brain* is self-contained, and we have seen that the structures spoken of by scientific psychologists will be structures in this self-contained brain. But the claim that the brain is a computer is fully compatible with the Wittgensteinian claim that mental characteristics like understanding words involve a bodily component. How could it not be? For it is one thing to say that my understanding of 'cat' is *made possible* by certain internal structures howsoever described, and quite another to say that it is *constituted* by them. Perhaps they are just necessary rather than sufficient conditions of understanding. In other words, Mentalism might contain the scientific psychological truths about the underlying causal conditions of the mind's activities, and Wittgenstein's view could be the correct description of mental activity from the point of view of folk psychology.

But to say that our uses of words constitute understanding is not to embrace Behaviourism. First, there need be no suggestion that ordinary descriptions of mental life such as 'X understands "cat" to mean *cat*' will have to be translated into descriptions of actual and possible behaviour: in so far as we adopt the view that understanding is a brute, given fact about us, not to be analysed in any other terms (chapter IV, section 5, and chapter VI), such ordinary descriptions have to be taken as they are. Second, as already remarked, a description of a technique with a word will not merely be a description of applications of it but also a description of characteristic belief-formation and inference. Third, there need be no suggestion that any old parrot or puppet or robot which mimicked our uses of words would thereby understand them too, *no matter how this mimicking was brought about.* We can consistently with the Wittgensteinian approach refuse to acknowledge that all such mimicking behaviour is genuine use or practice, and hence deny that it all amounts to understanding. So when is behaviour use? When it is brought about in the appropriate way. When is that? That is a problem for *any* anti-Behaviourist, not just Wittgenstein, and in particular it exercises workers in AI. Not all simulation of intelligent performance is real intelligent performance: it needs to have the right sort of causal structures underlying it. This is an issue on which all anti-Behaviourists need to agree, and it is quite neutral with respect to what divides

Wittgensteinians from Cartesians. All sides against the Behaviourist agree that what goes on inside is a *necessary* part of having a mind: that itself leaves open the question whether it is *sufficient*. (Note that this shows that even in-the-skin Wittgensteinianism is not a form of Behaviourism.)

A Wittgensteinian could even accept the broad outlines of Functionalism. Perhaps one *can* characterise believing in terms of inputs, outputs and other consequences. But this leaves it open to construe 'inputs' and 'outputs' and everything else in form-of-life terms: to believe that there is a cat present is something that e.g. (1) tends to come about on seeing or hearing a cat-like thing nearby, (2) combines with a feeling of helpless tenderness, (3) to lead one to encourage it to come closer by putting milk in a saucer, telling it that it is a nice little cat, and so on. The thought that mental characteristics need to be located in a broader framework in itself leaves all the hard decisions about how to describe the elements of that framework still to be made. For the same reason, Wittgenstein does not have to deny that folk psychological descriptions help explain and predict behaviour. Given the above functional characterisation, if I hear you saying 'What a nice little cat' then I can explain this, other things being equal, in terms of your believing a cat is present and your wanting to give it milk: and if I have reason to suppose you to be a cat-lover who believes that a cat is present, then I can predict, other things being equal, that you will fetch milk from the fridge and start saying 'What a nice little cat' and so on.

One aspect of Functionalism of which a Wittgensteinian has to be more wary is the claim that beliefs and desires are causal entities in their own right whose nature is exhausted by their causal liaisons.[5] However, this is not an independently given datum, but is an artefact of the determination to impose the Mentalism of scientific psychology on to our account of folk psychology, and is therefore optional. The game is given away by the implicit distinction between beliefs etc. and the behaviour they help to cause: this just is the scientific version of Mentalism, carried straight over to folk psychology (see further chapter VIII, sections 7 and 8). 'Behaviour' so understood is not, as remarked, what Wittgenstein means by the activities which, according to him, constitute belief and understanding. On the other hand, this does not mean that a Wittgensteinian has to deny that in describing someone as believing that such-and-such one is advert-ing to causally efficacious happenings. It may well be that folk psychology contains the idea that believing essentially involves causally efficacious mechanisms inside the body. But it is a further step, as we have seen, to go from this anti-Behaviourism to the Mentalistic claim that such mechanisms *constitute*, rather than simply *make possible*, belief and understanding.

To return to Descartes, we should now be able to see clearly why it obscures important questions simply to assimilate his view to Mentalism. In so far as he makes phenomenological claims, he can be taken as contributing to a description of the folk psycho-logical facts, and hence he is in direct conflict with Wittgenstein. But Mentalism in scientific psychology, we have just seen, is *compatible* with Wittgenstein's view, since it is not in itself a contribution to folk psychological description. Hence we need an argument, to the effect that scientific psychology and folk psy-chology really *coincide*, before the assimilation can be justified. And this argument would have to involve a refutation of Wittgen-stein: something that Mentalism itself does not provide.

So why is it so easy and tempting to move straight from Mental-ism in scientific psychology to Cartesianism with respect to folk psychology and the self-containedness of the mind with respect to the body? First, Descartes himself may have just assumed that folk psychology and scientific psychology coincide, which would explain his emphasis on both consciousness and the thought that the having of ideas constitutes reasoning and understanding. Second, one might simply make an unargued assumption that the proposed computational structures will be sufficient conditions for mental activity, rather than mere underlying necessary causal conditions. This would obviously be encouraged by unthinking Cartesianism: if we *simply* replace Descartes' immaterial sub-stance with the brain, then Cartesian self-containedness carries straight over, as we saw. Reflections on the vat-brain (chapter I, section 3) might have an effect here too, but we shall see in chapters VI and VIII that they are either question-begging or independently inadequate. Third, one might be influenced by a tendentious conception of what scientific psychology is supposed to help explain. The quick, unexceptionable answer is: *the observ-able folk psychological facts*. But the tendentious conception comes from the assumption that this means *behaviour*. For it need not. It may mean *the activities and forms of life of the sort alluded to by Wittgenstein*. And as we have seen, there is no reason to construe this as behaviour-as-understood-by-Behaviourists. Fourth, one can at this point be misled by a faulty analogy with other sciences. If we think of the theory of magnetism as an account of what magnets are like in themselves, then we can go on to say that it tells us what magnets are like no matter how they happen to strike us at the observational level, and we can evidently make sense of the realist thought that they might have been like that even if they had not impinged on our awareness. The misleading analogy is to construe behaviour as 'how the mind strikes us at the observational level' and thus to think of scientific psychology as telling us what the mind is like in itself regardless of how it happens to impinge on us by causing behaviour. The analogy is suspect simply because of the possibility of the Wittgensteinian position: although it makes little sense to think of how magnets strike us as part of how magnets are in themselves, it simply does make sense, as we have seen, to count practices and forms of life as part of how the mind is in itself, and not just aspects of its observable effects. The key *disanalogy* between the theory of magnetism and scientific psychology can thus be illustrated as follows. If you remove me from the world, then you remove any effects on my awareness which magnets might have, but you do not thereby remove the magnets. Similarly, if you remove me from the world you also remove any effects on my awareness which *your mind* might have. But you do not thereby remove your body and its activities, which can thus still count as an aspect of your mind left over when its effects on me are gone.

None of this is to deny that scientific psychologists can properly distinguish between mental structures and 'mere behaviour' for certain of their own explanatory purposes. The point is just that this has not been shown to be more than an idealisation, so that slipping in the thought that they thereby distinguish the essence of mind from its bodily effects is simply begging the question against Wittgensteinianism. But by the same token, of course, we must remain clear that the foregoing does not establish that a Wittgensteinian approach is correct. Mentalism in scientific psychology may not immediately deliver Cartesianism about the mind, and it may be compatible with a form of Wittgensteinianism about folk psychology. But it still could be that *all things considered*, it is better to opt for Cartesianism or some near relative rather than any form of Wittgensteinianism, even as an account of what suffices for folk psychological mindedness. This is still an outstanding issue, which we hope to resolve in Part Two (in Wittgenstein's favour). The key point for the moment is that the issue really is still outstanding, even when the powerful advances of Mentalism in scientific psychology have been fully acknowledged.

Before we start to resolve this outstanding matter, we are as well to have before us the usual Cartesian view of the relationship between folk psychology and scientific psychology, if only to spell out more clearly what Wittgensteinianism rejects.

4 Contemporary Cartesianism

Here is how Mentalism has tended to make its impact on philosophy. The ideological shift from positivism to realism manifested itself in the philosophy of mind partly by focusing on the signal failure of Reductive Behaviourism to come up with appropriate translations. There are three main problems with translating, say, 'X believes it is raining' into 'X is putting on her raincoat, glancing at the sky and making clucking noises, and if offered an umbrella she would probably take it...'. First, it is obviously incomplete (witness the dots), and no one has ever made much of a fist of showing how to complete it. Second, the behaviour described still seems to make covert reference to the mentality of the subject. Thus 'putting on her raincoat' is a description of an action which could be accomplished by a whole variety of bodily movements, and describing it as an action implies intent on her part. Third, believing it is raining only leads to raincoat-and-umbrella routines given e.g. that the subject *intends to go out* and *doesn't want to get wet*. If she had no intention to go out, or harboured a desire to get wet, then her behaviour would be entirely different. One might then try to translate descriptions such as 'X believes that it is raining and intends to go out and does not want to get wet'. But this is not enough. If all this were true of X, yet she also wanted above all to impress those about her with her Thesigerian indifference to personal hardship, then she might still not engage in the raincoat and umbrella routine.

Nor might she, say, if she thought that umbrellas kill on contact, or that people who wear raincoats are usually shot at, or that getting wet is a passport to fame and fortune, or ... It seems, then, that at best only a Behaviouristic translation of a person's total state of mind at a time could be offered. Given the paucity of the usual attempts at one-by-one translations, it is hard to be optimistic about the prospects for success in this.

In any case, the influence of realism encouraged the thought that there must be more to having a belief, say, than its manifestations in behaviour. For example, acquiring the belief that it is raining tends to lead not just to behaviour (in conjunction with any number of other mental states) but also to other mental states. Given that I also do not want to get wet, I might then acquire the desire not to go out, the belief that I had better find things to do inside, a feeling of foreboding about tomorrow's picnic, the intention to listen to the evening weather forecast, and so on without apparent end. This suggests that things like beliefs are entities in their own right, only some of whose effects are on behaviour. Given what we know about the role of the brain, this in turn suggests the Mind–Brain Identity Thesis – mental states just are brain states – and the thinking described earlier leads from here towards Functionalism. On this view, what makes a particular brain state a belief-that-it-is-raining are its causal liaisons with inputs (e.g. the sensory effect of rain), other mental states (e.g. the desire above all not to get wet) and outputs (e.g. bodily effects). This is perhaps the most common form of contemporary realism in the philosophy of mind. And it is often, though not always, understood as entailing the self-containedness of the mind with respect to the body and its material surroundings. Many who accept this picture are also sympathetic to the idea that everything mental about me now could be true even if my brain were floating in a vat of nutrients, as in Putnam's example (chapter I). This approach thus directly transfers the Mentalism of scientific psychology to (materialistic) Cartesianism in folk psychology itself.

This all sits very happily with the following account of the relationship between scientific psychology and folk psychology. Ordinary folk psychological talk of beliefs and desires belongs to a structure which we use to explain and predict one another's actions. Scientific psychology is the discipline which investigates the psychological (perhaps computational) mechanisms which underlie and explain this folk psychological structure. Thus scientific psychology could be expected to investigate what goes on when the information that it is raining passes through our sensory apparatus and we 'acquire' the belief that it is raining. What is 'acquisition'? What is it for a belief so 'acquired' and a desire already 'harboured', to 'combine' and 'produce' appropriate behaviour? On this view, the explanatory successes of folk psychology are evidence that the entities it apparently posits (beliefs, etc.) really do exist, and scientific psychology is the enterprise of displaying more fully the causal powers of these entities, for example by hypothesising about the workings of the Language of Thought. Thus in Fodor's words:

> A train of thought . . . is a causal sequence of tokenings of mental representations . . . To a first approximation, to think 'It's going to rain; so I'll go indoors' is to have a tokening of a mental representation that means *I'll go indoors* caused, in a certain way, by a tokening of a mental representation that means *It's going to rain*. (P: 17)

Given all this, it seems to follow that the medium of logic and thought is not our practice with words, or even spoken and written words themselves, but words or other items in the brain. Similarly, understanding a word of public language is not constituted by one's use of it, but is constituted by the workings of the element of the Language of Thought with which it is correlated. Actual uses of public language are now seen as mere signs of understanding, to be explained by the associated underlying psychological mechanisms. This is the rough shape of a very great deal of anti-Wittgensteinian orthodoxy.[6] The main point to bear in mind is that its construal of folk psychology is optional, and in no way forced by the acceptance of Mentalism in scientific psychology. This brings us back to our question: scientific psychology aside, which is preferable as an account of folk psychology, Wittgensteinianism or the materialistic Cartesianism? Part Two makes out a case for the former.

Notes and reading

Works referred to

PE   Fodor, J. A., *Psychological Explanation* (New York: Random House, 1968).

P   Fodor, J. A., *Psychosemantics* (Cambridge, MA: MIT Press, 1987).

LNA   McCulloch, W. S. and Pitts, W. H., 'A logical calculus of the ideas immanent in nervous activity' in W. S. McCulloch, *Embodiments of Mind* (Cambridge, MA: MIT Press, 1965); repr. in M. Boden, ed., *The Philosophy of Artificial Intelligence* (Oxford: Oxford University Press, 1990) (to which page references are made).

CSE   Newell, A. and Simon, H. 'Computer science as empirical enquiry: symbols and search' in *Communications of the Association for Computing Machinery* 19 (1976); repr. in M. Boden, ed., *op.cit.* (to which page references are made).

PI   Wittgenstein,, L. *Philosophical Investigations*, trans. G.E.M. Anscombe (Oxford: Blackwell, 1953).

Notes

1 See A.J. Ayer, *Language, Truth and Logic* (London: Gollancz, 1936).

2 See e.g. Paul Churchland, *Scientific Realism and the Plasticity of Mind* (Cambridge: Cambridge University Press, 1979).

3 See Thomas Nagel, 'What is it like to be a bat?', *Philosophical Review* 83 (1974), and Gregory McCulloch, 'The very idea of the phenomenological', *Proceedings of the Aristotelian Society* 93 (1993).

4 Thus: 'I saw this man years ago: now I have seen him again. I recognise him, I remember his name. And why does there have to be a cause of this remembering in my nervous system? Why must something or other, whatever it may be, be stored up there *in any form?* Why *must* a trace have been left behind? Why should there not be a psychological regularity to which *no* physiological regularity corresponds?' *Zettel*, ed. G.E.M. Anscombe and G.H. von Wright, trans. Anscombe (Oxford: Blackwell, 1967): §610.

5 Corresponding caution is also required where the word 'state' is concerned (this will be especially so in chapters VII and VIII below). A Wittgensteinian can go along with calling beliefs and desires 'mental states' if all this means is that 'X believes that P' describes a state or condition that X is in (in the neutral sense in which 'X is travelling from London to Coventry' might describe X's state or condition). But 'mental state' is often understood to mean something inside the agent, like a brain state. Wittgenstein would obviously object to this – rightly, as we shall see.

6 It should be noted that the description in the present section only

gives one, albeit common, way of seeing the impact of Mentalism in scientific psychology on folk psychology. There are for example different varieties of Functionalism which do not involve claims about the Language of Thought, and some of which do not endorse the mentioned claim about the vat-brain. Fortunately we do not need to delve into the details here, since the argument to come short-circuits most of the structure that they rest upon. For a large and useful sampling of influential materials, see William Lycan, ed., *Mind and Cognition* (Oxford: Blackwell, 1990).

Part II

We now move over from the history of the question of the mind's self-containedness to the proposed resolution. This distinction is moderately artificial: the history has not been comprehensive or philosophically neutral, and the resolution will require us to absorb a number of recent developments in the philosophy of language. These took place through the 1970s, and their implications have shaped one large area of both the philosophies of language and of mind ever since. The issues raised are continuous with those we have already encountered, namely, What is the nature of understanding? and Is the mind self-contained with respect to the material world? As the first shot in the battle, we shall develop a defence of an in-the-world Wittgensteinian approach to folk psychology. This will then be tested against the recent developments just mentioned, and seen to be superior to Cartesianism and related rivals.

CHAPTER VI

What it is Really Like

We start by returning to the point raised in the previous chapter, that one can usually distinguish between the way things strike us in everyday life, and the way they come to us as filtered through scientific theory. Thus there is the familiar table with its solid legs and brown top, and the (possibly colourless in itself) cloud of buzzing particles which occupies the same place in the kitchen. Similarly, we can speak either of the familiar facts about the mind as it strikes us in everyday life, or we can speak of the computations and what have you that, according to standard versions of Mentalism, go on in the brain. Even if the everyday facts are the same as the scientifically identified facts, as could be argued in the case of the table in the kitchen, the facts strike us in different ways depending on whether we are in the everyday or the scientific context. Hence the need for argument, as noted, to connect doctrines in scientific psychology with any particular conclusion about the everyday or folk psychological mind; and in giving such arguments one would be addressing the matter of phenomenology, as in the case of the everyday view of the table. Like the table, the folk psychological mind features in the phenomenology of everyday life, although it should be noted that the mind, unlike the table, does not appear as an object. Rather, folk psychological *mindedness* figures in the phenomenology of our existence. Just as we encounter the familiar table, so we encounter believings, desirings and other aspects of being minded. The secret to unlock if we are to give the right account of folk psychology is thus phenomenological: How does mindedness appear to us?

1 Ideas: communication again

We have noted that Descartes put a lot of emphasis on consciousness in his account, treating the mind as an idea-processing entity and ideas as objects of awareness or 'inner perception'. This at least suggests that he was interested not merely in the scientific question of how the mind works, but also in the phenomenological one of how the mind appears. And even if he did not conceive of what he was doing in this way, his claim that ideas are objects of awareness certainly is a phenomenological claim. This comes into sharper focus if we think of Locke, and the huge pressure we saw him to be under to treat ideas as mental images (chapter II, sections 3–5). One cannot help but see the imagist theory of ideas as an attempt at a model of the phenomenology both of material body and of minds. Question: How can we encounter a colourless cloud of buzzing particles as the familiar table? Answer: Partly because a little coloured image of it is produced in the mind. Question: How can we encounter the mind itself? Answer: Because we can 'introspect' or reflect on our own mental operations, and encounter the ideas of sensation that have passed into the mind.

In essential details this Lockean approach gives a standard model of the phenomenology of body and of mind which has persisted, in many circles, up to the present day. At the same time, however, it contrasts significantly with the Mentalistic tendency to treat the mind as a computational mechanism, even though this tendency gives rise to theories of the mind's workings which are strikingly like the theory of ideas in other respects. The crucial difference is that the supposed computational structures in the brain are not generally reckoned to be objects of awareness, and so the computational account does not purport to be as such a model of the phenomenology.

Why do I speak here of 'model'? The answer is that consciousness, its being like something, is normally reckoned to be an extremely puzzling feature of any system which exhibits it, and this puzzlement is thought by many to survive the mere observation that conscious systems have formidably complex information-processing capacities. Many consider this observation still to leave unanswered the question 'How can it be *like something* for the information-processing system?' What I am calling models of phenomenology are attempts to give the shape of an answer to this sort of question. From here, if you do not have a model of phenomenology, then whatever else you have, you do not have the most important thing you need as a philosopher of consciousness. Thus Locke suggested that some of the information was encapsulated in pictorial form. Others suppose that the special features of consciousness can be modelled on those of reflection: on this view, to be conscious that p is to believe that one believes that p. Others again cite pains, tickles and other sensations as paradigms of consciousness. Here our ability to feel our own bodies is taken as a model for all conscious awareness.

All of these models are quite mistaken, and more generally most approaches to phenomenology in the analytical tradition are hopelessly flawed because they are still far too close to the Lockean model, which we shall see is easy to discredit as a phenomenology both of body and of mind. One aim of this chapter is thus to suggest an approach to a more adequate model of phenomenology. But we should recall our dialectical situation. At the end of Part One we were left with a reason to compare Wittgensteinian with (materialistic) Cartesian approaches to folk psychology. We should also recall earlier unfinished business. In chapter III we upheld Frege's objection to Locke's theory of communication, but conceded that this did not in itself undermine the theory of ideas as a theory of the mechanisms involved in understanding, nor show that a notion such as Fregean sense was required in order to account for communication. In the following chapter we endorsed Wittgenstein's objections to *imagistic* (and immaterialist) versions of the theory of ideas as accounts of understanding, and set out Wittgenstein's positive view, remarking that it can be construed as a version of a Fregean approach. But we left it open whether non-imagistic, materialistic versions could provide the necessary dynamism for a theory of understanding. All of this unfinished business will be settled by exactly the same arguments that will settle the issue over the correct account of folk psychology. And this is because understanding itself has a phenomenological dimension, as indeed has communication.

The very idea that understanding and communication are anything to do with phenomenology may sound very surprising, but in fact the connection is intimate. Think again of Locke's view that to understand a word is to use it to signify an idea. On the face of it the *phenomenological* dimension of ideas – that is the doctrine that ideas are objects of awareness – might seem redundant here: as indeed it is once we modulate to the contemporary computational approach. But on second thoughts, things here are not so straightforward, as we can see by considering what happens in communication. Using language as a method of communication is itself a predominantly conscious enterprise. I am normally conscious of what I am saying to you as I speak, and when I understand what you have said to me that is usually because I was conscious of your saying that. Locke's account of this, mentioned in chapter II, section 2, involves the claim that words can come to excite ideas in the mind just as the things the words apply to can: your saying 'table' can make a table-idea appear in my mind just as a perceptual encounter with a table itself might. Given that all the ideas involved here are themselves phenomenological objects, it follows that when communication takes place, the exchange is treated as a conscious episode, as it should be: both speaker and hearer are aware of what is being said. Sadly, however, we already know that Locke's theory of communication is hopeless (chapter III), and is based on an unworkable theory of understanding (chapter IV). But none of this means that we do not need to worry about the phenomenology of understanding and communication. On the contrary, it means that we need to develop a correct model of it. And this will enable us to resolve the dispute between Wittgensteinianism and materialistic Cartesianism over folk psychology: the former can, and the latter cannot, deliver an adequate phenomenology of understanding and communication.

2 Ideas: phenomenology of body and of mind

So let us first consider Locke's imagist theory of ideas as a model of the phenomenology of *body*. The first thing to note is that on this approach, things like tables are not regarded, strictly speaking, as phenomenological objects, but instead as *indirect* objects of acts of perception whose *direct*, phenomenological objects are ideas. And as a model of the phenomenology of material body, this is soon seen to be inadequate. For it to work, experience would have to be purely contemplative, in that the world would literally pass by our view like a filmshow. But it does not. We live in the midst of our surroundings, moving and intervening, and this is how we experience them. Encountering the table as solid is a real experience, but it is not simply a matter of feeling skin contact and the inability to dispose our limbs as we want. The experience of the table's solidity is integrated into our sense of moving around it, our seeing its brownness, our hearing its creaking legs, and any other consciousness of it we may be having at that time. In the same fashion, we not only see and feel the squareness of the table-top, but also experience it as helping to dictate the way we move around it, lay the places on it and so on. One does not merely watch a square-brown-table filmshow in the visual part of the mind and feel accompanying tingles and other sensations in the tactile part.

The natural reply is that our rich, integrated experiences are in fact derived from a basis of image and sensation, but that through habit and inattention we have ceased to notice this basis, or perhaps have never noticed it. However, this reply is either possibly true and irrelevant, or false. First, in so far as this proposed basis of our experiencing the world is just supposed to be bodily processing of a package of incoming information – from irradiated retina and irritated nerve-endings, to representations in the brain – then the subject has been changed from phenomenology – how the world strikes us – to a science-based account of the alleged causal basis of the phenomenology. But to start talking in these terms, howsoever truly, is simply to give up on the present Lockean project, which was to provide a model of the phenomenology. To add that this physiological basis 'constitutes' the phenomenology would not be to the point, even if it were true. That would merely be to reaffirm commitment to the scientific picture of the mind's causal basis, and would not be to provide any model of the phenomenology itself. In effect, the reply involves the move from the traditional theory of ideas, which incorporates a phenomenological model, to something like the computational theory of mind, which does not. So much for the danger of irrelevance. Second, though, perhaps the suggestion about the basis of experience is intended in a phenomenological spirit. Perhaps the thought is that we are directly aware of images in the visual case, and of 'bare effects of power' (chapter II, section 5) in the tactile case, but that the organising and conceptualising powers of the mind quickly knit these elements together into the integrated table-experiences that we live through. And this suggestion connects, of course, with the idea that we can get a more accurate view of what this supposed phenomenological basis of experience is like by 'introspecting', or reflecting explicitly on its nature, ignoring the fact that we live through it as experience *of* the world. Thus we feel the roughness and think 'Table': but on this approach we can just forget the table and focus on the sensation of roughness. Similarly, we are aware of brown and think again 'Table': but we can just forget the table and focus on what some call the sensation of brown. In this latter case, introspection is modelled on the viewer of a painting turning attention on the painting itself as a patchwork of colours, forgetting the depicted items.

However, this suggestion is first, incoherent, and second – ignoring that – phenomenologically inadequate. As far as the tactile case is concerned, it is certainly true that there is something like a 'bare effect of power', in that we can indeed focus on the feeling at the surface of the body. Even here it is hard to experience it merely as a happening in the body, rather than as a dim sign of what is beyond the skin: but let that pass, since as we noted in chapter II, section 5, we can at least imagine creatures having such sensations without connecting them with any cause beyond. Sensations are not intrinsically representational. Still, what does it mean to say that the organising and conceptualising powers of the mind normally knit these bare effects into an integrated table-experience? One thing it presumably means is that our concept or way of thinking about tables somehow gets attached to the feeling and pulls it into line with visual awareness. And there is truth in this. But what is the concept or way of thinking about a table, on the current Lockean account? A table-image! So in the tactile case, the feeling becomes integrated into a full table-experience because somehow it fuses with a table-image. But this is a special case of what we were trying to explain in the first place: recall our problem was how disparate elements in the alleged phenomenological basis, such as an incoming perceptual table-image and a roughness-feeling, could be knitted together by the mind into the whole experience we normally have. Clearly, nothing has been explained at all by the introduction of concepts, if these are then construed, as they were by Locke, as more images. And of course this is even more obvious in the visual case. Presumably, once again, one's concept of a table is supposed somehow to fuse with an incoming perceptual table-image and thereby knit it into the full experience (just as seeing a patchwork of colour *as a painting of a table* involves one's concept of a table). But how can one table-image knit another into something else? Clearly, the most pressing phenomenological problem has been left completely untreated.

That brings out the incoherence of the account. But in the visual case there is also serious phenomenological inadequacy. Sensations of roughness we may feel in or on the the skin: but sensations of brown? We certainly do not experience these as being in the eyes, as one *can* experience sensations, say prickings through tiredness or soreness from acid. So when we forget about the table, and just focus on the brown, where do we experience it as being? Where we always did, over there in the middle of the kitchen. 'Introspection' in the visual case, that is turning attention to the given nature of the bare experience, just turns up the shapes and colours, etc. where they already were. This is nothing like forgetting about the table in a painting and just looking at the texture of the paint or the disposition of colours. Nor is it anything like trying to detach the sensory aspect, the 'bare effect of power', from one's tactile interactions with the table. It is true that careful attention might show up complexity in the appearance of the table that was unnoticed before – a stripe of light down the middle, a black stain on a leg, the grain of the wood. But they are still experienced as being over there, where the table is experienced as being, even when one is 'introspecting'. There is no such thing as a sensation of brown, if by this is meant a 'bare effect of power': or at least, there is no such thing at the phenomenological level in the visual case, even if there is one at the physiological level (cf. chapter II, section 5). We see the table as brown, and we can attend more carefully to the table's brownness. That is all.[1]

We should now note the very important point that it is not just the imagist model of the phenomenology of *material body* that is undermined by the foregoing. For 'introspection' was supposed to deliver us the phenomenology of *the mind*, on this approach: turning attention 'inside' was supposed to deliver awareness of our awareness. But there is no 'inside' in the appropriate sense, and 'introspection', in the visual case anyway, just delivers up the *world* again. There are no such things as Lockean ideas, if these are construed as image-like objects of awareness which are present in ordinary perception, apt to be revealed by 'introspection'.

The incoherence in the imagist account underlines the Wittgensteinian arguments that concepts, ways of thinking about things, cannot be images. Nothing as inert and itself in need of interpretation as an image could knit together the rich experiences that we know we have. In addition, the account's phenomenological inadequacy points up the fact that we now have no model at all for the phenomenology of material body or of mind, or indeed of understanding and communication. So where do we go from here?

3 Concepts and the fabric of experience

Locke, recall, suspected that even oysters and cockles enjoy some glimmer of sensibility which sets them apart from insentient nature. But here it is clear enough that no actual thinking or representation is involved: no oystery or cocklish sense of the passing show. If so, then the sensibility suspected by Locke is best modelled on bodily sensations as 'bare effects of power'. As remarked, it can be difficult for us to view our own sensations as such bare effects, and in any case sensation for us is integrated, normally, into complex experience. So we have no real idea what it can be like to be a cockle or an oyster, if indeed it is really like anything at all.

For a more challenging case, consider dogs. These lie somewhere between cockles and humans, though it is difficult to place them accurately. It is hard not to credit them with full-blown sensations somewhat like ours – tickles, aches, stings, burnings. It is equally hard not to credit them with a doggish sense of the passing show: dogs notice things, chase things, learn tricks, recognise people and words, make simple wishes plain. But recall now Wittgenstein's point (chapter IV, section 4) that although it is natural to credit a dog with simple thoughts and feelings, we soon run through the likely candidates: a dog cannot believe that his master will come the day after tomorrow. Nor can a dog daydream about winning the pools and buying a cat, or suspect that Napoleon, despite his heavy cold, should not on balance have handed over the conduct of the Battle of Waterloo to Marshall

Ney. So what is it like to be a dog? How does the passing show strike a dog? Here I again draw a blank: I can no more imagine what it is like to be a dog than I can imagine what it is like to be an oyster, although in the former case, but not the latter, I can at least make some sense of the thought that it must be like something.

Wittgenstein claimed that the huge gulf between ourselves and dogs depends on the fact that we have language. But we can accept much of this without having to go into the question about the priority of talk over thought, for the point can be made as follows: dogs do not possess many of the concepts or ways of thinking that we possess, and which we at least *exercise* through our use of language. And this much, which we have seen to be common to Descartes, Locke and Wittgenstein, seems undeniable: our intellectual superiority with respect to all other earthly creatures we have encountered is intimately connected to our linguistic ability, which correlates with conceptual sophistication. And this connects with the point of the previous section, that our conceptualising somehow knits together our integrated experiences. Our rich conceptual repertoire informs and conditions our conscious mental life, helping to make it the way it is. The richness and integration of my table-experiences is brought about by the fact that I have the concept of a table, can think about things *as* tables, with all that that involves. Correlatively, this is why I cannot really imagine what, if anything, it is like to be a dog: because I have no inkling of how the dog's conceptual repertoire, such as it may be, integrates its sensory awareness of the world, such as it is, into whole experience. I can gain no sense of the fabric of a dog's conscious life, cannot imagine how it lives through its experience of the world. It can, in some fashion, experience the table as an obstacle, or as something to hide under, and in time as a place where food (not for it) can be happened upon. But the table is involved in our form of life in all sorts of ways which are completely beyond the dog's ken, and our experience of the table is thus beyond anything the dog can manage, just as its experience of the table, such as it may be, is beyond anything I can imagine.

Obviously the key to the phenomenology of material body lies in getting a firmer grip on how our concepts thus organise our experience of it. Now we know that Locke's view that grasping a concept is contemplating an image is quite inadequate. This is not just for the usual Wittgensteinian reasons, reviewed in chapter IV, but also because the view does not deliver any intelligible account of how such images could integrate experience in the way that concepts do. But it is equally clear that retreating from Locke to the non-phenomenological view that possessing a concept is hosting a computational structure or word of the Language of Thought is to move in the wrong direction. Whereas Locke's view gives a bad phenomenological model, this view gives no model at all. Just as clearly, Frege's idea that grasping a concept is standing in a special relation to an abstract entity can be countered with a related dilemma: either the suggestion has no phenomenological dimension, in which case it is no use in the present context, or it does, in which case it is clearly unbelievable. In possessing a concept one does not seem to be lassoing something in the abstract realm. Of the options we have surveyed, this leaves Wittgenstein's view. And given the point about how our interactions with the table themselves contribute to the way we experience it, the following seems quite natural: we are aware of existing in the midst of our surroundings, moving and intervening, because our having the experience-informing concepts we do have is constituted, as Wittgenstein says, by our abilities to move around and engage with the things in our surroundings. In other words, the natural suggestion at this point is that a relatively mild form of in-the-world Wittgensteinianism about understanding or concept-possession is required to explain why we experience material body the way we do, to give substance to our model of the phenomenology of body.

I say the view required is a mild form of in-the-world Wittgensteinianism because there is nothing in the claim just made, which will be filled out in the following section, to take us much beyond the easily encounterable features of the familiar world. There is nothing here to tie form of life to anything more remote or arcane. That will come later, through chapters VII and VIII, when we investigate further the phenomenology of *mind*.

4 Embodiment

In coming to terms with the view just suggested, it is helpful to think of the existentialist critique of Cartesian conceptions of experience. Wittgenstein was chiefly concerned to argue for the bodily basis of the understanding of language, but the existential-ists argued for the bodily basis of many other kinds of mentality, including our experience of our surroundings.[2] Existentialist philosophy is founded on an approach to the mind which is as explicitly and strikingly anti-Cartesian, and as resolutely focused on our activities, as anything in Wittgenstein. Heidegger believed that the fundamental Cartesian distinction between mind and world is the root of much philosophical evil, resulting in faulty conceptions both of mind and of world:

> No matter with how many variations of content the oppo-
> sition between 'Nature' and 'spirit' may be set up ontically,
> its ontological foundations, and indeed the very poles of
> this opposition, remain unclarified; this unclarity has its
> proximate roots in Descartes' distinction. (B&T: 123)

In a similar spirit, Sartre called Descartes' view that minds are *things* 'Descartes' substantialist illusion' (B&N: 84), and he was equally hostile to the Cartesian claim that the mind processes ideas or representations, calling them 'idols invented by psycholo-gists' (B&N: 125).

Existentialism grows initially out of a reaction to the Phenom-enology of Husserl.[3] This style of philosophising, which has strong affinities with that of Descartes, is meant to lead us to an account of what consciousness is like. The basic idea is that the way to find this out is to withdraw from the 'natural attitude' towards experience, in which one just takes it unthinkingly to be experi-ence of material surroundings, and instead critically regard it in a special philosophical attitude akin to introspection in the Car-tesian framework. Given that our consciousness of the world is perhaps the most important or distinctive aspect of us, it follows that Phenomenology is a proposal about what *we* are like: or, we might say that Phenomenology is intended to deliver an account of our distinctively conscious existence or way of being. Now Heidegger accepts that this is a, if not the, respectable philosophi-cal enterprise. His concern, he tells us, is with ontology, the ancient problem of Being. He also retains the label 'Phenomen-ology' to refer to the philosophical exercise of attending closely and critically to our conscious way of being:

We [formally define] 'phenomenon' in the phenomenological sense as that which shows itself as Being and as a structure of Being. (B&T: 91)

But he has a very different conception both of what this exercise involves, and of what sort of account it delivers. For Husserl, the exercise is akin to introspection, and what it delivers is (in the first instance) something like a description of our mental representations regarded as such. For Heidegger, on the other hand, it involves something more akin to, although not the same as, the sort of observation and reflection gone in for by anthropologists, and it delivers an account not of representations but of various kinds of activity which we can come to recognise as part of our conscious way of being but which are or have become 'hidden' from us by, among other things, bad philosophy of which Descartes' approach is an example:

That wherein Dasein already understands itself . . . is always something which is primordially familiar. This familiarity with the world does not necessarily require that the relations which are constitutive for the world should be theoretically transparent. However, the possibility of giving these relations an explicit ontological–existential Interpretation is grounded in this familiarity with the world; and this familiarity, in turn, is constitutive for Dasein, and goes to make up Dasein's understanding of Being. (B&T: 119)

Here 'Dasein' means 'characteristically human way of being', and the sorts of activity which Heidegger believes to constitute this way of being he calls 'Being-in-the-world': Dasein, he says, 'is ontically constituted by Being-in-the-World' (B&T: 103). Again in much the same spirit, Sartre claimed that 'activity, as spontaneous unreflecting consciousness, constitutes a certain existential stratum in the world' (STE: 61).

Broadly speaking, then, the existentialist idea is that the bedrock of our experience of the world, as uncovered by Heideggerian Phenomenological reflection, consists not in the processing of representations, but in the exercise of a complex of abilities and ways of coping with our surroundings:

When Dasein directs itself towards something and grasps it, it does not somehow first get out of an inner sphere in which it has been proximally encapsulated, but its primary kind of Being is such that it is always 'outside' alongside entities which it encounters and which belong to a world already discovered. (B&T: 89)

One example Heidegger gives involves using a hammer. Imagine someone using a hammer in the normal way to knock in nails. The standard attitude of such a person, according to Heidegger, is a pre-cognitive mode of engagement with hammer and nails. Such a manner of engagement involves the application of all sorts of delicate skills, even where such a relatively crude form of activity is concerned: think of the difference between the clumsy efforts of the novice, and the practised fluency of the experienced carpenter. Now the episode of hammering is certainly part of the experience of the hammerer. Even when the carpenter is wholly absorbed in the job, and acting smoothly on the basis of well-instilled techniques, this is all deliberate, intended activity. This is not merely an episode involving things happening in and to the body: the doings are under the control of the agent, and are constantly modified in the light of his or her sense of them and the developing situation. In so far as we want a description of this person's experience of the surrounding world, then, the episode would have to be included. But according to Heidegger, this experience or 'understanding' of the world *consists in* the activity and the know-how displayed, and not in any of the underlying representation-processing episodes alleged by Cartesians:

> The kind of dealing which is closest to us is ... not a bare perceptual cognition, but rather that kind of concern which manipulates things and puts them to use: and this has its own kind of 'knowledge'. (B&T: 95)

In his illuminating commentary on Division I of *Being and Time*, Hubert Dreyfus offers a rather different, more culturally oriented example of this sort of knowledge or understanding of the world. He says that

> We have all learned to stand the appropriate distance from strangers, intimates and colleagues for a conversation. Each culture has a different 'feel' for the appropriate distances. In North Africa people stand closer and have more bodily contact than in Scandinavia, for example. These practices

are not taught by the parents. They do not know that there is any pattern to what they are doing, or even that they are doing anything. Rather, the children, always imitating the adults without trying, simply pick up the pattern. There is no reason to think that there are any rules involved; rather, we have a skilled understanding of our culture ... Of course, learning to do it changes our brain, but there is no evidence and no argument that rules or principles or beliefs are involved. Moreover, this is not an isolated practice; how close one stands goes with an understanding of bodies, intimacy, sociality, and finally reflects an understanding of what it is to be a human being. (BW: 18–19)

Exactly how do these examples bear on our discussion? First, it is clear that ordinary skilled coping with a hammer or with one's partners in conversation does not comprise elements all of which are accessible to explicit reflection. Normally I act and adjust myself to the things I am aware of without reflecting explicitly on this, and even if I do start to reflect while hammering or talking, lots of my ongoing intentional movements and adjustments will still not be available to me. Indeed, excessive self-consciousness can easily disrupt practical fluency. But nor will it do to suggest that the success in the activity is due to blind or non-conscious habit. As Sartre justly observed:

Now it is certain that we can reflect upon our activity. But an operation *upon* the universe is generally executed without our having to leave the non-reflective plane. For example, at this moment I am writing, but I am not [reflectively] conscious of writing. Will someone say that habit has rendered me unconscious of the movements made by my hand in tracing the letters? That would be absurd. I may have the habit of writing, but not at all that of writing *such* words in *such* an order ... In reality, the act of writing is not at all unconscious, it is an actual structure of my consciousness. Only it is not conscious *of* itself. (STE: 58–9)

Equally, reflecting on my beliefs about the situation and my place in it will not turn up everything that is going on to evince my understanding of it. It is not as if I have a fully articulable theory of hammering which I can consult at will. (Some may suggest that I must have a fully developed set of *unconscious* beliefs about hammering: but even if I do, that fact is, by definition, no part of my consciousness of hammering, except perhaps as a necessary causal underpinning: see chapter V, section 3.)

Now all of this is highly congenial to Wittgenstein's rejection of accompanying conscious 'hidden processes'. But more to the point, it is certainly obviously true that a vat-brain can neither hammer in nails nor adjust the distance between it and those it is talking to. So in this plain sense, a vat-brain lacks aspects of experience of the world which a normal human person is capable of having. It cannot have the distinctive experience of the surroundings of your average person. Nor, then, does it possess the understanding of being a person to which Heidegger draws attention. Embodiment is an essential ingredient of our way of experiencing the world, and a vat-brain is not embodied.

It may seem that there is some cheating going on here. For someone might *dream* that they are knocking in nails or having a conversation, and surely that is enough. First, one might say that dreaming that one is hammering nails is enjoying the essentially mental or at least experiential aspect of hammering. Then, second, it might seem that if a person lying asleep in bed can *seem* to him or herself to be doing these things, then surely so could a vat-brain, and this is everything the Cartesian needs.

Not at all. First, it actually needs an argument to get from the point about dreaming to the point about the vat-brain, since dreaming as we normally understand it is something that minded beings do, and simply to move from this to the Cartesian claim about the vat-brain is to beg one of the questions at issue, namely whether a vat-brain is a minded being. Still, it would be foolish to deny that someone might dream that they were hammering nails or having a conversation. True: but this is much less helpful than it might initially seem. For it is not even obvious that the dreamer would be in a position to *believe* he or she is hammering or talking: certainly *dreaming that one is X-ing* does not have the same functional role as *believing that one is X-ing*. And even if this were the case, the desired conclusion is still not reached. For the aim of the present suggestion is to show that the dreamer is enjoying the essentially experiential aspect of hammering or talking, and that what he or she is lacking is simply the bodily accompaniment. *But this rests on assumptions we have already seen reason to reject*. It may be that the dreamer enjoys the *introspectible* side of hammering nails – indeed, this is just to restate the basic claim that the dreamer seems to him/herslf to be hammering nails – but since we have already seen that not all aspects of the conscious activity of hammering nails are available to introspection, or even encapsulated in recoverable belief, the desired conclusion, that the dreamer is enjoying all the essentially experiential aspects of hammering nails, simply does not follow. Worse, it really only could follow if hammering were always accompanied by, as it were, an explicit inner filmshow which represented every experiential aspect of the hammering, and which could then re-run in the consciousness of the dreamer. But we know it is not: that was part of the point of the previous section.

One natural reply is to admit that this argument works against Descartes, since he puts so much store by the doctrine that ideas are phenomenological objects, but that it leaves materialistic Cartesianism intact, since this retreats to talk of the processing of representations in the brain, with no mention of consciousness. Surely if my brain can process the representations which purportedly underlie my hammering when it is in my skull, then it could do the same thing if it were in a vat? Yes, of course it could. But there is no argument here to the effect that the envatted brain has the essentially experiential aspect of hammering nails. We have already seen that admitting the necessity of brain-activity to mindedness does not amount to admitting its sufficiency. More, we have already noted that materialistic Cartesianism is not even intended as a model of phenomenology: the elements of the Language of Thought, to repeat, are not supposed generally to be available to consciousness. As we shall see further in chapter VIII, many are inclined to overlook these points when the chips are down on the basis of question-begging Cartesian intuitions about what it would be like for the vat-brain – that is, intuitions about the brain's subjective experiences. But this is not enough to disturb the existentialist approach, even if we forget about the question-begging. As we have already seen, even if the brain could have the appropriate dream experiences – and remember we have not conceded that it could – even so, this does not get us to the conclusion. There is more to consciously hammering nails than you can dream.

We suggested in the previous section that our experience is the way it is because it is shaped and informed by our concepts or ways of thinking. And this is a phenomenological claim: somehow, ways of thinking have to be a unifying factor in the fabric of experience. Now if, as we have just seen, the activity of hammering nails is itself a form of experience, it is completely mysterious how this form of activity could be shaped and organised by the concept of a hammer unless grasping that concept is itself a dynamic, action-involving affair. It is not as though we just need a causal account of the kind of brain-happenings that the ability to hammer rests upon. We need a model of how the concept-informed phenomenology we live through can be the way it is. In this sense, then, the existentialist conception of experience and the Wittgensteinian account of understanding are made for each other (as are, indeed, the Cartesian contemplative conception of experience and Locke's snapshot account of understanding).

The thought may still nag that it is at least possible to separate the strictly introspectible aspects of hammering nails from the mere bodily, non-introspectible aspects. And while it would be tendentious to say that this amounted to separating the mental from the non-mental (few now accept that all aspects of the mind are open to introspection), it would still be possible to claim that this would be a separation of the 'strictly so-called' *phenomenology* of hammering from its non-phenomenological accompaniments. And Heidegger himself sometimes seems happy enough with such a Cartesian model of 'strict' phenomenology, just so long as it is applied to a special kind of reflection which serves as the basis for scientific method (and Cartesian philosophy). But this is a mistake: as we saw in the previous section, 'introspection' does not deliver anything like the Cartesian phenomenology. And how could it? – we know already that we exist in the midst of our surroundings, moving and intervening and manipulating, and that this is how we experience them. As we saw in the previous section, the separation of the 'strictly introspectible' from the rest is simply a feature of the Cartesian model of experience, and has no actual basis in what our experiences are like. This thought, in effect, guides Sartre's procedure in *Being and Nothingness*. Sartre is sometimes accused of having grossly misinterpreted Heidegger as offering a theory of consciousness, and is thus charged with obscuring the true anti-Cartesian import of Heidegger's work (see e.g. BW: 13). But, in fact, this complaint is almost entirely back to front. Heidegger rightly offers skills and coping as the bedrock of our experience of the world, but sometimes seems to leave a 'strict' form of consciousness to the Cartesians. Sartre, on the other hand, sees more clearly that skills and coping are *forms* of the only non-reflective consciousness we are capable of: when I am hammering in nails, even with my mind on something else, *of course* I am still conscious of the hammer and nails. That is how I manage to tailor my movements in the light of the unfolding events. As even Heidegger says

> when we deal with [things] by using them and manipulating them, this activity is not a blind one; it has its own kind of sight, by which our manipulation is guided and from which it acquires its specific Thingly character. (B&T: 98)

What I need not be, as Sartre points out in many places, is *reflectively* conscious of the hammer and nails. And when I do reflect, this does not shift my attention on to a Cartesian, introspectible arena, but simply turns up the worldly objects of which I was previously unreflectively conscious. For Sartre, coping and the exercise of knowhow constitute (unreflective) consciousness of one's surroundings, whereas Heidegger tends to slip into thinking of them as constituting a preconscious substratum of our mental life. Heidegger, in effect, does not follow his own insight far enough. Sartre does not re-import Cartesianism into Heidegger's view, but expunges it more thoroughly. His approach may have arisen as a result of misinterpretation, but this was a very profitable misinterpretation.[4]

Be all that as it may, we now have before us a model of how embodiment informs our experience of the surrounding world by constituting our ways of thinking about and understanding it. In Wittgensteinian fashion, it seems true to the way experience strikes us to say that having a concept of a hammer is constituted by the kind of activity one is capable of performing with it, the form of life it makes possible, and that this is why our experiences of worldly things are the way they are: we experience the surrounding world in embodied form. We have also seen how Cartesian attempts to deal with these matters go astray, and in that respect have confirmed the objections to Cartesian phenomenology of material body mounted in the previous section. So much for the phenomenology of body. What of the phenomenology of mind?

5 Phenomenology of mind: communication

As soon as the subject turns to the phenomenology of the mind, contemporary analytical philosophers are apt to become reticent. Some will affect not to know what the issue is. Many will only talk here, if at all, about bangs and flashes, 'qualia', 'raw feels', sensations. This goes along with the unquestioned assumption that the phenomenology of the mind is to do with how (if at all) *my* mind appears to *me, your* mind appears to *you* and so on. The roots of this tendency, of course, are deep in the Cartesian tradition. Locke, recall, listed ideas of psychological matters, such as perceiving and doubting, as *ideas of reflection*, things got by turning attention on one's own mental operations, and to be contrasted with *ideas of sensation*, things got through perception (chapter II, section 1). We noted at the time this is not exactly innocent, since on the face of it one could perceive the perceiving etc. of others, and thus acquire the idea of perceiving as an idea of sensation. But these possibilities are ruled out by Locke's view that the mind is self-contained with respect to the human body (apart from, perhaps, the brain). This entails that the body cannot enter in any essential way into making the mind the way it is *qua* mind. The ideas of sensation I receive from you will all be ideas of body, so the only ideas of mind I receive will come from my own case when I reflect.

Also derived from the Cartesian tradition is the idea that *all there is* to the phenomenology of mind is what 'introspection' turns up, and closely related is the thought that what it does turn up is a limited manifold of sensory elements: shapes and colours in the visual case, bodily sensations like tingles and itches, noises in the ears. The limitation to colour and shape in the visual case is, obviously enough, derived from the thought that visual experience involves the inner perception of images, since when attention is turned on a non-mental image and its subject-matter is ignored, what is revealed is a patchwork of coloured shapes. We have been seeing that this conception of phenomenology has no basis in phenomenological reality, and it is clear that it survives simply because of tradition and unthinking commitment to Cartesianism. I mention it again just to remind the reader that the word 'phenomenology' here has quite different theoretical implications.[5] It is true that the position maintained here may leave room for some notion of a thin sensory type of phenomenology which is detachable from the concept-laden phenomenology we actually live through. We can perhaps imagine the primitive sort of sensibility which Locke attributed to cockles and oysters. Relatedly but differently, we can perhaps imagine a sensory but non-conceptual type of experience had by human infants, and differently again we could suppose such a sensory core to be mixed up in, and theoretically even if not phenomenologically isolable from, our own rich experiences. These ideas seem to me to be of doubtful intelligibility: I do not think that talk of its being like something for an organism can be detached from the idea of the organism's *knowing* that it is like that – and *knowing what it is like* is an achievement that requires conceptualisation. Unconceptualised streams of consciousness are, I suspect, entirely mythical. But I do not need to argue that here.

Now I encounter your body as one body among others, so up to a point your body strikes me as a solid, moving, coloured material thing, over there by the table. But we have seen that this phenomenology of body is not accommodated by Locke's Cartesian model. Rather, I have suggested, my experience of your body will be an aspect of my own embodiment, just as my experience of the table is: my experience of the world has an active, bodily basis. *But then so too will your experience of the world be an aspect of your manner of embodiment.* So why cannot I encounter your perceiving the table just as much as I can encounter your being next to the table? Both, after all, are aspects of your embodiment. If I can encounter one, the being next to the table, as part of my unified experience of the surrounding world, why cannot I encounter the other at the same time?

Well, I can, of course. I can see you seeing the table. I can see you trying to make it fit into the space beside the window. I can see you going off to get a screwdriver to remove the legs so that you can get it through the door. I can hear you saying that it's time we got a smaller one. Folk psychology, we have said, constitutes the way that mindedness in general is given to us in everyday life. And if we look at this matter through eyes untainted by

Cartesian models, then it is obvious that we see and hear meaning, intention and significance in the activities of other people. We do not just experience other people as coloured moving bodies, in polite society anyway: in addition, we apply the concepts of folk psychology to them. But this application of concepts informs our experience of them in just the way that any concepts inform experience. Just as my experience of the table is informed by how I can interact with it *qua* body, so my experience of you is informed by how I can interact with you *qua* minded being. Looked at from here, the phenomenology of mind is *not* just a matter of how (if at all) *my* mind appears to *me*, *your* mind appears to *you* and so on. It is equally a matter of how your mind appears to me, and my mind appears to you.

This takes us straight back to the theory of communication, shelved in chapter III, since in communicating we certainly do appear to each other as things with minds. Here we can lead off from Locke's account. One component of this, as already noted, is the claim that a word like 'table' can, like the things it represents, cause the table-idea to come into a mind. Since ideas are supposed by Locke to be phenomenological objects, this at least captures the thought that using language to communicate is usually a conscious activity. For Locke, this comes out as: when I speak meaningfully that is because I am aware of the idea(s) I associate with my words, and when you hear me and understand me, that is because you are aware of the ideas that my words cause in your mind. We can now ask: is this alleged causation of ideas in you by my words direct or indirect? For there are at least two possible mechanisms. On the first, my word 'table' causes an idea of *itself* (a word-idea) to appear in your mind, and this word-idea then causes a table-idea. On the second, the causation is direct, unmediated by the word-idea: my word 'table' immediately causes a table-idea in your mind, just as a table might. In fact, both mechanisms would seem to have application. Imagine here a spectrum of cases, with the following at one extreme: if someone speaks to you very slowly in a language you do not understand at all, then (if they speak slowly enough) you could acquire word-ideas, perhaps even well enough articulated to permit you to imitate the speaker. But no thing-ideas would be caused, except by accident, because you do not understand the language. Imagine now an intermediate case involving someone speaking slowly to you in a language you *can* understand but not very fluently. Suppose understanding ensues – you end up with the right thing-ideas – but you had to translate silently to yourself to get the meaning. Here it seems that the first mechanism mentioned above is appropriate, in that you first acquire word-ideas on which you do the translation to get the thing-ideas. Finally, imagine a case at the opposite extreme of our spectrum, where someone speaks quickly and at length on a familiar topic in your native tongue. Here the second mechanism seems appropriate: understanding is achieved on the back of direct causation of thing-ideas by words. There is not time or space to take up the words first and then grasp ideas they cause. If you start to try to listen to the words you will actually start to lose the message.[6]

In ordinary communication in our own language with our familiars, then, it seems that the transmission is direct: your words load their significance directly into my consciousness, and are in that sense themselves 'transparent'. (This is a phenomenological claim, of course, and is compatible with there being all manner of intervening events between the speaker's moving lips and the hearer's understanding. It is also compatible with many of these intervening events being capable of being brought into focus by a suitable shift of attention.) However, although this is correct, we know that the Lockean account of it is not: words do not signify ideas. So what happens instead? It is no help, of course, simply to reaffirm faith in the claim that some computational structures in the brain are activated, since this gives no model of the phenomenology involved. Frege's answer is that when you speak, your words express senses, so that when I understand you it must be that I latch on to these senses. But this is either an unhelpful redescription, or invokes an unbelievable mythology of the 'third realm'. What does Wittgenstein say instead? He says that the meaning you attach to your words is constituted by the abilities and practices involved in their use. So when my perception of your meaning is direct, as in the case under consideration, it must be because I experience your speaking-activity as meaningful in itself: there is no phenomenological intermediary, so your communicating behaviour must itself carry the phenomenology, be what I experience as meaningful.

And this is where we wanted to be. As noted above, if your

conscious life is an aspect of your embodiment, then since I can experience your bodily being, I ought to be able to experience your conscious life in what you do. And I do, for example when you speak to me, conscious of what you are saying, and I understand you in the normal run of things. In saying what you say you are conscious of what you mean, and in hearing and understanding you I am conscious of the same thing. This is the sort of thing it really means to say that we experience meaning, intention, significance in the activities of others.

The claim is compatible with the thought that learning to understand others is a slow and painful process, and that the resulting ability is highly sophisticated. To say that an ability contributes to the phenomenology, to what experience is like, is one thing: to say that it is simple or basic is something else entirely. Exactly the same point applies in the case of experiencing material things. Even learning to hammer in nails or walk around and lay a table takes time and application: but once developed, the hard-won skills contribute to the knitting together of the fabric of our experience. In Locke's account the two things – development and developed state – are run together: phenomenology is constituted by ideas which, howsoever sophisticated, are ultimately compounded from basic sensory elements which are pitched into the mind whole (chapter II, section 1). But this approach to phenomenology betrays his 'scientific' aspirations: he was concerned to say not just what it is like, but how it could get like that. It is perhaps the critical failing of the theory of ideas that it mixes up, under the influence of course of mechanistic science, these two quite different tasks. Recall the point of chapter V, section 3, that Cartesianism, taken as a contribution to scientific psychology, is compatible with Wittgenstein's claims, and only comes into conflict with them when it is taken as a contribution to the description of folk psychology.

Wittgenstein's contention that meaning is 'open to view' can now be seen to have a perhaps unexpected depth. It is natural to construe it simply as the point that our thinking, and understanding of language, show up in our overt practices, and so are in this sense observable, not hidden inside like ideas or brain-structures must be. If this is all it is construed as, then it is not difficult to see why it should appear to be in danger of collapsing into Behaviourism, even though this appearance is quite incorrect. But in any event, the real force of the point is this: it isn't just that understanding is constituted by observable events, *but that these events can be directly experienced as meaningful in themselves.* Your body is mostly empty space, a cloud of buzzing particles. But I do not experience it thus: in so far as I experience it as body, I experience it as coloured, solid and so on. Colour and solidity are aspects of the phenomenology of body, as we have seen. Equally, in so far as I experience you as minded, I experience your movements, and the sounds you make, as meaningful. *Meaning, then, is an aspect of the phenomenology of mind.* Meaning, as much as colour, is part of the structure of appearance. This should anyway be obvious from one's own case – thoughts can run consciously through the mind – but we have now seen that the same applies to the case of experience of others.

Note that this phenomenological argument enables us at last to endorse Frege's contention that communication requires sense and not just Meaning and ideas. We accepted that Locke's account of communication in terms of the matching of ideas is undermined by Frege's argument (chapter III, section 4), but conceded that this itself did not make a positive case for sense. This matter remained open even after our acceptance of Wittgenstein's point that understanding cannot be explained in terms of *contemplating an image* (chapter IV, section 1), since this leaves other versions of Cartesianism, such as those which posit a Language of Thought, in the field. However, the first step in our phenomenological argument supports Wittgenstein's positive account of understanding, in terms of practices and forms of life, since no other account can give an adequate model of the phenomenology we actually experience (sections 2–4). And this last step shows that understanding is not just a matter of each individual going it alone with words and deeds, but involves a genuinely public, objective, sharable dimension: in so far as we communicate, we experience each other's words and deeds as meaningful, and this meaningfulness is a shared, objective feature of experience. What you think and say is what I hear and understand. Nor is this a matter that could be accommodated just by the theory of Meaning, since it does not (just) concern the things we are thinking about, but also the way we think about them as manifested in our ways with words. If the names 'Istanbul' and 'Constantinople' figure in my understanding as if they were names of distinct things, that is because the practices and abilities which constitute my understanding of the first name are distinct from those associated with the second (see further chapter VIII, section 6). So Frege was right that the theory of understanding requires something sharable, over and above ideas and Meaning; and we were right to suggest that Wittgenstein's practice-based account of understanding can be seen as a spelling out of this Fregean suggestion. The objective, sharable dimension of understanding is constituted by our meaningful activities.

6 Where does this leave Cartesianism?

In my view, Cartesianism stands refuted by the arguments of the foregoing chapters. At most, its remnants, say in the form of the Language of Thought hypothesis, survive as a paradigm in scientific psychology: probably not even, contrary to what Fodor claims, 'the *only* available theory of mental processes that isn't *known* to be false' (P: 20),[7] but anyway no account at all of the folk psychological mind. To think 'It's going to rain; so I'll go indoors' is not *simply*, even to a first approximation, 'to have a tokening of a mental representation that means *I'll go indoors* caused, in a certain way, by a tokening of a mental representation that means *It's going to rain*' (P: 17). Even if it involves that, it is also e.g. to participate in the appropriate form of life, embodied, in the world.

However, the Cartesian Tendency is pervasive and long-standing, and characterises the work of many contemporary philosophers. So I do not expect choruses of agreement with this conclusion to ring out. What, then, must we do? Here it seems that the most fruitful way forward is to plunge into some contemporary issues that involve Cartesianism and its associated self-containedness doctrines, and try to show in detail how the morals of our story apply. This will be attempted in the final two chapters.

We shall be helped by the fact that we have brought into focus an important constraint: that sense, the proper object of understanding, has a phenomenological dimension. We now know that any credible account of it must respect this constraint, and we shall see how and why Cartesianism cannot. There is, of course, some irony in the fact that we have had to dredge the point out of the wreckage of the theory of ideas, since it was

155

present there already in the doctrines that ideas are objects of awareness and are signified by words. We have seen at length that neither doctrine stands up to scrutiny, and what seems to have happened in the history of this subject is that analytical philosophers, at least, in the stampede away from the imagistic theory of ideas, just forgot or never learned how to handle the topic of phenomenology. The influence of Behaviourism here was obviously crucial, and the Mentalistic reaction to Behaviourism, as outlined in chapter V, did not manage to shake this off. On the contrary, as we have seen, Mentalism in scientific psychology tends to accept the Behaviouristic distinction between overt behaviour and its inner causes, and simply reverses the Behaviouristic claim about the location of the mind. For Behaviourists, the mind is constituted by the behaviour, and the inner causes are not part of the subject-matter of the psychologist, whereas for the Mentalists, things simply go the other way round: behaviour is a contingent bodily manifestation of the internal psychological happenings. But the crucial shift in Cartesianism from images to e.g. elements of the Language of Thought left the phenomenology, or at least the phenomenology of understanding, in the dustbin to which the Behaviourists had consigned it. We have seen that the first step towards a credible model of phenomenology involves a reconceptualisation of the traditional distinction between overt behaviour and inner causes. Neither is sufficient for mindedness; both are necessary.

Notes and reading

Works referred to

BW   Dreyfus, H., *Being-in-the-World: A Commentary on Division I of Heidegger's 'Being and Time'* (Cambridge, MA: MIT Press, 1991).

P   Fodor, J. A., *Psychosemantics* (Cambridge, MA: MIT Press, 1987).

B&T   Heidegger, M., *Being and Time*, trans. J. Macquarrie and E. Robinson (New York: Harper and Row, 1962).

B&N   Sartre, J.-P., *Being and Nothingness*, trans. Hazel Barnes (London: Methuen, 1958).

STE   Sartre, J.-P., *Sketch for a Theory of the Emotions*, trans. P. Mairet (London: Methuen, 1971).

PI   Wittgenstein, L., *Philosophical Investigations*, trans. G.E.M. Anscombe (Oxford: Blackwell, 1953).

Notes

1 Thus see Paul Snowdon, 'The objects of perceptual experience', *Proceedings of the Aristotelian Society*, supp. vol. 64 (1990), V; and Jerry Valburg, *The Puzzle of Experience* (Oxford: Clarendon Press, 1992), ch. 2.

2 I shall, as is normal, treat Martin Heidegger and Jean-Paul Sartre as existentialism's chief proponents, although there are some problems even here: Heidegger repudiated the title, and in accepting it explicitly, Sartre commented that it had become so vague, in common parlance anyway, as to be useless (*Existentialism and Humanism*, trans. Philip Mairet, London: Methuen, 1948: 25–6). For existentialism in general see David Cooper, *Existentialism: A Reconstruction* (Oxford: Blackwell, 1990); for Heidegger see BW; and for Sartre see Gregory McCulloch, *Using Sartre* (London: Routledge, 1994).

3 See e.g. Edmund Husserl, *Cartesian Meditations*, trans. D. Cairns (Dordrecht: Kluwer, 1950) and David Bell, *Husserl* (London: Routledge, 1990), ch. III.

4 See McCulloch, *Using Sartre.*

5 Dictionaries define the phenomenological in terms of the objects directly noticed by the mind or the senses. This in itself is very obviously quite neutral with respect to any particular theory of what the mind's (direct) objects are: thus Gregory McCulloch, 'The very idea of the phenomenological', *Proceedings of the Aristotelian Society* 93 (1993). But contemporary analytical work is so shot through with Cartesianism that the word 'phenomenology' is usually taken without any thought at all to connote bodily sensations and their alleged counterparts in visual and other experiences. This is at least as crass as automatically construing, say, 'is a value judgement' as *is not really a judgement.*

6 Thus even Descartes: 'Words ... make us think of [the things they signify], frequently even without our paying attention to the sound of the words or to their syllables. Thus it may happen that we hear an utterance whose meaning we understand perfectly well, but afterwards we cannot say in what language it was spoken' (*The Philosophical Writings of Descartes*, vol. I, trans. J. Cottingham, R. Stoothoff and D. Murdoch): 81. He finishes the paragraph with 'Is it not thus that nature has established laughter and tears, to make us read joy and sadness on the faces of men?' The correct, invited answer is 'yes', although this is hardly available to Descartes given his self-containedness doctrine. (To be fair, his principal point in the passage is to illustrate the non-necessity for ideas to resemble the things that cause them.)

7 One possible opposition to this claim alluded to in the text comes from the attempt to understand the computational architecture of

the brain in non-symbolic terms. For a helpful introduction to the issues see Andy Clark, *Microcognition* (Cambridge, MA: MIT Press, 1989).

CHAPTER VII

Twin Earth

The route we have to follow takes us to the seminal work in the theory of meaning of the important American philosopher Hilary Putnam, whose vat-brain thought-experiment was mentioned in chapter I. Putnam's claim about meaning is still spawning a vast literature, although in the present chapter we shall focus mostly on his own discussions. The key matter we need to get hold of is Putnam's celebrated 'Twin Earth' style of argument, and the conclusion he draws: 'Cut the pie any way you like, "meanings" just ain't in the head!' (MM: 227). This, as we shall go on to see, really puts the cat among the Cartesian pigeons, and additionally allows us to show off the merits of our in-the-world Wittgenstein-ianism.

1 Stereotype and essence

The most convenient way for us into Putnam's arguments is through Locke's doctrine of substance. As we noted in chapter II, Locke supposed a substance like lead to have both a *real* and a *nominal* essence. The real essence, Locke said, is the hidden structure which causes samples of lead to have the superficial qualities they do have, and the nominal essence is the cluster of superficial qualities by which we typically recognise something to be a sample of lead. Given his views about word-meaning and definition, this means that the nominal essence of lead can be given by a definition of 'lead': say 'soft heavy dull whitish metal'. In addition, Locke makes two important claims about these essences. The first is that the real essences of substances are usually unknown, and perhaps in some cases unknowable, since

159

> The workmanship of the all-wise and powerful God in the great fabric of the universe and every part thereof further exceeds the capacity and comprehension of the most inquisitive and intelligent man than the best contrivance of the most ingenious man doth the conceptions of the most ignorant of rational creatures. (E:III,vi,9)

And the second is that what makes something a sample of a particular substance *is that it should answer to the substance's nominal essence,* that is, fit the substance-word's definition. Thus this piece of metal before me now is lead if and only if it fits the definition 'soft heavy dull whitish metal'. This in turn connects with a claim about what it is to understand the word 'lead': it is to associate with it the idea of a soft, etc. metal.

The first stage of Putnam's argument involves accepting a certain version of Locke's distinction between real and nominal essence, but disputing these two Lockean claims about the distinguished items, and in particular *disputing the claim about what it is to understand substance-words.* He considers a variety of what Locke would call substances and substance-words (he calls them 'natural kinds' and 'natural kind-terms' respectively, but we shall stay with the Lockean terminology for continuity). And he is perfectly happy with the idea that there is something about a sample of matter, to do with its inherent structure, which determines its superficial qualities:

> Normally the 'important' properties of a liquid or solid, etc., are the ones that are *structurally* important: the ones that specify what the liquid or solid, etc., is ultimately made out of ... and how they are arranged or combined to produce the superficial characteristics. From this point of view the characteristic of a typical bit of water is consisting of H_2O. (MM: 239)

This is close to Locke's doctrine of real essence. Putnam also accepts that in learning to recognise samples of a substance, and thus in coming to understand the substance-word, we need to be exposed to something like a Lockean nominal essence or, to use Putnam's preferred word, a *stereotype.* One gives the stereotype for a substance-word by describing the superficial qualities which typical samples of the substance possess:

In this view someone who knows what 'tiger' means... is *required* to know that *stereotypical* tigers are striped... Thus if anyone were to ask me for the meaning of 'tiger'... I would tell him that tigers were feline, something about their size, that they are yellow with black stripes, that they (sometimes) live in the jungle, and are fierce. (MM: 250–2)

Similarly, then, we might give the stereotype of 'water' as 'colourless, tasteless, odourless, thirst-quenching liquid which falls as rain and fills oceans, lakes and seas': and one can easily imagine a Lockean offering just this if asked for water's nominal essence. Conversely, Locke's definition of 'lead' would seem to be a good candidate for giving the metal's stereotype.

At this point, however, the first key difference between Locke and Putnam emerges. For far from accepting that a substance's stereotype gives any kind of essence, Putnam argues that fitting the stereotype *is neither necessary nor sufficient for being a sample of that substance*. It follows immediately from this that understanding a substance-word does not simply amount to associating the stereotype with it: the classifications we intend and effect with these words do not coincide with those which would be effected if we judged exclusively by reference to fitting the stereotype.

Fitting the stereotype is not necessary for being a sample of a substance, says Putnam, because there can be atypical samples of a substance or examples of a kind: a piece of discoloured lead is still discoloured *lead*, even if it does not fit the above definition. Similarly,

> Three-legged tigers and albino tigers are not logically contradictory entities... If tigers lost their stripes they would not thereby cease to be tigers, nor would butterflies cease to be butterflies if they lost their wings. (MM: 250)

Putnam goes on that fitting the stereotype is not sufficient to be a sample of a substance either, because what happen to be *different* substances may have the *same* stereotype. His celebrated and much-discussed thought-experiment designed to illustrate this involves imagining a liquid which is superficially indistinguishable from water, and which hence fits the water-stereotype, but which is in fact a completely different liquid. We shall examine this example in detail in the following sections. But in the spirit of Putnam's suggestion it seems we can easily envisage pairs of metals distinguishable only by special test (he offers aluminium and molybdenum as a possible example (MM: 225–6)), unrelated but superficially indistinguishable biological species (SP?: 151), and so on. In the same vein, Putnam points out that

> the term 'jade' applies to two minerals, jadeite and nephrite. Chemically there is a marked difference [underlying] the same unique textural qualities. (MM: 241)

But it does not matter to the point whether or not such pairs exist, any more than it matters to the previous point that atypical tigers and so on actually exist. All that is required is the thought that being a sample of a substance could come apart from fitting the stereotype in the envisaged ways. If so, then Locke's use of the word 'essence' here is out of place, and his doctrine about what it is for this piece of metal before me now to be lead is false. More importantly, Locke's claim about understanding substance-words has to go too, as remarked. We do not take 'jadeite' and 'nephrite' to be synonyms – that is, we understand them differently – even though they are associated with the same stereotype.

Note that although Putnam is attacking Lockean definitions, he is not making the Wittgensteinian point (encountered in chapter IV, section 2) that membership of a class is not determined by a feature or set of features shared by all the members, but rather by an overlapping set of similarities. In fact, he disagrees with this point as far as substances are concerned, as we shall soon see. All his present argument has in common with the Wittgensteinian one is a denial that the usual sort of Lockean definitions, which refer to familiar and relatively superficial features of paradigmatic examples of a kind, dictate (rather than loosely guide) our classifications.

But then what, according to Putnam, does determine whether something is a sample of a given substance? What do we understand, say, 'water' to apply to? Putnam, again disagreeing with Locke, answers simply: real essence. Something is water if and only if it has water's real essence. And according to Putnam, we *intend* our substance-words to make classifications which are sensitive to the regularities exhibited by these underlying factors. We understand 'jadeite' and 'nephrite' differently because, despite the coincidence in stereotype, they correspond to two different classifications at the level of microstructure. Not that we (or anyone) need know what these microstructural differences are. For Putnam holds that even *unknown* underlying differences can be involved in the understanding of words, even when stereotypes remain constant:

> I point to a glass of water and say 'this liquid is called water'... My 'ostensive definition' of water has the following empirical presupposition: that the body of liquid I am pointing to bears a certain sameness relation (say, *x is the same liquid as y* ...) to most of the stuff I and other members of my linguistic community have on other occasions called 'water' ... The key point is that the relation [*same liquid as*] is a *theoretical* relation: whether something is or is not the same liquid as *this* may take an indeterminate amount of scientific investigation to determine. (MM: 225)

His view is that chemistry just is the enterprise of discovering what (if anything) it takes to be e.g. water, biology the enterprise of discovering what (if anything) it takes to be e.g. a tiger, and so on. On this view, to do science, broadly speaking, is to try to find out what, if any, natural substances there are. In this sense our prescientific understanding of substance-words is supposed to be already sensitive to future or possible scientific discovery. According to Putnam, we understand these words as having their correct application ultimately determined not by the superficial characteristics which guide our day-to-day judgements, but by a supposed, perhaps unknown, unifying real essence. So if it had turned out that we had been applying 'water' to a mixture of two or more different but superficially indistinguishable chemicals, then we should have said that there is no *one* substance water, just as there is no one mineral jade and no one gas air. Equally, we should have said that our pre-discovery understanding of 'water' was to that extent defective: we thought we meant a single substance by it, but we did not.

I shall call this the doctrine that *the understanding tracks real essence*, and shall also, for reasons that are probably clear but which will be explained anyway, sometimes describe it as the view that *the understanding is not self-contained with respect to real essence* (that is: real essence is *NOT* Exterior to the understanding).

Now Putnam's approach plainly involves a forthright version of Scientific Realism as introduced in chapter V, and he is explicit in various places in urging this as against positivism (see e.g. ER; MM: 235–8). And in championing science in this way he is continuing a tradition with which Locke had great sympathy and on whose beginnings he was very influential, as we have seen. So why should there be such a strong disagreement? It may seem that the answer lies in the relatively primitive state of science in Locke's day. Thus his own observations of scientific practice led him away from Putnam's claim that the understanding tracks real essence. In reply to this suggestion, Locke answered

> that we find many of the individuals that are ranked into one sort, called by a common name, and so received as being of one *species*, have yet qualities depending on their real constitutions, as far different from one another as from others from which they are accounted to differ *specifically*. This, as it is easy to be observed by all who have to do with natural bodies, so chemists especially are often, by sad experience, convinced of it, when they, sometimes in vain, seek for the same qualities in one parcel of sulphur, antimony, or vitriol which they have found in others. For, though they are bodies of the same *species*, having the same nominal *essence*, under the same name, yet do they often, upon severe ways of examination, betray qualities so different from one another as to frustrate the expectation and labour of very wary chemists. (E:III,vi,8)

Clearly, refining techniques have come a long way since then! The relatively primitive state of science in his day also led Locke to describe real essences as unknown. Putnam, on the other hand, given the great advances in the study of microstructure, can say that we know full well what real essence makes it the case that this sample of liquid is water with the superficial characteristics it does have: namely, its consisting of molecules comprising two atoms of hydrogen and one of oxygen.

But even though there is something in all this, Putnam's idea that the understanding tracks even *unknown* real essence ought to indicate that it is not the heart of the matter. There is a much more fundamental source of what may so far appear to the reader to be a mere local dispute between Putnam and Locke on the role of definitions in the meaning of substance-words. To start to see this, note first that the real problem for Locke is that he cannot allow anything other than ideas before the mind to contribute to a person's understanding of a substance-word. But the relevant ideas, according to him, are precisely those whose names are included in the specifications of nominal essence. In adding that our understanding of a substance-word also includes an 'obscure and relative' idea of substance he is clearly making a gesture in the direction of an account like Putnam's (E:II,xxiii,3), but it is a gesture that he cannot really make on his own Empiricist principles. And this emerges very clearly when he gives his final reason for saying that it is nominal essence, rather than real essence, which determines whether something is a sample of a substance:

> Nor indeed *can we* rank and *sort things . . . by their real essences*, because . . . our faculties carry us no further towards the knowledge and distinctions of substances than a collection of those sensible *ideas* which we observe in them. (E:III,vi,9)

Given that the mind, according to Locke, is a self-contained dark room of ideas, whose life ultimately consists of compounded ideas of sensation, there is just nothing more that the understanding can do to represent the reality of things. Either the piece of metal before me now resembles my idea of it or it does not. If it does, then the idea is true of it. If not, not. But since the idea, on Locke's account, analyses into something like 'soft heavy dull whitish metal', then this piece of metal is lead if and only if it is a piece of soft etc. There just is no other possibility for Locke.

To put the same point slightly differently, the problem for Locke is not so much that real essences are unknown as that they are Exterior to the understanding, in the precise sense that the facts about the understanding (the entertaining of the ideas of the nominal essence) can remain the way they are in themselves whatever the facts about real essence, and even, indeed, if there are no real essences at all. Thus on Locke's account real essence *cannot* be tracked by the understanding: recall the point that Cartesianism makes the whole material world

Exterior, and hence essentially irrelevant to what makes us the kind of minded beings we are. To say that real essences are Exterior, to repeat, is to say that the understanding could exist just as it is in itself whatever form they take, if indeed they even exist. On Locke's theory, our minds cannot reach out beyond the ideas in them, and so cannot track real essence in the way urged by Putnam.

It now might seem as if Putnam's views about substance, if they are acceptable, merely give yet another reason for rejecting the Lockean theory of ideas as a theory of understanding. But that radically underestimates their importance. As we shall now see, they can be applied to various different kinds of theory of understanding in order to deliver the same sort of conclusion: that the role of real essence alleged by Putnam cannot be sustained by these theories since real essences turn out to be Exterior to the understanding according to the theories concerned. In this way, Putnam's claims ultimately lead to a very difficult dilemma: either we have to find a way of rejecting or reinterpreting them, or we have to modify fundamentally a number of apparently indisputable preconceptions about what it is for something to be Exterior to the mind. We shall aim to embrace the second horn, with the help of our in-the-world Wittgensteinianism.

2 Twin Earth and Exteriority

So let us turn to Putnam's 'Twin Earth' thought-experiment, which effectively started off a whole new philosophical technique. Underlying the technique is the following general strategy. On the one hand there is an account of what understanding a word consists in: in Locke's case, the entertaining of ideas. On the other hand are purported facts about understanding which outstrip the understanding's resources as provided for by the account: in this case, the understanding's tracking of real essence. The strategy then is to illustrate this by imagining parallel or 'twin' cases in which two minds, which ought according to the account of understanding to be understanding some word in the same way, are in fact understanding the word in different ways. If the case can be made out satisfactorily, then the account is shown to be inadequate.

Thus in the argument that associating the water-stereotype with

166

a word does not constitute understanding it to mean *water*, Putnam imagines, 'with the aid of a little science-fiction',

> that somewhere in the Galaxy there is a planet which we shall call Twin Earth. Twin Earth is very much like Earth; in fact, people on Twin Earth even speak *English* . . . One of the peculiarities of Twin Earth is that the liquid called 'water' is not H_2O but a different liquid whose chemical formula . . . I shall abbreviate . . . as XYZ. I shall suppose that XYZ is indistinguishable from water at normal tem- peratures and pressures . . . , tastes like water and . . . quen- ches thirst like water . . . that the oceans and lakes and seas of Twin Earth contain XYZ and not water, that it rains XYZ on Twin Earth and not water, etc. (MM: 223)

These stipulations ensure that XYZ, or twin-water, has the same stereotype as water, and so has according to Locke the same nom- inal essence, so that we Earthians should understand our word 'water' in the same way as Twin Earthians understand theirs. But this result is wrong, says Putnam. If I were to travel to Twin Earth and, pointing at a glass of twin-water say 'This is water', then I should have gone wrong, that is spoken falsely, since twin- water (XYZ) is *not* water (H_2O). My application of my word would not be in accordance with my prior intentions concerning it. A Twin Earthian, on the other hand, pointing at the same glass and saying 'This is water' would go right, that is speak truly, for XYZ *is* what Twin Earthians call 'water', and XYZ is what the glass contains. This Twin Earthian's application of the word would be in accordance with her prior intentions concerning it. Hence Earthians and Twin Earthians understand the word 'water' differently: we understand it to mean *our* liquid, they understand it to mean *theirs*. Our intentions concerning the word 'water' exclude XYZ and include H_2O, theirs do the opposite (whether or not the facts about real essence are known to anyone, recall). The problem, as we have seen, is that there is nothing in Locke's theory of the understanding to accommodate these differences of intention. If Earthians and Twin Earthians associate the same nominal essence with 'water', then their intentions with regard to it come out the same on Locke's account.

Of course, in the imagined case the Twin Earthians would take me to speak truly: but that is because they would misunderstand me, wrongly assuming me to be one of them. Also, if we knew that our stuff was H_2O and they knew that their stuff was XYZ, *and this could be incorporated into the respective nominal essences*, then the case would no longer be a difficulty for Locke. But that is irrelevant: this simply changes the subject to one where difference in understanding would correspond to difference in stereotype (assuming, what is far from obvious, that the Empiricist in Locke could accommodate ideas of hidden microstructure). Such a change of subject would not even show that real essence need not be Exterior to the understanding. For it would still be the supposed ideas of real essence, rather than direct tracking of the essences themselves, which would constitute the understanding. In any case, Locke's view has to be able to cope with all coherent examples, not just the favourable ones.

Now as already remarked, the Twin Earth strategy is not simply narrowly anti-Lockean: it generalises directly to other conceptions of the understanding. Thus consider the materialistic Cartesianism introduced in chapter V. On this view, understanding a word consists in processing mental words appropriately. If Putnam is right merely to the extent that associating a stereotype with a word does not constitute understanding it, then this materialistic Cartesianism has to show that processing mental words appropriately is not the same as associating a stereotype. But we do not even have to guess at the details to see that the Twin Earth argument applies anyway. All we need to imagine is that the Twin Earthians are the same as us as regards the processing of mental words. For example, imagine that their brains are computationally identical to ours. Then, since according to this form of Cartesianism the processing of mental words is constituted by what goes on in the brain, such that everything outside the brain is Exterior to the understanding, it follows that Twin Earthians and Earthians would understand 'water' in the same way, contrary to Putnam's claims. Obviously this result will apply given *any* version of the Mind–Brain Identity Thesis which identifies mental characteristics with internal brain characteristics: just imagine a case where Earthians and Twin Earthians have atom-for-atom identical brains.[1] Similarly, any form of Functionalism which construes 'inputs' and 'outputs' in terms of nerve activity will also fall prey: as will versions of Behaviourism according to which the mind is self-contained with respect to everything beyond the body's surfaces, and as will in-the-skin Wittgensteinianism. In each case, all we have to imagine are pairs of Earthians and Twin Earthians who are functionally or in-the-skin equivalent, and so equivalent from the point of view of the theory of understanding in question, but who differ in being related to H_2O and XYZ respectively. Then Putnam's claim will be that the members of the pairs differ in their understanding of 'water', despite the *ex hypothesi* equivalence.

It should be clear now why Putnam summarises his view with the slogan 'meanings just ain't in the *head*!' Given the point already noted that talk of sense or meaning and talk of understanding are correlative, in that talk of the meaning or sense of a word and talk of what is involved in understanding it come to the same thing, it follows that if the understanding tracks real essence in the way Putnam proposes, then understanding e.g. 'water', that is the meaning of that word, involves matters outside the head (and skin). Indeed, Putnam suggests that a Twin Earth argument could be generated even for a case in which

> I have a *Doppelgänger* on Twin Earth who is molecule for molecule 'identical' with me (in the sense that two neckties can be 'identical'), [who] thinks the same verbalised thoughts as I do, has the same sense data, the same dispositions etc. (MM: 227)

And we can agree, as long as the similarities Putnam mentions can hold even though the aforementioned substitution of XYZ for H_2O also holds. More generally, we can say that the Twin Earth argument works, if it works at all, against *any* conception of the understanding under which Earthians and Twin Earthians can share an understanding of 'water' even though this substitution is as described. If and only if the substitution is held to be Exterior to whatever facts are offered as constituting understanding, then the argument can be brought to bear.

That should do something to indicate the scope of the strategy. But just for good measure, we should also note that it can also be applied to at least some versions of the Fregean and in-the-world Wittgensteinian accounts of understanding we have considered.

Since we noted in chapter III, section 3 that a Fregean *could* adopt Locke's claim that understanding at least some words amounts to knowing a definition, it is obvious that the argument could get a grip, for example, on any Fregean account which entailed that grasping the sense of 'lead' consists in holding that something is lead if and only if it is soft etc. metal (cf. SP?: 139–40; MM: 218–19). But less obviously, we noted that Frege appears to countenance a form of self-containedness of sense with respect to Meaning. And this too threatens an inconsistency with Putnam's claims. For if the sense of 'water' is self-contained with respect to water, so that one could grasp the sense whether or not water existed, then it is hard to see how Putnam's claims about the understanding's tracking of real essence could be maintained. If grasping the sense of 'water' is indifferent to the existence of water then it seems that it would also be indifferent to the substitution of water for twin-water. Another way to approach this point is to recall the Fregean doctrine that *sense determines Meaning*. This is apparently inconsistent with the thought just mooted, that grasping the sense of 'water' is indifferent to the substitution of water for twin-water. For if Putnam is right, 'water' as used by Earthians has a different Meaning from 'water' as used by Twin Earthians. Hence it seems that either the senses are different too, or sense does not determine Meaning after all. But to say that sense does not determine Meaning is to say that one could understand a word yet it still not thereby be fixed what one was thinking about: an apparently nonsensical conclusion (but see the following chapter). In a way, of course, Putnam's claims about substance-words emphasise this point, since his idea is that the understanding *does* determine real essence and hence Meaning. But as he puts it,

> meaning [= sense] indeed determines extension [= Meaning]; but only because extension is, in some cases 'part of the meaning' [= part of the sense, tracked by the understanding]. (SP?: 151)

It is hard to see how Fregeans could go along with the idea that the Meaning of a substance-word is 'part of the sense' without *rejecting* the doctrine that sense is self-contained with respect to Meaning: and, predictably enough, contemporary Fregeans tend to do just this.[2]

At the very least, then, the Twin Earth strategy exposes a tension in Frege's overall position, and at most it applies in full force, as when grasping a sense is equated with knowing a definition. Can the strategy be applied to in-the-world Wittgensteinian accounts too? Here things depend crucially on what is packed into the Wittgensteinian notions of 'practice', 'form of life', and so on. We noted that Wittgenstein rejects the self-containedness of the understanding with respect to the body, since understanding a word is said to consist in the actual uses made of it, which of course involve much bodily contribution. We said that this approach would have to bring with it the objects of the body's surroundings too, so that credible versions of Wittgensteinianism will be of the in-the-world variety, although this may still leave room for some limited notion of self-containedness, for example as regards the form of life of cosmologists or ancient historians with respect to their 'official' subject-matter. But in fact the potential for self-containedness is not quite so limited as this makes it sound. We said that it was hard to see how one could give a decent account of a normal person's practice with 'cat' without making a good deal of mention of their interactions with cats. But imagine my *Doppelgänger* on Twin Earth whose biography runs exactly parallel to mine except that whereas mine involves interactions with cats, his involves superficially identical encounters with Twin Earthian *dogs* which fit the same stereotype as do Earthian cats (and are called 'cats' etc.) . . . Do we share a form of life or not?

One reason for supposing that we do is that we would have no apparent difficulty in interacting with and understanding each other should we come into contact. Moreover, were we to be switched unbeknownst while asleep neither of us, nor any of our friends and colleagues, would notice. God-like outsiders watching the two lives running in parallel would note the vast and undeniable similarities. It would be very much like watching two screenings of the same events, happening in parallel. And much the same goes, of course, for the ways in which water and twin-water are part of the weave of the life of Earthians and Twin Earthians respectively.

However, if reasons such as these lead ultimately to the conclusion that in the relevant sense of 'use' the Earthian and Twin Earthian uses of the words 'cat' and 'water' are the same, then the Putnam argument can swing into action: same use means same understanding, on the Wittgensteinian picture, whereas different kinds of animal or substance means different understanding, according to Putnam. Putnam's claims thus present a *prima facie* challenge even to our in-the-world Wittgensteinianism: either we must reject or reinterpret the Putnam contentions, or develop a conception of use which differentiates between my *Doppelgänger* and me in the imagined cases. What we shall eventually see is that this source of potential weakness is in fact a principal strength of in-the-world Wittgensteinianism. For the version of this approach which does so differentiate me and my *Doppelgänger* is the only account of understanding among those we shall have considered which can respect the phenomenological constraint argued for in the previous chapter. In this sense, Putnam is very much grist for the in-the-world Wittgensteinian mill.

But all that, of course, assumes that Putnam has at least made a plausible case to answer. So let us now ask: *does* Putnam's argument about substance-words have force? Has a worthwhile case been made for the claim that the understanding tracks real essence?

3 Positivism and realism

One key assumption of the argument is that twin-water/XYZ is not the same substance as water/H_2O. Putnam's reason for claiming this is that they have different chemical microstructures. It is thus natural to suppose that the principle underlying his strategy is that where there is a difference discerned by the relevant science – chemistry in this case – there we have to agree there is an ultimate, or absolute, difference. And this might seem unwarrantably deferential to science. For why not say that XYZ is just another type of water? After all there is dirty water, water with pieces of wood floating in it, water from Skegness, water that has had Putnam's hands plunged into it, and so on without apparent end: but these are still samples of water. So why not water with the chemical structure H_2O and water with the chemical structure XYZ? And we do recognise that something like this can happen, as when we say that a single substance can exist as two or more isotopes, where difference between isotopes is precisely a matter of difference in microstructure. If all this is right, perhaps Putnam's argument does not even get off the ground.

There is certainly no inconsistency in denying that science has the ultimate say in which classifications are correct in a language. If I am suffering from the affliction I have learned to call 'pounding headache', and some self-confident neurologist informs me that really my head does not hurt at all, because my brain is not showing the configuration that he has discovered pounding headaches to consist in, then I would be justified in laughing in his face (although it would hurt). As I (and other English speakers) use the phrase, any state of feeling the appropriate way is a state of pounding headache, regardless of neurological underpinnings. Our neurologist can tell us a lot about what causes pounding headaches, and correct our claims about such matters, but he cannot correct our classifications of feelings in the envisaged way. This is just how we use the phrase (of course we might change our usage in the light of his research, or for some other reason: but we are not already committed to). Similarly, if my walls look red in normal conditions then they are red, no matter how unusual or atypical or even inexplicable the micro-properties of the paint may be. In the same way, then, we can imagine a community who *have* decided to use 'water' in such a way that it applies to anything which superficially resembles typical samples. According to the practices of this community, XYZ would indeed be 'another type of water'.

So it might seem that Putnam's argument hangs on answering an empirical question about our practice with substance-words: are we in fact like this imaginary community, or are we not? He takes the answer to be beyond serious doubt:

> If we put philosophical prejudices aside, then I believe we know perfectly well that no [Lockean] definition does provide a necessary and sufficient condition for the application of [a substance-word]. (MM: 238)

But an objector, presumably, could find this confidence misplaced.

Fortunately, we can move on without having to settle the empirical question. All we need is the thought that there *could be* a community who understood substance-words in the way Putnam describes. For if such things are so much as possible, then we still have a challenge to accounts of the understanding according to which real essence is Exterior to it. A reasonable aim in giving an account of Xs is to give an account of any *possible* X:

this is why the method of imaginary counter-examples is so integral to enquiry, and why people who become irritated at such procedures simply have no proper grasp of what enquiry is all about. Nor is this just a point about *philosophical* enquiry: thought-experiment is an integral part of scientific theorising too. Only politicians and other simpletons who need the comfort of easy answers refuse to consider hypothetical questions. Thus as long as it is *possible* for substance-words to be understood in the way described by Putnam, then various accounts of understanding are faced by the charge that they are not adequate because they do not cater for all possible kinds of understanding.[3]

Putnam's mention in the above quote of 'philosophical prejudice' is a reference to a source of doubt about whether it is even possible to use substance-words in the way he describes. This is positivism, which as we saw in chapter V is at bottom an idealistic philosophy. Since idealism is the view that there can be no difference, at bottom, between how something really is and how it impinges on our awareness, it is clear that idealists would resist going along with Putnam: for an idealist, what makes water water cannot consist in something beyond our knowledge. Putnam thus tends to see his view about real essence, rightly it seems, as a natural consequence of realism, the view that things can have their own nature which goes beyond how they impinge on us. And if this is right, then his point about substance-words perhaps does not even require the deferential attitude towards science which he may display. For surely any realist must be prepared to admit that something could, possibly, impinge on our awareness in normal conditions in exactly the same way as water yet still fail to be water. To deny this possibility just is to embrace a very forthright form of idealism. Very well: let twin-water be such a possible substance, and let the argument proceed as before. If you like, consider Putnam's argument to be qualified with an initial 'If realism is correct, then . . . '.

We can move on then, since Putnam's argument only requires this denial of idealism, and the apparently consequential possibility of a community who understand substance-words as he describes. But for brevity let us proceed as though he has established the empirical claim that we are indeed such a community.

4 Embellishments

We now have to consider a number of embellishments which Putnam and others have added to the Twin Earth story as we so far have it.

First, we should note that not merely the *understanding of words* is implicated. When, after travelling to Twin Earth, I say 'That is water', pointing at the glass of twin-water, I thereby give expression to a belief or opinion of mine. But just as what I say is false, not in accordance with my intended meaning of 'water', so too what I *believe* is false. On the other hand, the Twin Earthian who points at the same glass and says 'That is water' both speaks truly *and* gives expression to a true belief. So it appears that our beliefs are different too: mine is false, hers is true. Similarly, if we both say 'Please give me a glass of water', then we shall be giving expression to different wants. If we are both handed a glass of twin-water, I shall not be given what I wanted (although I will not realise this): she, on the other, will get what she wanted. More generally, consider the class of *propositional attitudes*. These are folk psychological states which are standardly described by embedding a sentence thus

> Fiona thinks that *sparrows are brown*
> John wonders whether *the sun will come out today*
> Peter is afraid that *the sun will come out today*
> Joanna hopes that *the train will not be late*

In these examples the whole sentences say something about the state of mind of the named person: that they think, wonder, hope. And the emphasised embedded sentences specify, by way of their meaning, just what is thought, hoped and so on. If Putnam is right about substance-words, it seems that propositional attitudes which are specified by embedding sentences which contain these words will track real essence. Thus if X and Y are any Earthian and Twin Earthian respectively, and V any verb of propositional attitude, the sentences

> X Vs that water [= H_2O] is wet

and

> Y Vs that water [= XYZ] is wet

will describe different states of mind, no matter how similar X and Y otherwise may be. Thus any theory of mind which entails that propositional attitudes are self-contained with respect to real essence has to confront Putnam's argument.[4]

This aspect of Putnam's argument brings us square up against folk psychology, inasmuch as propositional attitudes are part of how the mind strikes us as a component of the everyday world. The key point here, as noted in the previous chapter, is that meaning figures in the phenomenology of mind. Given that a propositional attitude is specified by way of the meaning of an embedded sentence, as in the above examples, it follows that the tracking of real essence by these attitudes should somehow show up in our ordinary experience of the mind: this fact, apparently derivable from Putnam's argument, has to make a difference at this phenomenological level. This, as we shall see in the following chapter, is a crucial test of different responses to the Twin Earth challenge, including that of our in-the-world Wittgensteinianism.

Although he does not follow up the point at all clearly, Putnam notes that his view about substance-words is at odds with an assumption that is 'implicit in just about the whole of traditional philosophical psychology' (MM: 220). This he describes as

> the assumption of methodological solipsism . . . the assumption that no psychological state, properly so called, presupposes the existence of any individual other than the subject to whom that state is ascribed. (*Ibid.*)

To subscribe to methodological solipsism is clearly to embrace a form of self-containedness doctrine. As Putnam notes, the full-blooded version of this is that of Descartes, who supposes that no psychological state requires the existence even of the subject's body. But we have seen other versions. If the subject is identified with the brain, for example, and mental characteristics are identified with intrinsic brain characteristics, then no body or embedding environment is presupposed by the mental states enjoyed: and so on. Thus if we make the natural extension just noted, that propositional attitudes themselves track real essence, then plainly most traditional and many contemporary theories of mind are incorrect. Construing Putnam's word 'individual' so that it covers things like samples of substances, this extension of Putnam's conclusion suggests that many mental states – e.g. propositional attitudes about substances – *do* presuppose not only the existence of individuals other than the subject but also facts, possibly unknown, about the microstructure of the individuals concerned.

This sense in which a state of mind is held to involve the existence of other individuals besides the owner of the state should be carefully distinguished from others, where what is intended by 'individuals' is other *thinking subjects*. Of course, if humans count as substances, then they can be expected to yield examples conducive to Putnam's arguments just as water, tigers, cats and dogs can. But Putnam and others have suggested different possible involvements of others in a speaker's own understanding of substance-words. Here it is *their role as fellow-speakers* which is intended. Putnam suggests that it is natural to 'think of language as private property' (ER: 203). And this was certainly how Locke considered the matter, as we saw in chapter II: each person assigns meaning to the words he or she uses by associating them with ideas. Failure to do this results in the making of empty sounds only: other speakers are not involved at this stage at all. Against this, Putnam suggests that 'there is *division of linguistic labour*' (MM: 227). Where substance-words are concerned, this involves the fact that members of the linguistic community can use a word like 'water' or 'gold' without knowing what real essence it is that makes water water or gold gold. They can do this because they can 'rely on a special subclass of speakers' (MM: 228), presumably chemists or other experts, who know the relevant facts about real essence, can apply appropriate tests to distinguish H_2O from XYZ, and so on. As a supposed example of this, Putnam adduces his own situation with respect to the words 'beech' and 'elm'. Although he 'cannot tell an elm from a beech tree' (MM: 226), he claims that the words still mean different things in his mouth, and this, he implies, is partly facilitated by the division of linguistic labour. He sums up:

> there are two sorts of tools in the world: there are tools like a hammer or screwdriver which can be used by one person; and there are tools like a steamship which require the cooperative activity of a number of persons to use. Words have been thought of too much on the model of the first sort of tool. (MM: 229)

Now although there is of course something right about this

conclusion, it has to be said that Putnam's discussion of these points is confused. First, the existence of experts who can distinguish samples of a substance from superficially similar things is elsewhere said by Putnam not to be necessary for the understanding's tracking of real essence. As he puts it, 'the extension of the term "water" was just as much H_2O on Earth in 1750 [when no one knew this] as in 1950' (MM: 224). Indeed, it is not clear that this point requires even the *existence* of other speakers: on the face of it, it is just a claim about an individual's understanding tracking the unknown facts about real essence. Second, in admitting that he cannot tell the difference between an elm and a beech, Putnam is illustrating another point altogether, namely that speakers can get hold of words which they do not really understand. For in fact elms and beeches look quite different, have quite different types of leaf, provide wood of very different colour and smell and grain configuration, and so on. It is easy to tell them apart, *and one does not need to be a biologist or any other sort of 'expert' to do so.* One needs to know nothing at all about any microcellular or other related matter. So this case is quite unlike that in which two substances, H_2O and XYZ, are superficially indistinguishable. Putnam just does not understand the words 'elm' and 'beech' (does not know the stereotypes), whereas the whole point is that we do understand 'water' (know its stereotype) even if we do not know water's real essence, and even if we could not distinguish it from twin-water.

The confusion in Putnam's claims hereabouts condenses in the following passage:

> everyone to whom gold is important for any reason has to *acquire* the word 'gold'; but he does not have to acquire the *method of recognizing* if something is or is not gold. He can rely on a special subclass of speakers. (MM: 227–8)

Here the phrase 'method of recognizing' is ambiguous. It might refer to the ability of a non-specialist to e.g. tell the difference between gold and silver, or margarine. Or it might refer to the ability of the specialist to perform a test which reveals the presence of gold's real essence. If it is taken this second way, then Putnam is right that one can 'acquire the word "gold"' without having the ability. But if it is taken the first way, then surely not: in so far as 'acquiring the word "gold"' means gaining an understanding of it, then one cannot acquire it without learning how to recognise gold in the non-specialist's way, as when one is presented with a piece of gold and a piece of silver in good light and asked to select the gold. One need not be able to recognise an X in all possible circumstances, and distinguish Xs from all imaginable superficially indistinguishable imposters, in order to understand the word 'X'. But if one can do little more than parrot the word, and has no ability to apply it in even the most favourable of situations, then one simply does not understand it.

Of course, when Putnam utters the word 'elm' it does mean *elm* and not *beech*, and no doubt this is because the word has a fixed meaning in the language, thanks to the practices of others. But these others need not be experts who know the real essence of elms or anything like that: they just need to be people who *do* understand the words 'elm' and 'beech' and so can, for example, recognise typical specimens in the right circumstances. Even Locke could accept something like this point: in his terms, when Putnam utters 'elm' he may well be taken (by his audience) to be conveying its 'common acceptation', but he does not himself associate any idea (or any adequate idea) with it (cf. chapter II, section 2). It is true that Locke would also say that Putnam thereby utters a meaningless noise, but that is overstatement: what he should say is that Putnam utters a word which is pretty meaningless *to him* but which is nevertheless meaningful to appropriate English-speakers. This is quite a common phenomenon: children, incurious mouthpieces, parrots and tape recorders can be used to transmit meaningful linguistic messages which they do not themselves understand. More, as Locke points out,

> because words are many of them learned before the *ideas* are known for which they stand: therefore some, not only children but men, speak several words no otherwise than parrots do, only because they have learned them and have been accustomed to those sounds. (E:III,ii,7)

None of this has much to do with Putnam's doctrine about substance-words, since the above applies to any kind of word; and even if Putnam is completely wrong about substance-words, the mouthpiece phenomenon will still be with us. All in all, then,

Putnam's discussion of the division of linguistic labour, and its links with the doctrine that the understanding tracks real essence, obscures rather than elucidates his main point. We shall discuss some associated confusions in the following chapter.

One final embellishment of the basic Twin Earth story involves another way in which facts about fellow speakers can figure. This effectively involves trying to extend the scope of the argument from substance-words to others, such as the mode-words introduced in chapter II. Thus suppose that on Twin Earth things are very much the same as here, except that 'matricide' is so used that it can only truly be applied to acts of mother-killing carried out by males. Suppose too that Twin Earthian Louise is unaware of this fact about the word, so that when she hears of a woman killing her own mother, she accuses her of matricide. The accusation is not true, given how they use the word there. But suppose that Louise has a *Doppelgänger* on Earth, Thelma, who similarly accuses a woman in closely similar circumstances. This accusation is true. Relatedly, then, we might say that Louise has a belief which is not true, Thelma has one which is. Yet they could be in all relevant respects otherwise identical: the sole difference between them concerns facts about the use of a word by other speakers in their respective communities. There is not much relief here if we make the not implausible retort that in the circumstances Louise has an incorrect understanding of what she is saying. Even so, if, as might be claimed, her belief about the woman is not true, unlike Thelma's belief, then there appears to be a psychological difference between them which is somehow constituted by the speech practices of fellow speakers. Much the same goes even if we try to say here that Louise does not have any clear belief at all, due to her deficient understanding. This still leaves her apparently psychologically different from Thelma, who does have a clear belief.

In such examples a different kind of self-containedness for the mind is being denied: it is being denied that the mind is self-contained *with respect to the doings of other speakers.*[5] Note the difference from the Putnam case involving substances. This time there is nothing like a real essence which the understanding is said to track. But although this is clearly a very different claim from that made by Putnam, it conflicts with many of the same accounts of the mind. Thelma and Louise could be equivalent in respect of brain and the processing of mental words, peripheral nervous activity and functional relations between inner states, and so on.

To keep what follows relatively manageable, we shall concentrate on the straight Putnam case and possible replies to it, and ignore this latest embellishment. Even so, there is a large and growing literature comprising attempts to get to grips with Putnam's Twin Earth argument, much of it written from the midst of developed or developing theories of mind or of some range of cognitive phenomena. But it is just about possible to discern, at an appropriate level of abstraction, the kinds of option that are possible. One might argue that some feature of the Twin Earth scenario is illicit: that Putnam goes wrong in setting up the case, so that there is no need to think of responses. We rejected this in section 3. At the other extreme, one might accept that Putnam has shown that the understanding tracks real essence, and thereby refuted every model of the understanding we have so far considered except for a very strong form of in-the-world Wittgensteinianism, which so construes 'use', 'form of life' and so on that they too track real essence. We shall recommend this response. However, it is probably accurate to say that most theorists fall somewhere in the middle: they accept that Putnam has made a case and needs a response, but argue that the case does not force anything as radical as this in-the-world Wittgensteinianism. This, as we shall see, is often the way of those with the Cartesian Tendency, who typically try to show that Putnam's contentions about real essence are not, despite initial appearances, incompatible with Cartesianism. It is to these manoeuvres that we now turn.

Notes and reading

Works referred to

E   Locke, J., *An Essay Concerning Human Understanding*, ed. J. Yolton (London: Everyman, 1961).

ER Putnam, H., 'Explanation and reference' in his *Mind, Language and Reality: Philosophical Papers*, vol. 2 (Cambridge: Cambridge University Press, 1975).

MM Putnam, H., 'The meaning of "meaning" ' in *Mind, Language and Reality*.

SP?   Putnam, H., 'Is semantics possible?' in *Mind, Language and Reality*.

Notes

1 This requires some licence, given that human bodies actually contain H_2O! But it would be a severe failure of imagination to think that this matters: pretend that there is H_2O on Twin Earth, but only inside humans; or think of an example involving substances not found inside humans; or suppose the argument to apply to creatures which are very similar to humans except that they do not contain H_2O.

2 See Gareth Evans, *The Varieties of Reference*, ed. John McDowell (Oxford: Oxford University Press, 1982); Gregory McCulloch, *The Game of the Name* (Oxford: Oxford University Press, 1989); and John McDowell, 'On the sense and reference of a proper name', *Mind* 86 (1977). Frege is normally interpreted as willing to allow sense to words even given *global* failures of Meaning, so that the realm of Meaning is Exterior to the realm of sense: this was the suggestion made in chapter III, section 3 above. The Fregean texts just mentioned deny the very possibility of sense-without-Meaning, and hence deny the Exteriority claim. But an intermediate position would be to allow there to be some *local* examples of sense-without-Meaning, just so long as enough expressions in the language concerned had both sense and Meaning. This is probably better seen as a subtle denial of the Exteriority claim, rather than a qualified acceptance of it: see François Recanati, *Direct Reference* (Oxford: Blackwell, 1993): 222–5. A rather similar idea is to be found in Akeel Bilgrami, *Belief and Meaning* (Oxford: Blackwell, 1992).

3 In recent as yet unpublished work Jerry Fodor, whose published attempts to handle Twin Earth cases will be examined in the following chapter, has gone so far as to deny the need to account for all possible types of understanding (circulating draft of 'Chapter 1: If psychological processes are computational, how can psychological laws be intentional?' (28 September 1992), esp. pp. 10–17). His view seems to be that because Twin Earth probably doesn't exist, we do not have to worry about it. This is uncharacteristically desperate.

4 Note that this makes the argument somewhat independent of the understanding of words. If there can be creatures which lack language but which can e.g. believe or want things to do with water, then Putnam's argument will apply in their case too, and will similarly make trouble for any theory of these states of mind which has it that the facts about real essence are Exterior to them. But since we have tended to go along with Descartes' idea that mindedness requires at least the potential for using language, we shall ignore this point.

5 Thus see Tyler Burge, 'Individualism and the mental' in P. A. French, T. Uehling and H. Wettstein, eds, *Midwest Studies in Philosophy Vol. IV* (Minneapolis: University of Minnesota Press, 1979).

CHAPTER VIII

Internalism and Externalism

The key move among those who accept that Putnam has made a case to answer, but who still wish to uphold a theory of understanding apparently incompatible with his conclusions, is to adopt one or other version of the *Divide and Rule strategy*. This strategy enjoins attempts to divide up the phenomena treated by Putnam in such a way that the letter of his positive claims is maintained whilst the threatened incompatibility with the upheld account of understanding is avoided. Our aim will be to resist various common attempts to adopt this strategy, and thus to maintain the true spirit of Putnam's Twin Earth contentions. But before we see how all this works, it is desirable to impose some order on what is becoming an extremely tangled scene.

1 Methodological solipsism

Putnam himself has to take some of the blame for the tangle. Some of this accrues to his rather unhelpful remarks about the division of linguistic labour, which we have already criticised and will encounter again soon. But there is another factor, arising from his remarks on methodological solipsism. This, recall, is a self-containment claim, to the effect that no psychological state requires the existence of any individual apart from the subject who has it. Putnam says that although this is a standard assumption in philosophical psychology, it involves a significant departure from folk psychology:

> Making this assumption is . . . adopting a *restrictive program*
> – a program which deliberately limits the scope and nature

of psychology ... Just *how* restrictive the program is, however, often goes unnoticed. Such common or garden variety
psychological states as *being jealous* have to be reconstructed, for example ... For, in its ordinary use, *x is jealous
of y* entails that *y* exists ... Thus *being jealous* ... [is not]
permitted by the assumption of methodological solipsism.
(MM: 220)

He goes on to describe a distinction among putative psychological
states which has become practically orthodox: those permitted by
the assumption of methodological solipsism, and those not. The
first he calls *psychological states in the narrow sense*, and the
second *psychological states in the wide sense.* (*Ibid.*)

His talk of 'reconstruction' in the above quote adverts to the
fact that if jealousy and other wide psychological states are to be
accommodated by the restrictive programme, then we should
have to

reconstrue *jealousy* so that I can be jealous of my own
hallucinations, or figments of my imagination etc. (*Ibid.*)

And this is a very common move in philosophical psychology.
Thus if it is proposed that *x sees a dagger* or *x remembers going
to Skegness* are wide psychological states, in that one cannot see
a dagger unless there is a dagger present, or remember going to
Skegness unless one went, it is often replied that these states too
involve, as it were, a narrow core state which can be shared by
someone who merely hallucinates a dagger, or misremembers
going to Skegness. One motivation for this involves the idea that
a mental state's nature is exhausted by how it seems to its subject.
Since seeing a dagger could be subjectively the same as hallucinating one, the idea would be that these states ought to be lumped
together by psychology. This motivation is somewhat discredited
given the demise of introspectionist psychology (see chapter V,
section 1), part of the general move away from Descartes' focus
on consciousness. A superficially more respectable reason for the
move is noted by Putnam:

Only if we assume that psychological states in the narrow
sense have a significant degree of causal closure (so that
restricting ourselves to psychological states in the narrow
sense will facilitate the statement of psychological *laws*) is

185

there any point in engaging in the reconstruction. (MM: 221)

That is, the motivation is justified if the most comprehensive set of psychological laws involves ignoring the differences between e.g. seeing and hallucinating, since the similarities outweigh, for explanatory purposes, the differences. Thus one might argue that those who hallucinate daggers (and are taken in) *behave* in exactly the same ways as those who see daggers (and believe their eyes). Since the aim in psychology is to explain such similarities in behaviour, the argument continues, it is justifiable to posit a narrow state common to both seers and hallucinators. We shall return to this in sections 6–8 below.

Many suppose that the key to understanding Putnam's claims about substance-words, as well as to reconciling them with apparently conflicting accounts of the understanding, such as Cartesianism, lies in the distinction between narrow and wide states, or at least something akin to it. This distinction, in effect, is the inspiration for the Divide and Rule strategy. As for Putnam's own attitude to the distinction – that is very difficult to make out. On the one hand he expresses deep scepticism about the motivating assumption of methodological solipsism:

> the three centuries of failure of mentalistic psychology is tremendous evidence against this procedure, in my opinion. (MM: 221)

But on the other hand he proceeds to use 'psychological state' as synonymous with 'psychological state in the narrow sense' for the duration of his argument. Up to a point this is justified, since as he points out this is what most theorists of meaning have done too, and he aims to expose an inconsistency in their procedures (MM: 221). But consequently it has not really emerged as clearly as it might have done that one way of taking Putnam's claims, especially in the light of his scepticism about methodological solipsism, is as the joint proposal:

(a) that understanding a substance-word is, contrary to traditional preconception, being in a psychological state *in the wide sense*; and

(b) that *this state cannot be 'reconstructed' in accordance with methodological solipsism*.

But it will conduce to clarity if we keep this proposal in view (it is the proposal we shall recommend). Consequently, we turn now to the matter of distinguishing between *Internalism and Externalism* with respect to the understanding of substance-words.

2 Internalism and Externalism

Consider the Putnamian claim

{P*} Earthians understand 'water' to mean *water* [and not *twin-water*].

Does this describe a psychological state which Earthians can be in, or not? Clearly if it does describe such a psychological state, then it will have to be a wide one, since the whole thrust of Putnam's arguments is that *this* sort of understanding is not self-contained with respect to real essence, and hence is forbidden by the assumption of methodological solipsism. Just as clearly, then, the materialistic Cartesians of chapter V, for whom mental operations are self-contained with respect to anything beyond the brain, will have to deny that {P*} describes a psychological state which Earthians can be in (or deny that it does so 'strictly speaking'). So too will anyone else who subscribes to the Mind–Brain Identity Thesis and identifies mental characteristics with happenings in the brain, or to Functionalism which treats 'inputs' and 'outputs' in terms of nerve activity, or to Behaviourism which regards the world beyond the skin as Exterior to the mind, or to in-the-skin Wittgensteinianism. All such theorists must treat the sort of 'understanding' mentioned in {P*} as (strictly) a non-psychological phenomenon: {P*} cannot be considered a claim essentially about the mind, since it introduces matters (e.g. the difference between water and twin-water) which, on these approaches, are Exterior to the mind. Correspondingly, all such theorists will have to claim that *strictly speaking*, the real psychological state of UNDERSTANDING the word 'water' is a narrow state, subject to the restriction of methodological solipsism. To the extent that understanding, ordinarily so-called, is a wide state (like jealousy), it will have to be reconstructed on these approaches.

Contrast this attitude to {P*} with that of someone who rejects methodological solipsism and so is willing to countenance wide psychological states. Such a person is not so far precluded from accepting {P*} as *making a claim essentially about the mind*, a claim which entails that real essence is not Exterior to it. If this is done, understanding 'water' to mean *water* [and not *twin-water*] can be accepted without reservation or qualification as a wide psychological state. Imagine here an in-the-world Wittgensteinian (perhaps Wittgenstein himself) who so construes 'form of life' that the Earthian form of life involving the word 'water' is not the same form of life as the corresponding Twin Earthian one. On this approach, actual uses of 'water' and interactions with water *constitute* understanding, in a sense of 'understanding' which is both full-bloodedly psychological and the same as that involved in {P*}. On this approach, to have a mind is to participate in certain forms of life which themselves, besides of course involving bodily and other factors, track the differences between e.g. H_2O and XYZ, even when these are unknown to the speakers. Those of us sympathetic to this in-the-world Wittgensteinianism can thus affirm that the genuine psychological state is (wide) understanding, and deny a role to UNDERSTANDING, the narrow state postulated in accordance with methodological solipsism.

This involves a certain amount of stipulation: in taking this line we do not, as we saw in chapter V, have to deny that there are e.g. self-contained brain-states which underlie the understanding of words; nor deny that scientific psychologists might develop fruitful ways of describing these as the processing of elements of the Language of Thought or whatever. But it would muddy the waters rather badly to take over the word 'narrow psychological states' for these putative inner states: it would give the impression of a shy commitment to methodological solipsism in *folk psychology*, rather than a mere acknowledgement that it might be appropriate in *scientific psychology*. So we are best to regard this in-the-world Wittgensteinianism as including the joint proposal of the previous section:

(a) that understanding a substance-word is, contrary to traditional preconception, being in a psychological state *in the wide sense*; and

(b) that *this state cannot be 'reconstructed' in accordance with methodological solipsism*;

and we should reserve the term 'scientific psychological state' for any e.g. Language of Thought processing state that might accompany this wide state.

The position just described is Externalist, and the position described before that is Internalist. That is, as far as the issue of substance-words is concerned, anyone who denies that {P*} describes a psychological state which Earthians can be in (or denies that it describes one 'strictly speaking') is an Internalist; and anyone who accepts that it does is an Externalist. To be precise, one might be an Internalist with respect to some aspects of mind, and an Externalist with respect to others. But to keep the argument simple we shall ignore this. We shall focus on Internalism and Externalism with respect to {P*} and parallel doctrines about other substances, without constantly making this relativisation explicit.

The labels 'Internalist' and 'Externalist' are useful, if not essential, for grouping theories and keeping the issues manageable. But they do have their dangers. Clearly enough, the 'external' means *external to the human individual*, so that anything beyond the skin is external in this sense. But the danger here is that 'external' will be taken to mean *external to the mind*. And this is ridiculous, since the whole point of Externalism is that e.g. such things as real essence are not external to the mind, in that the mind is not self-contained with respect to them![1] The main source of this confusion is the traditional idea of the 'external world', which is almost indifferently (and sloppily) taken to mean either the world surrounding the mind *or* the world surrounding the human individual. Given Cartesianism, of course, the two things almost exactly coincide. But that is all the more reason why the necessary distinction should not be blurred when Cartesianism itself is being assessed. This is one reason why it has been necessary to use the word 'Exterior' throughout: the other, recall, was that the doctrine of the 'external world' is an epistemological doctrine, whereas we wanted an ontological one (chapter I, section 4). So be clear: Externalism is the view that some things which are external to the human individual are *not* Exterior to the mind. For example, it is an external fact about me *qua* human individual that I inhabit a world which contains H_2O rather than XYZ, but according to Externalists this fact is not Exterior to my mind.

The 'internal' has its problems too. For it is normally said that

Internalists believe that the mind is in the head. And Cartesians do.[2] But if *Behaviourists* (or Functionalists or in-the-skin Wittgensteinians) who simply assert that everything beyond the skin is Exterior to the mind are also Internalists, it seems that they would be committed to the absurd claim that e.g. the arms and legs are in the head. The usual lame reply is that 'in the head' is intended metaphorically, as a term of art. But that in turn covers up more potential for grotesque confusion. Suppose someone somehow refuted Externalism. They would thereby have established that the mind is in the head *metaphorically speaking*. But suppose now one forgets about the metaphor in the excitement. It then would seem that refuting Externalism is tantamount to showing that the mind is (literally) in the head, so that (ignoring Dualism) materialistic Cartesians were right to claim that brain-activity constitutes understanding, and that the vat-brain is a thinking subject. But clearly, forgetting the metaphor is tantamount to ignoring the other versions of Internalism just mentioned, and so begs the question about the vat-brain, embodiment and related matters.

Still, as long as these reservations are borne in mind, it is helpful to polarise theories of mind with the use of these two terms.[3] So from now on, we shall classify responses to Putnam's claims about real essence as either Externalist or Internalist.

We have rejected already the suggestion that Putnam has not made a case to answer. So Internalists, then, are committed to explaining away his claims about the tracking of real essence by the understanding. And this is where we come to the Divide and Rule strategy. There are, as we shall now start to see, various versions of it, but they all involve the thought that Putnam has demonstrated a hitherto overlooked need for a major distinction in theories of language and/or mind. The general idea is that by dividing up the phenomena in some way, the sting can be taken out of Putnam's contentions, and Internalism upheld. After that it would be just a matter of deciding which Internalistic theory of mind to adopt. We shall now describe the more common varieties of this strategy, and argue that they invariably suffer from crippling defects: they are badly motivated or not motivated at all; they beg the question against Externalism; most of all, they fail to meet the phenomenological constraint argued for in chapter VI.

3 The semantic and the cognitive

One implementation of the Divide and Rule strategy involves a certain way of distinguishing *semantics*, the study of language and linguistic practices, from *cognitive studies*, the study of the mechanisms involved in understanding. Although there are different ways of filling out the idea, the broad proposal is that Putnam's observation that 'water' as used by Earthians does not apply to the same stuff as 'water' as used by the Twin Earthians is a semantic thesis, a fact about *the workings of public language*, to be assessed and if need be accepted as such, regardless of any puzzles that it may generate for traditional theories of understanding or of the individual. These are held to involve topics for cognitive studies.[4]

This approach is bound up with an influential anti-Fregean movement to which Putnam's arguments about substance-words contributed. Recall that Frege distinguished between the study of word–world relations (theory of Meaning) and the study of word–mind relations (theory of sense). But he saw them as working together in a fully integrated theory of language and understanding, a feature underlined by e.g. the doctrines that it is senses, rather than the words which express them, that represent things in the world, and that sense determines Meaning. This integration was emphasised even more by what became the orthodox interpretation of Frege, namely the view that one gives the sense of a word by offering a definition: thus the sense of 'lead' might be given by 'soft heavy dull whitish metal'. In a similar fashion, Frege was construed as holding that the sense of a proper name such as 'Aristotle' could be given by a definite description, say 'The famous philosopher born in Stagira'. The reason why these construals of Frege emphasise the integration between the theories of sense and of Meaning is that such proposals, although themselves doctrines about sense, nevertheless amount to semantic theses, that is theses about the workings of public language: thus 'lead' represents *whatever 'soft heavy dull whitish metal' represents*; 'Aristotle' represents *whoever 'the famous philosopher born in Stagira' represents*.

Arguments like Putnam's, which show that e.g. 'lead' does not work in the alleged way, can thus seem to show that Frege had the wrong conception of how this part of public language works.

191

Similarly, Kripke was at around the same time arguing strongly and influentially that proper names do not come paired with definite descriptions in the way that the above construal of Frege requires (see NN; Putnam notes some of the parallels at MM: 229–35). This gave a strong impression that Frege had been on the wrong track regarding the workings of proper names too. If it is now further assumed – as it still often is – that there is no other way to construe Frege's apparatus of sense and Meaning, then it can seem that the whole idea of an integrated theory of language, incorporating a theory of understanding and a theory of word–world relations, is just a mistake. Instead, the thought goes, two separate theories are needed: semantics, to deal with the public aspects of language, and cognitive studies, to deal with the impact of language on the individual. This tendency was certainly present in the search that both Kripke and Putnam instigated for the ways in which the relevant parts of public language actually do work. Putnam, as we have seen, tended to stress, if not particularly coherently, the role of the division of linguistic labour (chapter VII, section 4), while Kripke urged that the question of who (or what) a proper name applies to is to be settled by investigating the causal history of the use of the name, rather than by (fruitlessly, in many cases) seeking a definite description which competent users take to give its sense:

> Someone, let's say, a baby, is born; his parents call him by a certain name. They talk about him to their friends. Other people meet him. Through various sorts of talk the name is spread from link to link as if by a chain. (NN: 91)

All of this, of course, leaves outstanding some of the issues which Frege introduced the theory of sense to address, such as the question 'What is it to understand a word?', and the problem of how words equivalent in Meaning (e.g. 'Istanbul' and 'Constantinople') can figure in the understanding as names of distinct places. But with the perceived failure of the Fregean programme, such questions tend either to be reconstrued as questions about the sorts of social and causal mechanisms mentioned by Putnam and Kripke, or else left on one side to be dealt with in cognitive studies. Putnam's conclusion ' "meanings" just ain't in the head' is interpreted as a claim about semantic mechanisms, and his baffling tendency to speak of what *is* in the head as 'conceptual' or 'cognitive' (see e.g. MM: 245) is interpreted as the claim that a psychology of narrow states is required to take up the residual questions that Frege's theory of sense addressed. Hence, on this approach, there are two sorts of question to be asked about speaker S's use of 'water'. The semanticist or theorist of public language will ask what social and/or causal mechanisms ensure that the word as used by S applies to the stuff it does apply to rather than e.g. other, superficially indistinguishable substances. This, as we have seen, may well involve matters of which S is entirely ignorant. The other sorts of question to be asked about S concern his or her 'cognitive economy': what narrow processes underpin these uses of 'water'?

Such a diagnosis of Putnam's claims obviously suits Internalists very well. Internalists are almost certain to be committed to the view that semanticists are not engaged in a psychological enterprise at all, but are concerned with public and/or other manifestations and accompaniments of the mind's doings. For semantics is typically about things beyond the skin, whereas for practically all Internalists the psychological concerns only what is within.[5] By the same token, residual questions to do with the individual's own grasp of words fall nicely, on this approach, into the hands of narrow psychology, which is what cognitive studies becomes or at least comes to include. Indeed, on this construal of things, *Locke's* theory of mental processes may still be a candidate treatment! For on the present approach, all Putnam has shown is that Locke gave an inadequate account of how words apply to things in the world (his talk of definitions, and ideas resembling objects). But once this enterprise has been taken away from the philosopher of mind, it requires different arguments to show that Locke's theory of ideas is not an adequate account of thinking processes themselves (this is one reason why it is possible, as we have already remarked more than once, to regard the Language of Thought hypothesis as a version of the theory of ideas).

In sum, the approach just outlined is clearly one natural way for Internalists to try to Divide and Rule. But – and this is the first of three crucial points – the above is not the only way to construe the *in itself* unexceptionable division between semantics and cognitive studies. Externalists, for example, consider the public and other semantic mechanisms spoken of by Putnam to concern the proper subject-matter of the theorist of *mind*. On this view not only meanings, but also the mind itself, ain't in the head; nor even does it stop at the body's boundaries. If use of language constitutes understanding, and this kind of understanding is accepted as a (wide) psychological matter, then semantics is part of the study of mind. At the same time, we have also seen that Externalists do not have to deny such things as the Language of Thought hypothesis, or claims that the brain is a computer, or the idea that these matters belong to scientific psychology or cognitive studies. All they need to deny is that these alleged computational matters *constitute* the mind and the understanding, i.e. are sufficient for mindedness: it does not also have to be denied that they are necessary causal conditions. Consequently, Externalists do not have to resist the idea of a division between semantics and cognitive studies. But they will insist that this division does not coincide with the division between non-mental and mental studies in the way described above.

Obviously, then, unless and until some further, independent argument can be given for Internalism, this first application of the Divide and Rule strategy is unmotivated and potentially question-begging. But, second, things are worse than this. Let us return to the thought that this implementation is heavily involved with the idea that Frege's programme has failed. In fact even this is not justified by arguments such as Putnam's. It is true enough that any attempt to explain grasping sense in terms of knowing definitions and definite descriptions is seriously compromised by them (as well as by Wittgenstein's family-resemblance arguments): but these are not the only ways of carrying forward Fregean ideas. In particular, as we remarked in chapter IV, Wittgenstein's *meaning-is-use* view can itself be regarded as an attempt to spell out what grasping the sense of a word amounts to. Since we have now seen that Wittgenstein's view can be construed as a form of Externalism, and hence as compatible with Putnam's conclusions, it follows that *Frege's* can too. True, as remarked in the previous chapter, the view that sense is self-contained with respect to Meaning is put under pressure by Putnam: but a view does not cease to be Fregean when just this component is abandoned. All of the other distinctive Fregean theses can remain: that each word has a sense and a Meaning; that the senses and Meanings of complex expressions are determined by the senses and Meanings of their constituents (and their manner of combination); that sense determines Meaning; that senses are grasped by the mind (as glossed by Wittgenstein, say); that Lockean ideas, even if they exist, are irrelevant to the understanding; and so on. It is in fact a very serious distorting influence on contemporary philosophy of language and mind that Frege's views should still be widely but wrongly regarded as discredited by the arguments of Putnam and Kripke. A whole lopsided literature of Divide and Rule sets off from this false premiss.

The third point to make against the above implementation of the Divide and Rule strategy is that it is seriously at odds with the phenomenology of understanding. Corresponding to Frege's idea of an integrated theory of language is that of a unitary notion of meaning (sense): we say things with words, and we entertain beliefs, and on the Fregean approach both saying and believing involve the same thing – what we say with 'Istanbul is a city' is what we believe when we believe that Istanbul is a city. And this certainly fits the way our thinking and use of language strike us. We do not normally suppose that giving verbal expression to a belief somehow involves us in saying something different from what it is we believe. I may think something, say what I think to you, and you may hear directly what I say, as we saw in chapter VI. At the phenomenological level, the entire episode concerns one content of belief, which is first thought and then expressed and grasped simultaneously. Yet it is hard to see how this phenomenological unity can be preserved given the above Divide and Rule manoeuvre. On that view, in speaking I project, as it were, beyond the cosy cognitive circle of my thoughts, and hazard something that turns on semantic, causal and other public matters which are Exterior to my understanding. Making a move in the language game is thus comparable to throwing a bottle I cannot open into an ocean I cannot enter, all the time hoping somehow that somewhere out there the desired impact on someone else's desert island will ensue (not that they are any better placed than me to open the bottle containing the public message I am supposed to have sent). Note a version here of the severe tension we found in Descartes and Locke (chapter II), between their stifling conception of the self-contained mind on the one hand and their expansive talk about the role and workings of language on the other. At least Locke, with the doctrine that ideas are objects of awareness, had some inkling that communicating is an open, conscious, communal event. How this is meant to be captured by the bottle-and-ocean model is something which has probably not even occurred to its proponents.[6]

These phenomenological points are best pressed home by way of a discussion of another very popular implementation of the Divide and Rule strategy: so we shall now turn to this.

4 Wide and narrow content

Let us focus more closely on the point that it is not just the *understanding of words* that is involved in the issues raised by Putnam, but also propositional attitudes such as belief and desire. According to Externalists, such attitudes themselves track real essence; and Internalists must deny this. But here they encounter a strategic difficulty. Imagine a pair of atom-for-atom *Doppelgänger*, Liz_1 and Liz_2, the first contemplating a glass of H_2O on Earth and the second a glass of XYZ on Twin Earth. And suppose it is the case that both

1 Liz_1 believes that water [= H_2O] is a boring drink

and

2 Liz_2 believes that water [= XYZ] is a boring drink

are true. Now the insertions in the square brackets indicate that in specifying these beliefs, we are using 'water' with the Earthian meaning in (1) and with the Twin Earthian meaning in (2) – as we should, given that we have accepted that these are different meanings, and we are assuming that Liz_1 and Liz_2 are typical members of their respective communities, and so understand their words in the appropriate ways. But if we now note that the phrases which follow the 'that's in (1) and (2) specify the beliefs we are attributing *in virtue of what they mean,* or their content, then it seems that we are attributing different beliefs to Liz_1 and Liz_2. This is exactly in order for the Externalist, of course, but an embarrassment for the Internalist.

Now in the pre-Putnam days, when it was considered plausible to claim that Liz_1 and Liz_2 shared a meaning for their words 'water', Internalists could move to deal with the matter as follows. If Liz_1 and Liz_2 have a shared understanding of 'water', it ought to be possible to spell out exactly what they each take it to mean.

And this is where Lockean definitions come in handy: one can say they both believe themselves to be confronted by e.g. *odourless, tasteless, thirst-quenching liquid that falls as rain.* If the giving of such a definition is now transposed into a Fregean context, and so taken as giving the sense which each associates with 'water', it becomes possible to rewrite (1) and (2) respectively as

1′ Liz_1 believes that the odourless, tasteless, thirst-quenching liquid that falls as rain is a boring drink

and

2′ Liz_2 believes that the odourless, tasteless, thirst-quenching liquid that falls as rain is a boring drink.

And hey presto!, we see from (1′) and (2′) that Liz_1 and Liz_2 really have the same belief,[7] as Internalists require. The problem, though, is that post-Putnam it is no longer permitted to rewrite (1) and (2) like this in order to display the shared belief posited by the Internalist. For Putnam's key point is that there is no such shared definition or description which will adequately convey what is understood by 'water'.

Internalists often try to respond to this difficulty as follows. What Putnam has shown is that public and related mechanisms guide our words on to the appropriate substances. So whenever we use a word like 'water' we cannot help but speak about the substance that the mechanisms home in on: and this goes even for cases of describing the contents of someone's belief. So naturally, when using Liz_1's own word to describe her belief, as in (1), we cannot help but describe her as having a belief about *Earthian* water (H_2O). By parallel reasoning, we cannot help but describe Liz_2 as having a belief about *Twin Earthian* water (XYZ). Hence the result that (1) and (2) apparently ascribe different beliefs to our agents. But if Internalism is true, this appearance has to be misleading, since Internalism entails that (1) and (2) ascribe the same belief to Liz_1 and Liz_2 in the circumstances. So what we have to do as Internalists is distinguish between the *wide contents* which we inevitably must use to specify beliefs, and the *narrow contents* which these beliefs actually have. This distinction between types of content is obviously derived from the distinction between wide and narrow psychological states. According to the usual forms of Internalism, all psychological states are narrow (can exist as they are in themselves independently of what is external to the human individual). Given that a propositional attitude has to have a content (i.e. be specifiable by a meaning) which makes it the propositional attitude it is, it follows then that the contents they have must also be narrow (independent of anything external to the human person).[8] A narrow content is perhaps to be identified in computational terms, or in some other way which does not mention matters external to the individual. Wide contents, on the other hand, are the ordinary meanings which words and sentences have which we actually use when specifying beliefs, as in (1) and (2). We can say if we like that this fact shows that beliefs have wide contents, but if we are Internalists we cannot say that this is an essential feature of a given type of belief: for according to Internalists, Liz_1 and Liz_2 have the same type of belief, but the two beliefs have different wide contents.

Externalists, on the other hand, can happily accept that wide content is essential to type of belief, since Externalists are committed to the view that since belief tracks real essence, change in real essence (and hence wide content) amounts to change in belief. Note that the epithet 'wide' might be strictly redundant here as far as the Externalist is concerned, since it is not clear that Externalists should have to recognise narrow content at all. It is true, as we have seen, that Externalists need not deny the importance or relevance of computational brain-studies and the like, but it is not obvious that they need to accept that such accounts of how brain states function in the production of our behaviour, linguistic and otherwise, are accounts of a narrow kind of content (and this is just as well, given the forthcoming criticisms of the notion).

The Internalist way with (1) and (2) is another illustration of the Divide and Rule strategy. Faced with the semantic facts about the ascription of propositional attitudes which Putnam's arguments deliver, and which appear to be inconsistent with Internalism, they just divide up the phenomena. In effect, the standard Internalist view is that within each widely *described* belief there lurks a narrow content, which unlike the wide content is essential to the type of belief it is. Think of these narrow contents as a sort of potential which a propositional attitude has, a potential for having one or the other wide content depending on which context (if any) it happens to inhabit. To use the word of Jerry Fodor, an influential proponent of this doctrine,[9] a propositional attitude needs to be 'anchored' in a context before it has a wide content, and the wide content it thereby gets will vary from context to context (see P: ch. 2). Thus Liz_1's belief as reported in (1) has a wide content concerning H_2O since it is anchored in the Earthian context which Liz_1 actually inhabits. But if she had instead been born and raised on Twin Earth then her belief, with the same narrow content as in the actual case, would instead have had a wide content concerning XYZ, since it would then have been anchored differently.[10]

How ought Externalists to respond to such suggestions? We should first be clear that this reaction to Putnam is not obligatory unless you are an Internalist. What is more, making the distinction between wide and narrow content is not what Putnam's argument at bottom amounts to. Further, to repeat, Externalists have no obvious need for the notion of narrow content. And more to the point, making the distinction is not an *argument for* Internalism. This is all worth stressing, since it often appears to be overlooked by contributors to the literature on Putnam. Defensively, then, Externalists can reply that this application of the Divide and Rule strategy still requires independent, Internalist, motivation.

Aggressively, though, they can point to the fact that it cannot accommodate the phenomenological constraint argued for in chapter VI. This has actually emerged, albeit unwittingly, from the conclusions of Fodor himself. As we noted above, post-Putnam it is not permissible to specify the belief allegedly shared by *Doppelgänger* like Liz_1 and Liz_2: in (1) and (2) this supposed shared belief is ascribed using *different* wide contents. Fodor makes this point by conceding that narrow contents, such as the one he would claim to be shared by the beliefs of Liz_1 and Liz_2, are 'radically inexpressible' (P: 50). But this means that such narrow contents cannot figure in the phenomenology of understanding and communication. For recall that what I think is both what I say and what you hear me say, phenomenologically speaking. If narrow content is inexpressible, then obviously I cannot communicate such a content to you, which means that such a content cannot figure in our conscious thoughts either. This in turn means that in so far as our beliefs are conscious and capable of being communicated in language, they are not made to be the beliefs they are by their purported narrow contents. Instead of saying 'inexpressible', Fodor might just as well have said 'unthinkable'.

The failure to accommodate the phenomenological facts is bad enough, but the very idea of an unthinkable content is bizarre. In so far as we have any grip on what contents or meanings are, it is as the expressible content or meaning *of* this or that expressive item: say a piece of language, or a gesture, or an episode of thinking or experiencing. It is true that e.g. unconscious beliefs and gestures have content too, but these are contents which can be brought into consciousness, either that of some observer or therapist or even the subject concerned (if only for denial). A content which cannot *in principle* be expressed, thought or brought into consciousness is a different matter altogether (rather like that of an *unfeelable* pain).[11]

The next idea, then, is that the proponent of narrow contents had better find a way of expressing them after all. But now there is a fatal dilemma. Either these contents can be expressed in the normal direct way in public language, or they cannot. But if they can, then it is clear that Putnam's anti-definition arguments can be applied to them. For these purposes, we may as well stay with (1') and (2') above as attempts to express the narrow content allegedly shared by Liz_1 and Liz_2. Putnam's whole Twin Earth point is that an ascription such as

1' Liz_1 believes that the odourless, tasteless, thirst-quenching liquid that falls as rain is a boring drink

does not adequately capture the state of mind described by

1 Liz_1 believes that water [= H_2O] is a boring drink.

To reply, as under the present suggestion, that this is correct at the phenomenological level but that there is some narrow-state level of analysis at which the point does not hold, is mystery-mongering. For we have no other way of understanding (1') except at the phenomenological level, as a statement of ordinary English. This is not question-begging, since if the point is meant to be that we UNDERSTAND (a narrow state) (1') differently at a non-phenomenological level, then clearly we are no further forward: the same may as well be said about (1), *and that was the problem we started with!*[12] That is one horn of the dilemma.

Internalists become impaled on the other if they try to suggest that narrow contents can be expressed in some special way, rather than by way of a sentence of ordinary language. On the face of it this may seem easy: why not introduce a special operator 'N[ ]' and stipulate it to be such as to yield a phrase expressing a sentence's narrow content when it is applied to that sentence? Then we might take an ordinary sentence, say

(a) Water is wet

and convert it into an expression of that sentence's narrow content thus

(b) N[Water is wet].

Or so it may seem. But in fact this idea is confused. Suppose we interpret 'N[ ]' to mean 'the narrow content associated with the wide content that [ ]'. Then (b) comes out as

(c) The narrow content associated with the wide content that water is wet.

And this is, at best, a name or description of a narrow content, not an expression of it. It no more expresses a content than does

(d) The claim with which Mary responded to Bob's claim that London is pretty.

We might successfully use (d) to pick out a content, but we have not thereby given expression to it (we still do not know *what*, if anything, Mary said to Bob).

So inexpressible narrow contents are not really intelligible, and expressible narrow contents are just not available. For our final flourish, we should now wonder how Internalists might propose to deal with the phenomenological facts which the theory of narrow content does not accommodate. It is clear that they cannot simply concede our in-the-world Wittgensteinianism as a correct account of the phenomenology, but still claim that Internalism is a correct account of the mind. For this is just to redefine 'mind' so as to exclude such things as what *consciously* goes on when language is used and understood: and why should we change our use of 'mind' in this way? It is quite easy to show that all humans are male if it is stipulated that *being female* is not a way of being human! Nor can they get away with the bland announcement that the phenomenology is constituted by wide contents appearing before consciousness, and that wide contents are yielded when states with narrow contents are appropriately anchored in a context. For everything difficult is hidden by the words 'appear before consciousness', 'constituted' and 'yielded'. What these words cover up is the need for a positive conception of what it is to grasp or understand a wide content. And if the idea is to leave that to the in-the-world Wittgensteinians, in the light of the advantages for this approach set out in previous chapters, then this is just to give up the ghost. The standard claim of Internalism, that a state of mind is made to be the state of mind it is in virtue of its narrow content, would have dwindled to the claim that states of mind have an internal, non-phenomenological, perhaps computational, core. But this, we have seen more than once, is not something with which the Externalist has to quarrel. For the Internalist to retreat to this would not be to make a concession, but to capitulate totally.[13]

Yet what else can the Internalist do? Given the correctness of Putnam's Twin Earth claims, it seems that only the form of Externalism which comprises in-the-world Wittgensteinianism can cope with the facts about meaning. For as we saw in chapter VI, meaning and understanding are phenomenological notions, and the phenomenology only came out right when we moved to this form of Wittgensteinianism. But Putnam's doctrine is a doctrine about meanings too, and is hence also a phenomenological doctrine: that of which we are conscious when we understand language tracks real essence. So not only do we arrive at in-the-world Wittgensteinianism, but we arrive by default at the version which construes 'form of life' etc. so that they too track real essence. Nothing less than this will square with Putnam's claims about the likes of Liz_1 and Liz_2. If (1) and (2) really do ascribe different wide contents – contents which track real essence – and wide contents are phenomenologically available, then only the strong in-the-world Wittgensteinian account of these matters is going to fit the facts. By way of their embodied interactions with H_2O and XYZ respectively, Liz_1 and Liz_2 come to engage in different forms of life.

How does this, a phenomenological claim,[14] square with the fact that Liz_1 and Liz_2 might be switched unbeknownst and still rub along as before, apparently communicating and all the rest with their fellows? Here we should recall the point of chapter III section 4, that differences in sense need not always show up, but may lurk as a potential for crossed purposes. However well a switched Liz₁ might get by on Twin Earth, the fact is that while her ties to Earth remain (they would weaken as time went by, of course) she is labouring under misconceptions: asking for water (= H_2O), she wrongly thinks she gets what she wants on being handed a glass of XYZ. Believing the rivers and lakes on Twin Earth to be filled with water (= H_2O), she unwittingly trades in falsehoods. All of this would come out if she were notified of the switch and the facts about microstructure came to light. There is thus no sense in which these are the illusory undetectable differences of meaning that afflicted Locke's account of communication. If Putnam is right about Twin Earth, the understanding tracks real essence. If we were right about the phenomenology in chapter VI, then this gives strong in-the-world Wittgensteinianism. There is no future in the Divide and Rule strategy or in Internalism.

5 Vat-brains

That concludes the positive case for Externalism. But we now have to consider some arguments which are popularly supposed to establish Internalism. Our case will not really be complete until we have shown that these arguments establish no such thing. We shall begin with the vat-brain, although we have seen that this does not have to be the issue at stake between Internalists and Externalists. For it certainly is the issue when the form of Internalism in question is the materialistic Cartesianism introduced in chapter V, and this is a very common form of Internalism.

We have to leave aside, however, unargued inclination. Many people just find it obvious that the (human) mind is the brain, and so find it obvious that a vat-brain identical to mine would be a mind with exactly the same mental properties as mine. For such people, this Cartesianism is not something that needs to be argued for. However, given our arguments for Externalism (and the possibility of other forms of Internalism), it is clear that argument is needed. Nor should it be thought that Cartesianism is, as it were, the default position, which it is legitimate to stand firm on unless opponents can produce inescapable arguments to the contrary. Arguments for Externalism have already been given, and attempted Internalistic reinterpretations of these conclusions have been rebutted. Internalism is itself on the back foot, and badly needs some arguments.[15]

Here is a direct argument for Internalism. Imagine a clever scientist constructing a vat-brain on a waterless world. At time t_1 this brain is atom-for-atom identical with mine (forget, as before, that brains contain water), and at t_1 I am drinking water and thinking that water is a boring drink. It seems that the materialistic Cartesian is committed to the view that the vat-brain embodies a subject who shares this (and all other) propositional attitudes with me. Since the brain is not connected to water by the right sorts of causal and social mechanisms (which will not even exist on the waterless world) we cannot *describe it* as thinking that water is a boring drink, but as we have seen, the Internalist can claim that that does not prevent it from having propositional attitudes with the same narrow contents as mine, among which is one which would be a thinking that water is a boring drink were it anchored in the appropriate way (for the space of this argument let us generously waive the problems we have unearthed with the notion of narrow content).

Imagine now that we transport the brain to Earth, and eventually transplant it into a body atom-for-atom identical with mine at the appropriate time (assume I'm asleep). Throughout the entire process we ensure that the brain remains atom-for-atom with mine, and the morning after the operation we ensure that the new individual, $G.W.McC_2$, comes to in the same way as I do in a matching environment, so that the atom-for-atom parallels remain. This would all be quite difficult to arrange, but presumably not absolutely impossible. At t_2, after I have awakened, I suddenly remember that I was thinking that water is a boring drink yesterday at t_1 (imagine I'm very thirsty and enjoying a delicious glass of water). Since $G.W.McC_2$ is atom-for-atom with me, he too will be thirsty and enjoying a drink of water and – surely – *remembering thinking exactly the same thing yesterday at* t_1! Of course, if we tell him the real story about yesterday, he will accept that not all of his apparent memories are correct: he was not actually lifting a glass to his lips and pouring water into his mouth, since yesterday he had no lips or mouth, since his brain was in a vat. Nevertheless, he will insist that *it seemed to him* yesterday that these things were happening, as his present memory now attests, and the Cartesian will no doubt be happy enough with this. If the vat-brain seemed to itself yesterday to be drinking water and thinking that water is a boring drink, then surely that is enough to show that yesterday it shared the relevant narrow psychological states with me. And that is all Cartesianism requires. This thought-experiment seems to confirm what the Cartesian needs to say about the vat-brain (think also of the claims that might be made by the persons resulting from the brain-swap case mentioned in note 15 above).

But the argument has no force. An apparent memory can be *completely* delusory, rather than partially so. So perhaps G.W.McC$_2$ is wrong about yesterday in every respect, and not just about whether he had lips and a mouth then. Perhaps it did not even seem as though he did yesterday: his present memory may be a total delusion. This is clearly what the Externalist has to say: but can anything more be said to support the proposal? Yes. Let us take the story back to t_0, a time before the vat-brain was assembled but when all the materials required to assemble it were stored in various bottles and jars in a cooler. At t_0 let us suppose that *I* was thinking to myself that water is better drunk cool than warm. At this stage no vat-brain exists which is atom-for-atom with mine at t_0, although as we said the materials for G.W.McC$_2$'s brain are all in the cooler. Later, at t_3, I recall thinking at t_0 that water is better drunk cool than warm. By now, of course, G.W.McC$_2$ is up and running too, and we can suppose that he remains atom-for-atom with me. So he too will apparently recollect, at t_3, thinking at t_0 that water is better drunk cool than warm. But it is quite obvious that this *does* involve a total delusion. Not even G.W.McC$_2$'s brain existed at t_0, although the material for it was all together in the cooler. And not even (materialistic) Cartesians are going to say that these materials stored in their bottles and jars constituted a subject of propositional attitudes, so that a ghostly G.W.McC$_2$ lurked unsuspected in the cooler. Hence if some of G.W.McC$_2$'s apparent recollections concerning times before t_2 are total delusions, perhaps they all are, including the one at t_2 previously discussed.

The natural reply is that there is a big difference between t_0 and t_1. At the earlier time we just have a lot of organic materials in bottles and jars, whereas at the later time we have *an organised mechanism*, processing information and what have you in exactly the way that my own brain is processing information at t_1. As this shows, what we have in the vat at t_1 is something which, *if* it were properly connected to an appropriate body, *would be* involved in the having of thoughts about water. Things are quite otherwise at t_0, when all we have are separate parcels of material. It does not even make sense to imagine *this* ensemble properly connected to a body. So the two cases are quite different.

Of course. But where is the argument? In fact, the preceding paragraph simply involves a restatement of the Cartesian position, dressed up with a rhetorical flourish. The fact that at t_1 we have materials organised into an information-processing structure which would be involved in thinking if appropriately embodied is no decisive difference at all unless we have already accepted that Cartesianism is true. But that is the issue at stake. So an Externalist, who denies that the above vat-brain constitutes a subject of propositional attitudes, will be unmoved by the preceding paragraph. Only a Cartesian will find it compelling: *there is no independent argument for Cartesianism there at all.*

Imagine now a different kind of case. If you cut off my legs but take care to keep me alive, I do not cease to be a subject of propositional attitudes. Nor will I if you then proceed to remove my arms, my ears, my torso . . . and finally my skull. As long as the right sorts of life support mechanisms are set in place throughout, surely I survive each operation as a subject of propositional attitudes. But of course what remains as the result of iterated amputation is a vat-brain. Now imagine an atom-for-atom identical vat-brain which was got not by amputation but direct construction: this vat-brain has never been in a body. Surely if the result of iterated amputation is a subject of propositional attitudes, then so is its *ab initio* replica?

Again, only a Cartesian will be impressed by the rhetorical flourish at the end of the preceding paragraph. Possible Externalist replies could run as follows. First, one might reply that the amputee's ability-losses are overridden by the fact that the brain has been adequately linked to water and the rest of the world in virtue of its history in the body prior to the amputations. If so, one can take these historical facts as decisive in ensuring that the result of iterated amputation is indeed a subject of propositional attitudes. But in the case of the *ab initio* replica, there are no parallel reasons for claiming there to be a subject of propositional attitudes. So an Externalist can quite consistently deny that there is such a subject in the *ab initio* case. Only a Cartesian will find reason enough in its information processing and the like: and we have seen that there is no independent argument here. Or, second, one can deny that the amputee remains as a subject of propositional attitudes once enough of the body has gone. For with the body goes the basis of a lot of the abilities which Wittgensteinians take to constitute understanding. Reversing the amputation by putting the brain back into an appropriate body and asking the resulting person what he or she was thinking while in the vat would not demonstrate anything, as the previous example shows. Overall, it seems that if you hack someone about enough then it starts to go indeterminate whether they are still capable of having propositional attitudes. The situation here resembles what happens when brain-damage or chemical imbalances or other changes result in mental impairment of the subject, so that it becomes impossible confidently to affirm or deny that propositional attitudes remain.[16] We all live through such a predicament at least once. The new-born baby has no propositional attitudes, and most full-grown adults have some: but there is no magic moment when the lights come on. On this approach, as the amputations proceed there becomes less and less plausibility in attributing propositional attitudes to the patient. And from the Externalist perspective, there never was any plausibility in attributing them to the *ab initio* replica brain.

It is hard to imagine a more direct attempt to establish Internalism. So let us turn now to some slightly less direct ones.

6 Explaining behaviour (1)

The arguments we are about to consider take off from the idea that wide contents, howsoever interesting they may be from the phenomenological point of view, are *no use when it comes to the explanation of behaviour*. But one might suppose that one feature of a propositional attitude psychology is that it should enable us to explain behaviour (section 1 above). Narrow contents, it is said, are on the other hand eminently suitable for this job. Hence, the thought concludes, we have need of narrow contents. As we shall see, there are different ways of taking this conclusion.

Why should it be supposed that wide contents are no use when it comes to the explanation of behaviour? Here we first have to remove a quite general misunderstanding, linked to the anti-Fregean movement mentioned in section 3 above. One of the reasons for distinguishing sense from Meaning in Frege's manner, recall, is that what happens to be one thing can figure in the understanding as though it were two. Linked to this is the idea that senses appear to have a role in the explanation of behaviour, for to say a thing can 'figure in the understanding' as though it were two has implications for the behaviour and states of mind of the subject. Someone might go in for an elaborate enquiry into how to get from Istanbul to Constantinople. And part of the explanation for this initially bizarre-seeming behaviour would be

1 This person does not realise that Istanbul is Constantinople.

Once (1) is known, things become clearer, and the attempts to make travel arrangements do not seem so bizarre (although, of course, one might still find this an odd misconception to labour under: but that too could be made clearer by a fuller description of the person's predicament). In any case, (1) is a very different ascription from

2 This person does not realise that Istanbul is Istanbul.

Even if it is possible[17] to be in the state described in (2), there is no clear reason to suppose that someone of whom (1) is true is also someone of whom (2) is true. So (1) and (2) appear to ascribe different propositional attitudes to the person concerned, even though they are both attitudes towards the same city and a question of identity. Frege, of course, claimed that this difference in propositional attitude is to be put down to the difference in sense between 'Istanbul' and 'Constantinople'.

Now given Putnam's claim that what makes something a sample of a certain substance is that it should have the appropriate real essence, it follows that a piece of ice is in fact a sample of water. As he says, 'Gold in the gaseous state is still gold' (SP?: 140). But we can imagine an incurious group who know water from the hot plain and later encounter ice on the cold mountain, who have never seen the former freeze or the latter melt, and who suppose that water and ice are as different as Chablis and cheese. Asked why a thirsty group of them marooned on the mountain do not simply suck ice, we reply

3 They do not realise that ice is water.

Again, this is quite a different thing from saying

4 They do not realise that ice is ice,

and once more Frege would say that this is down to the fact that 'ice' and 'water', even if they Mean the same substance, have different senses.

But what are these different senses? Here we might recall the idea of giving the sense of a word by offering a definition. On this approach, we could spell out more fully the state of mind of the persons mentioned in (3) by rewriting it as

3′ They do not realise that the cold translucent solid on the mountain is (the same stuff as) the thirst-quenching liquid found on the plain.

But the problem with this, of course, is that Putnam has shown that such ways of spelling out senses are not available, and *if it is further supposed that there is no other way to explain what it is for a word to have sense*, then it appears that this whole Fregean approach to ascriptions of propositional attitude must be abandoned.

This conclusion is often combined with the following reflection. The semantic upshot of Putnam's arguments is that when we use substance-words the implicated public and causal mechanisms automatically see to it that we are talking about the stuff with the appropriate real essence. This goes even for the case of describing someone's propositional attitudes: as we noted in section 4, the contents involved in propositional-attitude ascriptions are wide. But then how *can* there be any difference between (3) and (4), as we had supposed? Given Putnam's arguments, we can elucidate them as follows:

3* They do not realise that ice [= H_2O] is water [= H_2O]

and

4* They do not realise that ice [= H_2O] is ice [= H_2O],

letting the inserts in square brackets indicate which substances are involved in the ascribed wide contents. But as we see, we have the same substance (H_2O) involved throughout. So surely the wide contents ascribed in (3) and (4) are the *same* wide contents, so that (3) and (4) amount to saying the same thing. So how could one of them figure in psychological explanations in which the other does not figure? How could there be a difference in explanatory power between (3) and (4) if they both ascribe the same wide content to the subjects concerned?

The invited answer, of course, is that wide content does not have explanatory powers, because explanation needs a distinction between 'Ice is water' and 'Ice is ice', yet the above arguments seem to show that they have the same wide content. Once more, then, it seems that we need to appeal to the Divide and Rule strategy: in so far as we *do* use sentences like (3) and (4) in psychological explanations, the thought might go, this can only be because there is some implicit indication of lurking narrow contents which do differ in the way required.

Given the problems we have unearthed with the notion of narrow content, this threatens paradox. Fortunately, then, we can report that the above argument is completely useless, despite its popularity. Its failure lies in its assumption that the *only* way to construe Frege's claim about senses is as a claim about definitions. For we have seen this to be false: there is also the in-the-world Wittgensteinian way. On this approach, to say that one associates a certain sense with a substance-word is to say that the word is part of a practice or form of life involving the substance. But even when this is intended, as here, so that forms of life track real essence, it does not follow that forms of life have to be sensitive to *nothing but* real essence. Hence it does not follow that the 'water'-involving practice has to be identified with or include the 'ice'-involving practice, even though they both in fact track the same real essence. And of course, on no sane interpretation of 'ability' do the members of the group described above acquire just the one ability in acquiring 'water' and then 'ice'. Down on the plain they are inducted into one practice involving water in liquid form, then later up on the mountain they begin or are inducted into an entirely distinct practice involving water in the solid form. Clearly they could engage in either practice without engaging in the other. Obviously to supplement one by the other is to extend their linguistic repertoire and hence their scope for forming propositional attitudes. On our Wittgensteinian approach, then, their uses of 'water' constitute one exercise of understanding, and their uses of 'ice' constitute another. In other words, the contents ascribed in (3) and (4) are distinct contents, even though they are also wide and track the same real essence. So there is no reason to suppose that they have the same explanatory powers. Hence the above argument that wide contents are useless for explanatory purposes fails. It suffers from the distorting misinterpretation of the impact of Putnam's arguments on Fregean doctrine which we mentioned in section 3.

7 Explaining behaviour (2)

It is possible to accept this, however, yet still argue that these wide contents have the *wrong* explanatory powers. The argument here involves Twin Earth once more. Imagine as before that Liz_1 and Liz_2 are atom-for-atom *Doppelgänger* on Earth and Twin Earth respectively. Their environments, in fact, are entire duplicates of one another except that XYZ replaces H_2O on Twin Earth. Looked at from the outside, their lives would appear to follow the same course: this would be another case like the one mentioned in chapter VII, section 2, in which to a God-like outsider it would be just like watching the very same events unfold on parallel screens. Liz_1 is thirsty, she walks across to the tap and fetches a drink. Looking across, we see Liz_2, who is of course thirsty too, do the same. Most times when Liz_1 believes there is rain falling and wants to remain dry, she takes an umbrella if she goes out. On all and only the corresponding occasions, Liz_2 takes an umbrella too. Liz_1 and Liz_2 are like two peas in a pod.

One thought now is that as they act out their parallel lives they are performing *exactly the same kinds of actions*, that is displaying exactly the same behaviour. It is therefore reasonable to suppose that their parallel behaviour indicates that they are equivalent from the psychological point of view. Think of mechanics. If two metal balls react in exactly the same way to the same forces then, perhaps by definition, they are mechanically equivalent: they obey the same mechanical laws (otherwise they would not react in the same way to the same forces). Similarly, if they react to the same chemical manipulations in the same way then they are chemically equivalent, that is obey the same chemical laws. Now Liz_1 and Liz_2 are atom-for-atom duplicates, so it seems assured that they are not merely equivalent from the point of view of physics, but also from the point of view of chemistry, mechanics, physiology, neurophysiology and so on. In each case we can expect the same inputs to produce the same response, at the appropriate level. And nothing seems to change when we ascend to the psychological level: as remarked, they respond in tandem to parallel circumstances as they come up. The problem, however, is that they are not equivalent in respect of the wide contents of their propositional attitudes. Recall the case where they each contemplate a glass of what they would each describe as 'water' (section 4 above). It could be that both

1 Liz_1 believes that water [= H_2O] is a boring drink

and

2 Liz_2 believes that water [= XYZ] is a boring drink

are true. But as the inserts in square brackets indicate, these beliefs have different wide contents. Hence Liz_1 and Liz_2 are not psychologically equivalent if we reckon the matter from the point of view of wide states: from this point of view, they are psychologically different, since they are in different (wide) belief-states. But (the argument goes on) surely this is a difference that makes no difference. As we saw, there is every reason to suppose that they are psychologically equivalent, just as they are physically equivalent, chemically equivalent and so on.

Note that this argument can be pressed even if it is accepted, as urged in the previous section, that wide contents involve more than real essence alone. The argument now is not that wide contents have *no* explanatory powers, but that they have the *wrong ones*. Nor does this claim seem to be affected by our point that there are differences between Liz_1 and Liz_2 which could show up if the right facts came to light. The point is that the observable parallels between them are themselves evidence that common explanations should be given, and hence common mental states ascribed.

Once more some version of Divide and Rule seems available: wide contents might figure in our ordinary descriptions of propositional attitudes, but the job of classifying agents from the psychological point of view is best left to narrow-state psychology. Otherwise we see psychological differences where none exist for explanatory purposes.

There are different ways of taking this conclusion. On one construal, it indicates that our folk psychological ways of classifying propositional attitudes do not really implicate wide contents in the supposed way. On this construal, the argument brings it home to us that not even folk psychology is committed to the idea of wide *psychological states* (or not as far as substance-words are concerned anyway), but only, given the truth of Putnam's semantic theses, to the idea of wide propositional attitude *ascriptions*. If this line is taken, the present argument suggests that Putnam is wrong to suppose that adoption of methodological solipsism involves 'reconstruction' (see section 1), at least in these cases. On this view, folk psychology implicitly works with a notion of narrow content.

This way of taking the conclusion is refuted by our phenomenological findings, however. In so far as we appear to each other under the concepts of folk psychology, the contents that we think and communicate are wide. Taken another way, however, the conclusion merely suggests that the reconstruction be undertaken. Even if folk psychology does work with wide contents, it ought not to. And this last prescription can itself then be taken in one of two ways. It could mean that *folk psychology* needs to be reconstructed, or it might merely mean that scientific psychologists need to reconceptualise in terms of narrow content before they get down to serious scientific business. Here we are invited to leave folk psychology as it is for ordinary purposes, but clean up our act for serious explanatory ones (given the problems we unearthed with narrow content, however, it is moot how clean our act could be made).

The question of what to do about scientific psychology will be left to scientific psychologists, as it surely should be. The idea that folk psychology should be reconstructed will be dealt with briefly in the final section. But first we should ask: does the foregoing argument against wide contents work anyway?

8 Self-containedness again

An initial reply is that it does not work since it rests on a false premiss, namely that Liz$_1$ and Liz$_2$ *perform the same actions*. For in fact they no more perform the same actions than they have propositional attitudes with the same wide contents. Just as when Liz$_1$ has a water-belief, Liz$_2$ has a twin-water-belief, so when Liz$_1$ goes swimming in water, so Liz$_2$ goes swimming in twin-water. But these are different actions: an Earthian would have to set about things in quite different ways in order to obey the two instructions 'Go and swim in some water' and 'Go and swim in some twin-water'. Obeying the first would still leave the second to do, and this would require a journey by rocket. Doing the first twice over would not be the same as doing both. Of course, there may be a way of describing the careers of Liz$_1$ and Liz$_2$ so that they perform the same actions. Both *go swimming in the odourless etc. stuff that falls as rain;* both *drink whatever stuff it is comes out of the tap when thirsty*; and so on. But why should these similarities be deemed to be more important than the above differences, unless it is simply being assumed that psychology should be insensitive to differences in real essence? Why not use their own words to describe what they do (when they succeed, of course), just as we use their own words to describe their beliefs and intentions (when they are sincere, of course)?

However, one can reply that all this misses the point. To say that two metal balls are mechanically equivalent is to say that they obey the same mechanical laws, give the same outputs in return for the same inputs and so on: abbreviate this to *they have the same causal powers with respect to mechanics*. But two individuals can have the same causal powers in this way even if they do not duplicate one another's careers. The fact that one ball is melted in a furnace and the other is not hardly shows that they differ in causal powers. All that is required for sameness of causal power is that the second would have melted if it had been treated in just the same way as the first one. In other words, sameness of causal powers requires only same reaction *given the same context*. The thought now is that Liz$_1$ and Liz$_2$ have the same causal powers in this sense. Although, as we saw above, their careers are actually different (Liz$_1$ drinks and swims in water, Liz$_2$ drinks and swims in twin-water), it is also the case that they live in different contexts. But imagine that (say) Liz$_2$ had been born and raised on Earth (forget about Liz$_1$). Then she would have followed much the same career as Liz$_1$ actually did follow, and as far as her dealings with water (H$_2$O) are concerned, there is no doubt that they could have been exactly the same. But this indicates sameness of causal power after all: just as two metal balls have the same causal powers if and only if they would react the same in the same contexts, so presumably the same goes for agents too. Liz$_1$ and Liz$_2$, it seems, have the same causal powers as far as psychology is concerned, since they would react the same in the same contexts (thus compare Fodor in MA).

This is neat, but it begs the most important question of all. We are willing to allow that two metal balls are mechanically equivalent if they have the same (mechanical) causal powers because we have already accepted that causal powers are all that matter from the point of view of mechanics. This is linked to a more broadly metaphysical view that a thing like a metal ball has a sort of mechanical (and also physical, and chemical etc.) context-free nature which it can carry around with it from context to context, at least in the sense that we can imagine the ball remaining exactly the same as it is in itself, mechanically speaking, even though transported to a different context. Here it is now colliding with something, and suffering a certain distortion as a result: this result is partly due to the context-free causal nature of the ball in question. The point is that we can imagine that this very same nature could have contributed to the same distortion even if the context had been different, for example, even if some other kind of thing had collided with our ball. Perhaps in the first case the distortion resulted from a collision with a piece of aluminium, perhaps in the second from a collision with a piece of molybdenum, of the same mass though perhaps different shape and size in order to compensate for the differences in density, elasticity and so on between aluminium and molybdenum. The thought is not that the piece of molybdenum is mechanically equivalent to the piece of aluminium – it will not be. The thought is only that it is *all the same as far as our metal ball is concerned*: in each case it brought its own contribution to the collision, its own mechanical nature at that time, and despite differences beyond its surfaces, helped bring about the same effect. Mechanical nature is in this sense self-contained with respect to context:

215

the ball can retain its own mechanical nature even though the context is varied. The pieces of aluminium and molybdenum are mechanically Exterior to the ball.

In comparing Liz_1 and Liz_2 to metal balls in the above way, the Internalist argument clearly begs the question against the Externalist. To assume that sameness of causal power in the above sense is tantamount to psychological equivalence is just to assume that the mind is self-contained with respect to changes in context such as that between Earth and Twin Earth. But that is precisely the question at issue. The whole point of Externalism is that the mind does not have a context-free essence whose causal powers explain the bodily accompaniments in this or that context. Our in-the-world Wittgensteinianism, for example, sees the differences in actions performed between Liz_1 and Liz_2 not as inessential reflections of their difference in context, but as part of the stuff of the psychological difference between them. It is no argument against this to make the comparison with metal balls: that is just to beg the question about self-containedness. No one who has really understood Externalism and the Wittgensteinian position could intelligibly press the causal power argument against them.

It may be that the metal ball analogy at least shows that there has to be some form of narrow-state psychology if psychological causal powers are to take their place in the hierarchy of causal explanatory sciences, and that Externalism is at best an account of folk psychology. This may be right, although given the total physical replicahood of Liz_1 and Liz_2, the extent to which they are like two peas in a pod is not at all surprising. So we need some further argument even here, presumably along the lines of the presumed or expected successes of Mentalism in scientific psychology and AI mentioned in chapter V. But this may still leave room for some work for some kind of wide content to do, even in scientific psychology: and this is one line of investigation that recent work explores.[18]

Be that as it may, it is clear that the foregoing explanation-based arguments are powerless to establish Internalism, just like the preceding reflections on the vat-brain. They either misconstrue the nature of wide content, or beg the question against the Externalism which we have established on independent, phenomenological grounds.

9 Naturalism and scientism: a sting in the tail?

On the face of it, many could view the results of the foregoing with quite a measure of equanimity. Externalists, and especially in-the-world Wittgensteinians, have been vindicated. But in arguing that such a position is compatible with Mentalism in scientific psychology, we have left room for many of the cherished views of Internalism, particularly those of a computational nature. Even Behaviourists can claim to have had a partial grip on the truth. So if these arguments are correct, there is no need for a dog-fight between Externalists and Internalists: one side has all it wants, the other can go for most of what it needs. Much of the dog-fighting in the literature seems to assume an incompatibility between broadly Wittgensteinian approaches and Mentalism, or between Putnam on Twin Earth and scientific approaches to psychology. We have seen these assumptions to be unwarranted. But before we get too cosy, we had better finish off by noting one residual issue.

Think first of the problem discussed in chapter IV, section 5, of accommodating the normativity of understanding: How can our thinking and reasoning practices enshrine rightness and wrongness, given – what is surely not to be questioned – that we are thoroughly natural creatures, whose every nook and cranny is a fit object of scientific investigation? At the time we noted three possible replies: first, that we do not really understand anything at all; second, that understanding is a primitive, unanalysable fact about us; third, that a suitable account of the brain's workings would disclose the dispositional base of our behavioural capacities and thereby account for the normativity of understanding.

The phenomenological argument of Part Two is best seen as a defence of the second option and a rebuttal of the third. Given, as we have seen, that the phenomenological facts about understanding cannot be accommodated by Internalists, Externalism is a correct account of the mind; more accurately, strong in-the-world Wittgensteinianism is the only account which gets the phenomenology right. There is no hope of analysing away these phenomenological facts in terms conducive to Internalism. Only if there were would it be possible to give a reductive analysis of what it is to understand a word, and hence what it is for a practice

217

to enshrine this rule rather than that one. Since it is not possible to account for understanding within Internalism, it is not possible to reduce the phenomenological, rule-governed facts to anything else. Alternatively, consider the fate of causal theories of representation. What we have seen is that merely fixating on causal relations between the things we think about and alleged representations in the mind or brain delivers no account of what is *representational* about representation: to represent X is not simply to host the bare effects of X's power. In the context of the Lockean theory of ideas, we saw that enriching the causal account of representation with the notion of *resemblance* seemed to be to move in the right direction, and this because to do so introduces the notion of phenomenology (ideas-as-images). Once the inadequacies of the imagistic theory as a theory of understanding are appreciated, however, phenomenology has to be accommodated in the Wittgensteinian way described in chapter VI. The common alternative, that of the materialistic Cartesianism discussed in chapter V, retreats even further from phenomenological adequacy, and so gives even less of an account of what is representational about its posited representations in the brain. This is not to say that there are no such representations, nor even that the notion of cause has no role to play here. The point is that the only way to see these bits of brain as representations is to appreciate the role they play in underpinning the practices, the form of life, of their hosts. So understanding the hosts as understanders comes first, the causal stories about their insides come second: which is just to say that in seeing them as understanders we see unanalysable, primitive facts about them. Piecemeal explanation of the causal basis of this or that practice, we have agreed, will no doubt be forthcoming aplenty. Across-the-board reductive analysis will not.

Such points stick in the craw of most contemporary analytical philosophers, which of course brings us to the first option mentioned above: that of claiming that we do not really understand anything at all. This is one formulation of *eliminativism*, the view that folk psychology should be 'eliminated' because it is a false account of what we are like.[19]

Now there are one or two mildly respectable currents of thought hereabouts. As we saw in sections 6–8 above, there may be reasons for thinking that the proper development of explanatory laws in scientific psychology requires reconceptualisation in narrow terms. If this is right, then the notion of understanding will be pushed aside in scientific psychology, because its proper object – (wide) content – has no role to play. The folk psychological will thus be eliminated from scientific psychology. But even so, the point here should not be exaggerated, even if we once again graciously waive the difficulties with narrow content. As we saw, it is still possible to argue that even scientific psychology will have some use for (wide) content: and anyway, given the point of the paragraph before last, narrow reconceptualisation for scientific purposes will take place under a necessary phenomenological umbrella of understanding.

Be that as it may, these mildly respectable currents run in a great torrent of, well, less respectable thought. Many who work in this area are manifestly either hag-ridden by the fear, or alternatively exhilarated by the prospect, that folk psychology may have to be eliminated *altogether*. But what can this mean? One claim is that although, as it were, we can't really stop ourselves reasoning and understanding, and seeing each other through the concepts of folk psychology, we shall have to accept, in our more lucid moments, that this is all *wrong*: at best a somewhat tawdry acquiescence in a second rate, rough and ready conceptual scheme. This claim is mostly empty posturing, however, where it is not incoherent. Deciding that really there are no witches has (should have) practical upshot. Acknowledging that a certain theory of Xs, still in use, is actually only useful-but-false, requires a background conception of how a different theory of Xs, more faithful to the facts, could at least in principle answer the purposes to which the false theory is put. But can anyone really believe, after giving it just a bit of thought, that the only purpose to which we put folk psychology is the explanation and prediction of one another's movements: a purpose which might better be served by scientific psychology? Just reflect on how you put in the folk psychological time. This brings us to a more sinister idea: that to do the elimination properly we shall have to *change ourselves*, and get out of the habit of being folk psychologists altogether. Think here of lunatics who stop using and even talking about furniture (because furniture-talk doesn't describe the true and ultimate structure of reality); or who stop up their eyes and ears to keep out the false imaginary glare (because colours and other secondary qualities are not really in the objects); and who stop seeing other humans as persons (because folk psychology is false). Can anyone really believe that all this would constitute an intellectually responsible, sane and balanced reaction, even in the face of the fantastic advances of mechanistic science?[20]

So where is this great torrent coming from? The short answer is: scientism – the tendency to accord exaggerated respect to the scope and power of natural science. Analytical philosophy, especially philosophy of mind, is currently awash with scientism. But there is perhaps a real issue over folk psychology. Given that we have no choice but to acknowledge that we are natural beings, perhaps we really do find it difficult or even impossible[21] to comprehend how we could also reason and understand, that is enshrine standards of rightness and wrongness in our practices. And how can there be all this phenomenology that we live in the midst of? How can it be like something for a natural, material being? It is not at all *surprising* or even (initially) disreputable to approach these questions with the assumption that natural science can deliver satisfying answers. But if the arguments in the preceding chapters are going in the right direction, this assumption will not bear fruit: understanding comes first, piecemeal scientific explanation second. If so, then the issue over folk psychology is still outstanding, and I perhaps leave you with a residual problem: how is understanding possible in a natural world? But if this needs an answer, and we are able to give it, then it will have to come from outside science. There is no scientific answer; and scientistic elimination is not an answer either. To destroy something because you don't understand it is simply to lapse into barbarism.

Notes and reading

Works referred to

MA   Fodor, J., 'A modal argument for narrow content', *Journal of Philosophy* 88 (1991).

P   Fodor, J., *Psychosemantics* (Cambridge, MA: MIT Press, 1987).

NN   Kripke, S., *Naming and Necessity* (Oxford: Blackwell, 1980).

MM   Putnam, H., 'The meaning of "meaning" ' in *Mind, Language and Reality: Philosophical Papers*, vol. 2 (Cambridge: Cambridge University Press, 1975).

SP?   Putnam, H., 'Is semantics possible?' in *Mind, Language and Reality*.

Notes

1 A recent example is to be found in John R. Searle: he tells us that Externalists, or people who believe in mental states with wide content (see section 4 below), hold that this involves 'relations to objects outside the mind' – *The Rediscovery of the Mind* (Cambridge, MA: MIT Press, 1992): 80. This is one example of the strikingly Cartesian tenor of a work which nevertheless proclaims little sympathy with current orthodoxy: see also 'All my mental life is lodged in the brain' (*ibid.*: 162), and the remarks on supervenience (124) and capacities (137).

2 Descartes, in claiming that immaterial minds have no spatial characteristics, perhaps intended that they cannot even have a spatial location. But he also held that such minds nevertheless causally interact with a very specific part of the brain (the pineal gland), and there seems little wrong with the further thought that a dimensionless mind could be situated at a point in space, and thus inside the head, for example at the centre of gravity of the pineal gland.

3 For most practical purposes it suffices to consider atom-for-atom *Doppelgänger*, since given reasonable assumptions (and ignoring immaterialism, as ever) all the Internalisms discussed in the text will claim that such pairs are psychologically equivalent. Could there be any other forms of Internalism? Yes: imagine in-the-world Wittgensteinianisms which fall short of making form of life track real essence, so that the Earthian form of life involving water is the same as the Twin Earthian one involving twin-water. Such positions are ruled out by the arguments of section 4 (note here also a further unfortunate feature of using the word 'internal').

4 Something very like the described approach underlies a great deal of the 'Californian' work on reference and semantics: see e.g. the contributions of David Kaplan and others in J. Almog, J. Perry and H. Wettstein, eds, *Themes from Kaplan* (Oxford: Oxford University Press, 1989). See also the collections of Perry's and Wettstein's own papers, respectively, *The Essential Indexical and Other Essays* (New York: Oxford University Press, 1993) and *Has Semantics Rested on a Mistake?* (Stanford: Stanford University Press, 1991). The approach is perhaps most explicit in Wettstein, who joins it to the bizarre idea that Wittgenstein's talk of practices and the like is 'just' semantic, with no intended bearing on the nature of the mind (*op.cit.* e.g. ch. 10).

5 The exceptions are the intermediate in-the-world Wittgensteinianisms mentioned in note 3.

6 This gives us another illustration of the fact that purely referential theories of communication are inadequate (see chapter III, section

4; and chapter VI, section 5). It is very easy to slip into thinking that since communication is a matter essentially to do with public language, it can be adequately handled by factors unearthed by the semanticist. If this is then added to the view outlined at the beginning of the present section, that semantic studies concern extra-mental matters, it can seem obvious that a purely referential theory of communication *must* be right. But theoretical prejudice is exerting an extraordinary grip here, since it surely ought to appear simply ludicrous that (cognitive) factors to do with one's own understanding of language are to be separated in this way from factors to do with one's understanding of others.

7 These rewritings reflect Frege's doctrine that when words are used to specify propositional attitudes, they do not have their usual Meaning, but instead serve in those contexts to attribute their senses to the person described. See 'On sense and Meaning' in P.T. Geach and M. Black, eds, *Translations from the Philosophical Writings of Gottlob Frege* 3rd edn (Oxford: Blackwell, 1980): 66–7.

8 Again, intermediate in-the-world Wittgensteinians could try to introduce a type of content which is not wide (to reflect their denial that form of life tracks real essence) but also not narrow (to reflect the fact that this is a form of in-the-world Internalism).

9 In the unpublished work mentioned in note 3, chapter VII, Fodor contemplates life without narrow content. But since he still wants to make the kinds of Internalist claim that narrow content is supposed to facilitate, he proposes that we ignore Twin Earth since it probably does not exist anyway. And philosophy does become much easier if we refuse to consider counter-examples.

10 This is still compatible with the Fregean point that sense determines Meaning as long as it is understood that this determination is *relative to context*. Thus the narrow content of 'water' determines H_2O *on Earth* but XYZ *on Twin Earth*: thus Fodor in P: ch. 2. In this, substance-words are sometimes said to be similar to *indexicals* like 'here' and 'I'. It is plausible that in some sense of 'meaning', my use of the sentence 'I am here' means the same as yours: this is often called *linguistic meaning*. But if you say it whilst in London and I say it whilst in New York, then, equally, we *say different things* (what you say is true if and only if you are in London; what I say is true if and only if I am in New York). For some dangers involved in making this comparison with indexicals, however, see note 12.

11 Here I am in general sympathetic to John R. Searle's contention that mental facts can only be understood *as mental* because of their ultimate links with the notion of consciousness: see *Rediscovery*.

12 It may be suggested that narrow contents are not really inexpressible after all. Consider the point introduced in note 10 that our two utterances of 'I am here' share a common (linguistic) meaning, even though we say different things by them. Why not say that simply by using this sentence one *thereby* 'expresses' this linguistic meaning, even while one *also* expresses the communicable content which varies

from context to context? And if so, why not say that there is yet a third sense of 'expresses' in which one expresses a narrow content simply by using a sentence which has it? Rather than quibble about the correct employment of the word 'expresses', we should focus on the main fault in this suggestion. This is that neither linguistic meaning nor narrow content can figure in the phenomenology of communication and understanding in the way that (wide) contents specifiable in sentences of the form 'X thinks that P' can figure. Thus even if narrow contents (and linguistic meanings) are 'expressible' in some special sense, they are not the contents that figure in our phenomenology, so they do not make our beliefs the beliefs they are in so far as we can consciously think and communicate them, and so they are, in this straightforward sense, *unthinkable* even if not inexpressible. Thanks to Tim Williamson here and elsewhere in the present chapter.

13 Recall here the failure of Locke's causal theory of representation (chapter II, section 5). The problem there was that by construing ideas as 'bare effects of power', like stinging feelings, Locke missed completely the fact that, say, *seeing something as red* is intrinsically representational, whereas stinging feelings are not. In order to accommodate this in the theory of ideas, we suggested, one should appeal to the notion of *resemblance*: an idea (image) of red, but not a stinging feeling, would then come out as at least *purporting* to represent its cause. The inability of narrow contents to figure in the phenomenology of understanding is the exact correlate of this failure to capture what is *representational* about a representation: words in the Language of Thought are 'bare effects of power' in an even more thoroughgoing sense than stinging feelings (they do not figure in the phenomenology *at all*). This is very bad news for the many supporters of causal theories of representation. What it means is that such approaches are exactly back to front: if there are any mental representations, they refer to what they refer to not in virtue of their causal relations to 'external' things, but in virtue of figuring in the causal underpinnings of believings, desirings and so on *as identified from the phenomenological, content-recognising point of view.* For more on this, see section 9 below.

14 Note that in order to understand this sentence as intended, one must not read 'phenomenological' in the discredited sense deriving from the Cartesian tradition: see chapter VI, especially section 5.

15 We can imagine switching the brains of human persons X and Y, and it is plausible, though not obligatory, to claim that the person goes with the brain, so that such a case would be a case of X and Y swapping bodies (see Derek Parfit, 'Personal identity', *Philosophical Review* 80 (1971); contrast Bernard Williams, 'The self and the future', *Philosophical Review* 79 (1970)). This may encourage the thought that a person just is a brain. But the point is not conclusive, even if the description of the matter as a body-swap can be sustained. If all the staff of University A move to the buildings of University B,

and *vice versa*, then perhaps this is a case of two universities swapping buildings. But it does not follow that a collection of staff without any buildings is a university. Perhaps a university is a-collection-of-staff-with-appropriate-buildings, and a person is a-brain-in-a-body. The resolution of this last matter depends on, among other things, deciding the issue between Internalists and Externalists, and so it provides no independent leverage.

16 Thus compare Steven Stich, *From Folk Psychology to Cognitive Science* (Cambridge, MA: MIT Press, 1983): 54–60.

17 One must distinguish here between cases involving flagrant self-contradiction, and others. See Saul Kripke, 'A puzzle about belief', in A. Margalit, ed., *Meaning and Use* (Dordrecht: Reidel, 1979); and Gregory McCulloch, *The Game of the Name* (Oxford: Oxford University Press, 1989), §§80–1, and 'Making sense of words', *Analysis* 51 (1991).

18 See e.g. Martin Davies, 'Individualism and perceptual content', *Mind* 100 (1991).

19 For examples see Willard V. O. Quine, *Word and Object* (Cambridge, MA: MIT Press, 1960), chs II and VI; Stich, *Cognitive Science*; and Paul Churchland, *Scientific Realism and the Plasticity of Mind* (Cambridge: Cambridge University Press, 1979). Or practically any recent book in the philosophy of mind and/or language.

20 This is not meant to undervalue a good scientific education. As Churchland (*Scientific Realism*) points out, coming to adopt science's 'superior and (in the long run) profoundly different conception of the world, *even at the perceptual level*' (2), helps us to become 'properly at home in our *physical* universe for the very first time' (35): 'the possibility of a dramatic modification and expansion of the domain of human consciousness ... becomes quite real' (15). Indeed. But one wonders what happens to all this expanded consciousness, and how at home we are supposed to feel, once 'the familiar ontology of common-sense mental states' has been eliminated, or '[sent] the way of the Stoic pneumata, the alchemical essences, phlogiston, caloric and the luminiferous aether' (113–14). In a nutshell, Churchland's position incoherently combines Externalism (the case for science is based on the fact that the 'objective intentionalities' of our representations 'is a relational matter' (25)) and Internalism (folk psychology is a 'moderately detailed ... *theory* of what makes people tick, ... their inner goings on' (92)).

21 For an interesting recent exploration of this idea see Colin McGinn, *Problems in Philosophy* (Oxford: Blackwell, 1993), esp. chs 1 and 4.

Index